Leurena,

I hope you enjoy reading about my journey from Tehran to Miami.

— Donya

TEHRAN TO MIAMI

Written by Donya Ziraksari
Illustrations by Ali Baghban

TABLE OF CONTENTS

INTRODUCTION

I have written this book with the intent of providing an honest account of the difficulties experienced by the Iranian generation born during the 1980s, after a bloody national revolution led by an uncompromising, upstart political opportunist gifted in attracting sycophants. The generation that lived through a damaging eight-year war with neighboring Iraq, which shrewdly began with the bombing of Tehran's national airport while its citizens were still shuffling through the rubble of the aftermath of the 1979 revolution. I am stating the truth without exaggeration as seen by me, a religious minority who experienced and witnessed inhumane treatment in Iran, especially during the eighties.

To better understand the before and after of the revolution, reasons behind the revolution, and Islamic Republic of Iran's structure, goals, and plans, I recommend you read *The Persian Night*, written by Amir Taheri. *The Persian Night* provides a complete, detailed, yet simple-to-follow explanation regarding the Islamic Republic of Iran's regime.

It has been a challenge to speak on behalf of the 1980s Iranian generation and capture all the difficulties that our parents and we faced and eventually adapted to. Our generation has suffered a great deal of emotional abuse and has been brainwashed throughout school and society. The new Iranian regime misrepresented the symbols of the Western lifestyle, morals, and political views to provoke hate, anger, and worst of all, resentment for European countries and especially America.

1

DEDICATIONS

I dedicate this book to my mother, a hardworking, smart woman, a member of a religious minority, someone who lived through the revolution and the Iran Iraq war and continued to spend her life serving mankind. She is a true role model for everyone, and I wish there were more people like her in this world. To me, she has been a mother, a father, a sister, and an honest friend, and she has always encouraged others and radiated positive energy to everyone who crossed paths with her.

This book is written in honor of religious minorities in Iran, who have been scared to practice their beliefs, fearing for their family's lives and future, before and after the revolution. Most people mistakenly believe that the persecutions of the Baháʼís only started after the revolution, but the persecutions existed even before the revolution, and only got worse after the Islamic Republic of Iran was established in 1979. Due to their beliefs, Baháʼís have not been able to attend universities, acquire a job in the public sector, start or keep their businesses open, or stay out of prison for tens of years. Many in the Baháʼí community in Iran have been imprisoned and suffered emotional and physical abuse for years. Some mothers gave birth and raised their children inside prisons because they were persecuted. Baháʼí men, the family's providers, were either executed or imprisoned, and their families were left to survive without financial support.

Iranian women have been oppressed and stripped of their rights by the Islamic Republic of Iran since the 1979 revolution. Too often they cannot get a divorce from their cheating and abusive husbands because the government give divorce rights to only men, so she is forced to stay with him for years and reluctantly accepts her husband's misdemeanors. Women are compelled to wear the hijab, and are often stopped on the street, lashed in public, or imprisoned for their lack of a decent hijab, for taking a walk with a male friend, or even for riding a bicycle in public. The hijab is defined by the extremists, followers of the new regime, and enforced regardless of your beliefs.

I dedicate this book to all of my Iranian War brothers and sisters, the 1980s generation, and the children of war. The ones who lost their brothers and fathers to the non-stop deadly eight- year war. We all suffered, together, from emotional torture, and food scarcity, and we learned to have empathy and stay strong.

I write this book to honor the refugees around the world. As a refugee, I too endured immense emotional distress, and I know that other refugees around the world are facing the same, if not worse, emotional and physical distress, longing for a better future. Some refugees that have reached their final destination and are confused and unsure about their future as an immigrant and foreigner and are craving a place to call home. Some refugees are currently facing scarcity of food and other necessary supplies as you read this book. I want to thank the host countries that took us in, with open arms, even if they were instructed by the United Nations to do so. I condemn all kinds of wars—emotional, religious, and political—that lead to mass migrations and refugee camps.

The purpose of this book is to tell untold, pre- and post-revolution stories about my Faith, family, and country. I would like to open the door to Persian homes, demonstrate some of the cultural, geographical, and religious facts and history, observed by me, to the people who do not know about Iran or Iranians. People who may be confused about what happened during the 1980s and 1990s and what life was like for the new generation living under the oppressive government of the Islamic Republic of Iran. These stories are based on facts that I know, while others may have experienced a different life in Iran depending on their family's political and socioeconomic status.

MY HOME

Iran, my homeland, has a population of 80 million, comprising mostly young people, because many children were born during and immediately after the Iran-Iraq war.[1] I am from that young generation, the 1980s, and experienced the after-war consequences and witnessed the transformation of the new society.

Iran experiences a variety of climates ranging from arid deserts in the central areas to luscious rainforests in the northern provinces. The Caspian Sea, on the north side of Iran, provides humidity to the surrounding cities and trees and vegetation keeping them green year-around. I remember visiting the Caspian Sea several times, from where I have collected large seashells to take back to Tehran, where I would spend time listening to the sounds of the ocean from my bedroom, and caught fresh small shrimps, using a metal strainer that my mother had handed to me, to later dry under the burning sun and save to eat as snacks. Most people in the north have lighter skin colors and green or blue eyes.

Northwestern Iran has a dry climate with very cold winters and annual snowfalls. I have never visited those provinces and have only passed through them by train but have heard they have a beautiful landscape that must be seen. As we get closer to the center of Iran, we approach the deserts of Lut and Kavir. These deserts can reach up to 70°C (160F) surface temperature, making it one of the driest and hottest places on earth. I have

---

1 The war started on September 22, 1980, and ended on August 20, 1988.

passed through these deserts many times, traveling to my mother's hometown to visit family for the holidays and admired their beauty and powerful silence. People living in the southern region, close to the Persian Gulf, have a darker complexion and they mostly eat fresh spicy seafood food caught from the gulf. In the south, by the Persian Gulf, it is hot and humid, and it never snows. Some parts of Texas that face the Mexican Gulf remind me of southern Iran, and if I press my eyelids shut and hyperactivate my sense of smell and touch, I can imagine myself there, on the shores of the Persian Gulf.

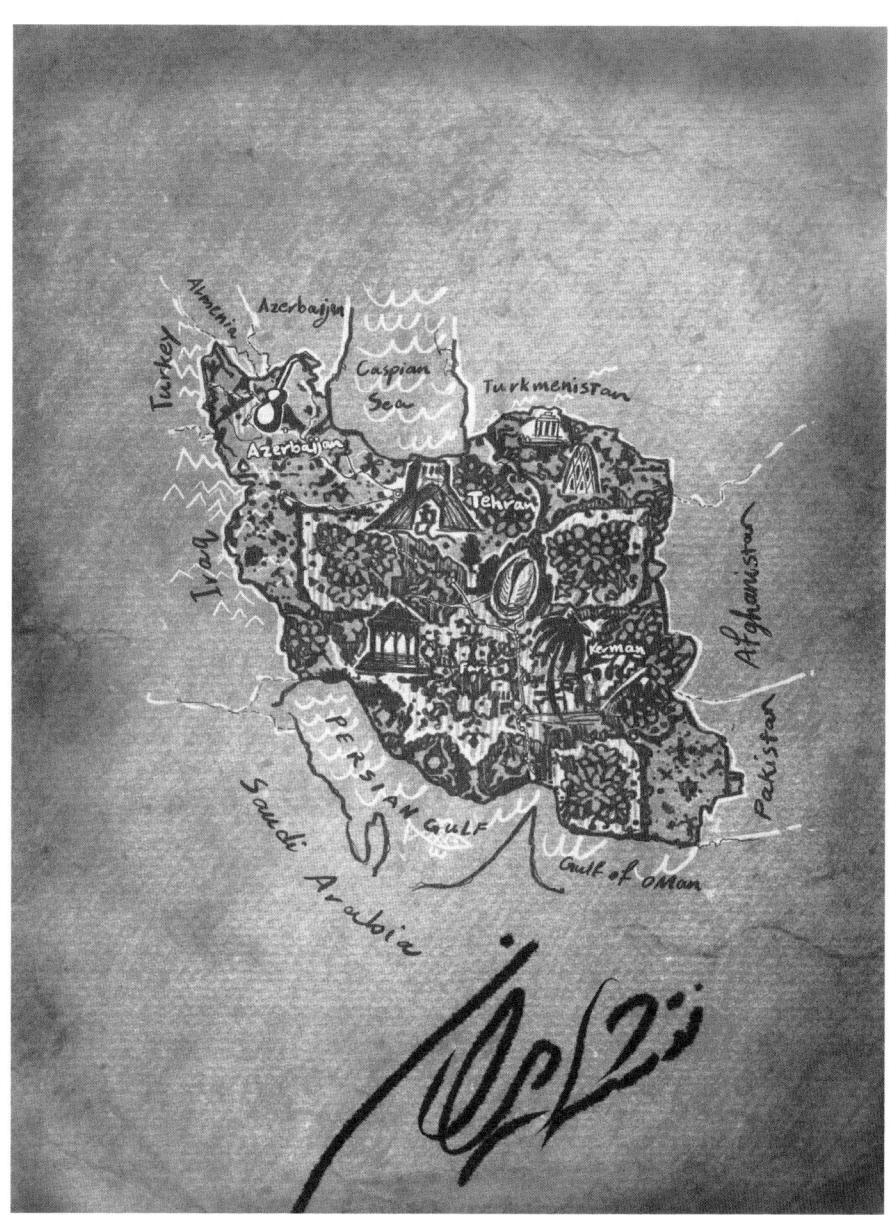

Tehran, my birthplace, is the capital of Iran. This city is flanked on the northeast side by the mighty Damavand Mountains and experiences all four seasons equally. The Damavand Mountain gives Tehran its mighty and confident appearance that shouts, "I am the Capital!" Spring days are cool in Tehran, and the afternoons are filled with occasional heavy rains that emit a sweet aroma from the flower blossoms and cool down the city before nightfall. The rain helps with the air pollution that has been plaguing the city for years.

I liked the spring because it would begin with at least thirteen days off of school in observation of Nowruz[2], the beginning of the Persian calendar year. House visits in the beginning of spring were a great way to start the year. My parents would visit their siblings, and I was able to play with my cousins. Sometimes we would travel out of Tehran to visit family in other states and get away from the constant air pollution in the capital. I did not enjoy taking final exams in late spring, but the final exams were a promise of three months of summer.

Summers in Tehran are hot with low winds. The native Iranian white mulberries are the summer's treat, sweet like honey, only available for a few weeks in the summer, and hard to find in other parts of the world. Being forced to wear a hijab in the hot summers of Tehran is not a woman's favorite choice of clothing, but it is a mandatory rule to wear a hijab in Iran, whether or not you are a Muslim and whether or not you are about to pass out from heat exhaustion. The hijab that women wear in Iran is not as extreme as what the Muslim women in Saudi Arabia wear. Iranian women are permitted to show their face and some hair, and dress in colors, not just in black as it is common in Saudi Arabia.

Fall, my favorite season in Tehran, is just charming and wondrous. Trees experience a sudden change in weather and change colors. It rains

2 Persian New Year.

often throughout the three months of fall as the temperature drops rather considerably throughout the months. Fall is the season for lovers to go out and walk down the streets as they watch the leaves fall on the ground. The first day of fall, is also the first day of school and my favorite day of the year, as I would reunite with my friends and catch up with them on the summer events.

Winters are cold in Tehran, but since we, women, are forced to wear a hijab, it keeps us warmer than men. Our hijabs act as a mandatory winter shield, and we do not complain much about it in the winter. It used to snow a lot more in Tehran when I was younger compared to now. It seems like Iran is under sanctions from Mother Nature as well as the United Nations and the United States. When it would snow in the winters, I was allowed to go on the roof and hang out for a short period of time. If it was the third or fourth snow of that winter, my mom would allow me to get a bowl of snow and eat it with the jam syrup that she made from the sweet cherries or strawberries in the summer. It was one of the most memorable things to do as a child since my generation did not have any sort of medium of entertainment after the revolution and the recent war. My brothers and I made many snowman sculptures on the roof and dressed them with a hand-knitted winter scarf.

The country was referred to as Persia up until the Persian New Year in 1935 as it had been for several thousand years, when the new government of the king, Reza Shah[3], declared itself to be known as "Iran," which is the name of the country in the native language, Farsi. This symbolic change was interpreted as the country's efforts to distance itself from its historically cantankerous relationship with the United States and the Great Britain, built over nearly a century of disagreements over who should ben-

---

3 Reza Shah Pahlavi was the king of Iran from 1925 until he was forced to abdicate by the Anglo-Soviet invasion of Iran, 1941.

efit from its vast oil reserves: the men and women who discovered and refined it or the men and women who felt a geographic right and were not satisfied with the extreme disparity in material lifestyle in Iran compared to the West.

Iran is divided into thirty-one provinces, each with its own unique culture and dialect. Prior to Tehran, other cities such as Shiraz, Ecbatana, and Isfahan served as Iran's capital. I would say Farsi has changed so much throughout the years, and people have begun using more English and even some French words than before. Iranians were forced to adopt the Arabic alphabet in the ninth century after the Arab Islamic invasion, and as a child growing up, the Islamic Republic of Iran tried hard to hide the bloody events that lead to this change and never touched on the old Persian alphabet.

In Iran, weeks start on a Saturday. People go to work and school from Saturday through Thursday, and Friday is the only day off. Government offices, banks, universities, and schools are closed on Fridays and most religious holidays, which total at least one month a year, not counting the cultural or New Year's holidays. The government gives less attention and value to the cultural events and holidays compared to the Islamic religious holidays, which are always celebrated lavishly in public.

My Iran is a country with beautiful people and nature whose essence is acutely reflected in its cosmopolitan capital city, Tehran. The vibrant city is located on the slopes of the Elburz Mountain range and is flanked by Mount Damavand in the north, whose peak extends to more than 18,000 feet. Tehran's 8 million men and women mostly align with liberal Western attitudes and are open-minded, which is too often in strong contrast to their government.

In Iran, we dress ourselves with outstanding precision and follow fashion more than the French and the Italians. Walking along the streets, one will notice men dressed like they walked out of a European catalog and women like elegant and flashy fashionistas. Boys and girls, being forced to wear the hijab, have gotten used to the idea of covering up in modest yet trendy ways. The unbelievable amount of money that men and women spend on clothing, cosmetic surgeries, makeup, haircuts, and hair dyes keeps increasing each year, and it makes me sad that my fellow countrymen and women are becoming more materialistic each day and numb towards the sufferings caused by the Islamic Republic of Iran.

Tehran is a crowded and loud city where people migrate from other provinces with dreams of getting a better and a higher-paying job, and a luxurious life. Everyone is constantly seeking better opportunities and striving to improve. Even though the majority of people, especially women, are educated in Iran, they do not have decent jobs. Almost all adults have at least a bachelor's degree but are not working in the field in which they studied meaning education and industry are not connected. People in Tehran do anything to survive the current social and economic situations. They could have a doctorate degree but buy an inexpensive car and start transporting people around for income. They do not need to be an official trained taxi driver to make money off of transportation, and some people work multiple jobs just to make ends meet.

Tehran has many tourist attractions and is a town of technology with great above- and below-ground transportation, Tehran is Iran's New York City, and there are tall, exotic buildings that are breathtaking. Architecture in Iran is astonishing, and I enjoyed walking around the city and checking out every detail of the old and new buildings. Amazingly designed and jeweled mosques in cities like Shiraz, Isfahan, Tabriz, and Mashhad are like no other mosques in the world. One would want to spend hours in a mosque to relax and meditate regardless of their religion or beliefs. Even as an Iranian living in Iran, one does not get tired of visiting the unique mosques and historic structures to admire their beauty. Interestingly, the types of mosques that were built in Iran are significantly unique to Iran because the mosques are built by Shia Muslims and not Sunni Muslims, and therefore, their structures are different from the Turkish or most of the Arabic mosques.

Iranians keep the inside of their homes clean, well-decorated, color-coordinated, and chic. As one enters the well-ornamented homes in Iran, one feels welcomed and quite comfortable, as if they were at their own home. Remarkable and unique Persian rugs are the center of attention in every house.

Famous, well-respected Persian rugs always brought our families together as we hosted many celebrations throughout the year. Persian rugs do not just serve as decorative objects in our homes. They also offer a playground for children and a soft yet thin ground for adults to rest on. I remember playing with my cousins on the unique rugs and trying to make up stories from the rug patterns. When we played house, one corner of the rug was my property, and the other corner would be theirs. The rugs watched us grow up and find ourselves, listened to our secrets, and comforted us on many occasions.

Persians use any excuse to get together and party, laugh hard, stay up into the night, and put on a show. Music and dancing have always been a major contributor to these private events, especially after the 1979 revolution, when the new regime announced music and dancing were religiously forbidden. I remember many gatherings involving my family, neighbors, and friends that went well into the night, and our guests danced to loud, illegal music and we would be worried and careful about the local police finding out, for fear it would lead to arrests and more serious legal consequences.

Iranians live in tall buildings and large apartments, but they all know their neighbors and care about them as if they were family. We do not just live in our apartments and keep everything to ourselves; we live together and share what we can with each other. Relationships do not end when people move away. They just get stronger.

Iranians take pride in their culture, history, poetry, rugs, cuisine, sense of humor, and the unity they once had. There are at least two palaces in Tehran that housed the last dynasties and kings of Iran. They have marvelous interior and exterior designs, but many valuable and historic items were looted during and after the 1979 revolution. I heard that, in 1979 when the latest Shah[4] left Iran, the revolutionary followers forced their way through the palaces and pillaged the furniture, gold, paintings, and other valuable items from the palace. Many of the possessions that were in the king's palace had been gifted by foreign kings over centuries, in admiration for the Persian kingdom's glory and might. Some of these items turned up in European museums, and others are still missing. The Revolutionary Guard[5] and new leaders rejected the material status of the king's belongings and collections. As a young teenager, I visited the palaces in Tehran and saw the glory and glamor in which the kings lived. Not sure if I agreed with the wealth they kept in their palaces, but they sure seemed mighty and untouchable.

Sometimes I wish we had the archives and museum collections in our own museums for the world to see, but currently, I am happy that museums in other countries, such as the Louvre in Paris, host many ancient Persian artifacts and are taking care of them for the future generations to appreciate. If the Islamic Republic of Iran had these items in their possession, they would have already been destroyed out of spite. I know this because growing up I have witnessed the hate and disrespect that the government had for the ancient artifacts and history of Persia. They once announced they would be building a dam in a location that would result in burying

---

4 Shah means king
5 A branch of Iranian armed forces protects political system of the Islamic Republic of Iran

an ancient artifact under water. Many protests that took place to stop the government from building the dam, and many people were injured and imprisoned for protesting. I am ashamed to admit that I believe the current Iranian regime would rather destroy the history of the Persian monarchies and wipe out our pre-1979 revolution culture, replacing it with superstition, prejudice, and Islamic history.

Ancient Persian poetry is well known around the world, with famous authors such as Rumi, Hafez, and Saadi being the subject of university courses. I have met many people who admire Persian poetry, which sounds amazing when recited in Farsi and carries its wisdom even when translated into other languages. Iranians have a strong sense of pride in their culture and literature. Many of us often brag about our ancient history such as how Cyrus the Great expanded his empire to become the largest empire in the world and published the world's first declaration of human rights. However, most of the bragging about Persian history and accomplishments stops right around the 1979 revolution.

Iranians are very empathetic, generous, and giving people by nature. Most of the time, they do not pass by one another without offering help. They offer their seat on the metro or bus to mothers, children, and seniors. If someone is carrying a heavy load, they offer to help them to carry it. People help one another, financially, physically, or emotionally. Iranians are great cooks, and they tend to express their love for one another by preparing and sharing food. There is always more food than can be consumed at parties, and often neighbors share their food with one another regularly. I have not met anyone who has tried Persian food and has not liked it.

Iran has changed a lot over the past forty years, but change seems to be moving much more quickly, especially over the past twenty years. Iran has many modern, towering buildings that one would not find in most places in the world. Tehran has many places to visit such as Tehran's grand bazaar, art and rug museums, and expansive public parks with entertainment and food for visitors. There are a lot of underground coffee shops serving exotic desserts and non-alcoholic drinks. Tehran has become a modern town; people have the latest and newest phones, laptops, and cars. They follow the Western culture as much as the Islamic Republic of Iran's government allows, and people are constantly pushing the boundaries while they strive to live day by day, and I once was one of those people.

SOCIETY AFTER 1979'S REVOLUTION

Iran's last revolution occurred in 1979. The revolutionary leaders had laid the groundwork for years, which culminated in the overthrow of the monarchy. There are many books that attempt to describe or justify the series of events that led to the revolution, but I think every writer has his or her own understanding and biased opinion. I was not born during the years leading up to the revolution to witness those events, but it is clear that the public's demands for social change were not heard by the government of the Shah. Change was much needed.

My parents experienced it firsthand, and the post-revolution life was not pleasant. Revolutionaries reminded citizens of the injustices at the hands of the Shah's government and especially targeted the feelings of uneducated and underprivileged people, urging them to join and expand the revolution. However, the promises made by the revolutionary leaders during this time were not kept. Newspapers and video recordings from those times feature Khomeini in a defiant and determined tone as he promised free housing and bus transportation and a constant monthly income for every Iranian citizen to win the heart and support of the poor. These benefits were to be paid by nationalizing the oil industry, a similar approach that was attempted by the government of Mohammed Mosaddegh, who shortly served as prime minister before being ousted via coup d'état led by the American CIA[6] and British MI6[7] in 1953.

The post-revolution atmosphere was devastating to those citizens who did not actively participate in the overthrow of the Shah's government. Those who led and participated in the revolution were gifted swaths of land and rewarded with highly paid, distinguished government positions; most others that were not a supporter of the new regime were left out. Many people did not think highly of the Shah's monarchy before the revolution, but conditions within the country overall were much more stable and the country was more respected internationally. My mother was among those who had a better life before the revolution than after, and the Shah's regime had fueled the career she development as a woman and a member of the religious minority.

Unfortunately, I believe Iran is one of a few countries that has managed to travel backward in time as it has become more isolated from its neighbors, prejudiced, superstitious, and narrow-minded. It has pressured its citizens for over forty years to forget its pre-Islamic historical significance, succeeded in becoming much less popular internationally, and has nearly altogether lost its tourism industry. Iran has suffered a brain drain, as many people during the past twenty years have emigrated to live healthier lives and to provide better futures for their children.

Many religious, social, and political minorities have left Iran in order to practice their beliefs freely. They had to leave their relatives, homes, friends, and childhood memories behind, though they still carry the hope to go back someday, to a better Iran. Many have died hoping the regime would change and that they could be re-united with their loved ones, and I do not know if I will witness this change during my lifetime.

---

6 Central Intelligence Agency
7 Secret Intelligence Service of United Kingdom

After the Shah left, many people rushed toward the borders to leave the country. From what I have heard, the first group of people who left were referred to as "people of the crown" and they were close to the Shah. Their family's lives were in danger. This group was made up of the royal family, political advisors, military generals, and high-ranking pilots. Most left their belongings behind as they fled hastily, hoping to one day return as many thought the revolution would fall apart and fade away. Some important members of the court stole or high-jacked airplanes and left the country in order to seek asylum elsewhere. Those who did not leave were captured and executed, some publicly, while others were gruesomely tortured and interrogated to confess their sins. Most of the properties owned by the affluent were confiscated and recommissioned into offices for the new regime officials or sold to revolutionary supporters at a small fraction of their value.

After a few years of leadership by the new government, Islamic Republic of Iran, a second wave of people left the country. It was becoming clear by then that their hopes of governmental failure or the return of the Shah would not come to fruition. Shah had died in 1980 from cancer and was buried in Cairo. It was unsafe and obvious that his family was not planning on returning to Iran to take back their kingdom. My mother believes most of the second wave of people who left the country were either from the educated class or true Muslim believers who were out of work and watched from afar as enthusiasts took over and influenced the government. During this time revolutionary supporters received higher ranks in government, created new restrictive laws, and wrote a new constitution that closed paths for those who did not support the regime or shared the same beliefs. The new laws were written solely for the benefit of the authors and the like-minded. Virtually the entire constitution was culled from Islamic law, with much stricter interpretations, and ideas such as equality and free will were not taken into consideration. It appeared at this time that the revolution was dragging the country backwards in time instead of progressing forward with the developing world.

The belligerent intolerance of the new ruling class imposed harsh punishments on religious minorities, especially the Bahá'ís. This group had experienced mistreatment under the Shah's regime as well, but not to the extent of that meted out by the new government. After the revolution, their temples were bulldozed, and they were forbidden from practicing or speaking about their religion in public or private. An organized effort was made to confiscate every worldly possession from this group of people and capture and imprison them. Many Bahá'ís were unfortunately executed without any trial or proven crime. Most minorities were forbidden from receiving passports to leave the country; therefore, they escaped through the border with Pakistan to avoid the much worse consequences of imprisonment or death. It is difficult to estimate the numbers of Bahá'ís who remained in Iran, as they are not officially recognized; some stayed behind owing to lack of choices, and endured the hardships created by the new regime.

Bahá'ís were no longer allowed to attend public or private universities or have a job. Again, before the revolution, there were some restrictions on what Bahá'ís could and could not do, but after the revolution their living situation was much worsened. Those who had jobs were informed that they would be terminated unless they switched their religions to Islam and my mother was one of them. Many private business owners lost their private businesses; many stores were burnt to ashes, and some clerics forbade the public from shopping from "the Unclean," Bahá'ís. The revolutionary leaders had not advertised that they would target a specific religion after gaining power, but once they were in charge, they were merciless.

Another group of people who were slaughtered by the Islamic Republic of Iran was called Mujahedin-e khalq of Iran.[8] The Islamic Republic of Iran almost wiped out their entire organization. The ones that did not get executed and were left to live left the country to seek asylum. Growing up in Iran, we were brainwashed about Mujahedin-e khalq, their purpose, and the events they were involved with, leading up to the revolution. They were portrayed as evil, anti-Islam and professional killers. In my opinion they were trying to change the regime, just like Khomeini's followers but they were not successful.

---

8 An Iranian Marxist political–militant organization in exile that advocates for a violent overthrow of the ruling system in Iran.

MADE IN IRAN

My father was born and raised into a large Muslim family in the early 1950s in Tehran. Back then Tehran was a bustling city with ample opportunities. He had six brothers and two sisters, and since he was born twenty some years before the revolution, he experienced and enjoyed Tehran cabarets and dance clubs. My paternal grandfather was from Tehran and used to work for the national airline. He was much respected at his work, and his oldest son, from his first marriage, later worked for the same company.

My grandfather was married twice and had a son and a daughter from his first marriage. I do not know why his first marriage did not work, but in a time when divorce was the absolute last resort and extremely uncommon, he divorced his first wife and retained custody of his children. In Iran, fathers typically retain custody of the children if the children are over the age of seven. The court may allow them to stay with their mother when the children are younger, but the courts generally favor men for every aspect of marriage and divorce, especially the final divorce ruling. The majority of the laws are male-favored in Iran, and it is very difficult for a woman to prove that the father is incapable of raising their kids in order to win custody. Consequently, many mothers do not file for divorce when they otherwise would, just because they do not want to be separated from their children.

Soon after my grandfather's first divorce, he married my grand-mother. My father is the first child from my grandfather's second marriage, and after him my grandmother had five more sons and a daughter, not in that order. My father and his siblings had a tough childhood. Their father used to physically abuse and threaten them. Once he attempted to cut my father's head off in the front yard next to a small pool that used to be in the middle of the yard, which was used for washing clothes and dishes. He only let my father go because my horrified grandmother begged him to. After years of alcohol abuse, my grandfather became a Dervish[9] and tried to better himself by not drinking or abusing his children. He died a few years later from lung complications due to heavy smoking. He had never given up the cigarettes. My father was young at that time, and since he was the oldest child, he had to support the whole family and take care of his younger siblings.

My paternal grandmother's origins are from Tabriz, a city in the northwest part of the country that shares a border with Turkey. She too had a very hard childhood. Her parents separated when she was a young child, and she was raised by her paternal grandmother. My grandmother did not have many childhood memories of her mother who had remarried and had more children from her second marriage, and later in her life my great-grandmother moved to the house next door to my grandmother.

I remember my grandmother's mother. All of us grandchildren, would call her "Nane," which means mother. She was very skinny and had a wrinkled face due to heavy hookah and cigarette smoking. She spoke Azeri[10] as her primary language and because we did not speak her language I never understood what she was saying to us or to my grandmother, and most of the time, I just guessed what she meant from her hand gestures. I could see that beyond those wrinkles was a woman similar to my grandmother, a woman who had experienced many difficulties in her life and

---

9 One who accepts material poverty and lives a simple life.
10 A Turkic language spoken by Azerbaijani people, who live in Iran in the northwestern states neighboring Turkey

22

had patiently tried to make the best decision as a fearful divorced woman living in Iran. A divorcee would have been considered used goods during those times. I now know that Nane did what she had to do to survive the male-dominated society of Iran in the early 1900s. She had no choice but to leave my grandmother with her ex-husband and remarry another man shortly after her divorce. A remarried woman had to have children from her second marriage to prove her love, commitment, and loyalty to her new husband. She would not have been welcomed back to her childhood home after divorce because women were not the breadwinners of society and would not have financially contributed to the household, and divorce was so uncommon and harsh that a family's reputation was in danger.

Sometimes my grandmother and my father would speak in Azeri around me so I would not know what they were saying. I knew they were talking about my mom, but could not understand what they were saying, and that made me nervous. Their conversation was usually followed by a loud fight, and my father would storm out of the house to the front yard and immediately light a cigarette. I would usually sit in the corner of my grand-mother's one-bedroom home and watch him through the white-laced window curtains as he continued to smoke and bicker with my grandmother in a low tone. My grandmother would look at me reluctantly and whisper to herself in Azeri. In my little head I would ask, "Is she talking about me?" I grew up despising their secret language that was used to gossip about us in our presence, not knowing that one day life would require me to master both Turkish and Azeri as well.

When my grandmother married my grandfather, his family told her that his first wife had serious mental issues, and he divorced the woman to save himself and his children from her abusive behavior. My grandmother's stepson would act very rude towards her because he saw her as the other woman, not his stepmother who was there to take care of the entire family. She was arranged to be married to my grandfather. There was no love before or after their marriage, only duty. I felt bad for my grandmother because she endured hardship as a child and as a married woman, taking care of two stepchildren, tolerating my grandfather's insane behavior and addiction to alcohol, as well as giving birth to seven children, of which six of whom were rambunctious boys.

My grandmother was illiterate, and when she would visit us, I would try and teach her the alphabet so she could read and write. Using a white board marker, I would give her lessons on the bedroom's glass balcony doors as she sat on the floor, on the red, handmade, detailed Tabriz Persian rug in my bedroom. She would always try to learn the alphabet during my few-hours long lessons but would have forgotten everything by the next time we saw each other, and we would have to start over again. She would mostly participate in my Farsi lessons to make me happy and keep me entertained, I know now that she knew she was not going to learn how to read and write at the age of sixty-seven.

My mother was always very nice to my paternal grandmother, her mother-in-law. I remember that every time my grandmother was sick, my mom would bring her to our house and nurse her as though she was her own mother. My mother would cook healthy foods for my grandmother and give her a room with a bed, so she was comfortable. My grandmother usually slept on my bed when she would stay overnight. She loved my mother, who held a special place in her heart, even though they did not share the same beliefs.

My mother was born in Rafsanjan, a town in the province of Kerman, located in southeastern Iran. It never snows in Rafsanjan, and the weather is usually dry and hot with occasional heavy rains, which cause floods throughout the city and nearby villages because the dry earth cannot absorb the large amount of rainfall all at once. The city of Rafsanjan is located near the desert and welcomes the snakes and scorpions into the city and often into homes. My mother had seen many snakes and scorpions in her childhood home, and she had many stories to tell us growing up.

My mother was the second child of six: she has three sisters and two brothers. Her father owned a mechanic shop that had a great reputation in Rafsanjan; her mother was a stay-at-home wife. If I ever decide to write about her parents, it will be a nearly endless book about their love and respect for each other. When my grandfather got sick, he wished on his death bed that he would not see the day that mullahs take over the country and he did not. My mother's father died ten months after my second brother was born, which was the night before the Islamic Republic of Iran claimed complete governmental authority. The wish of that pure-hearted man came true.

My maternal grandfather was the youngest of five siblings. His father had thirteen wives, which was a norm at the time if one was a wealthy man. He lost his mother when he was an infant, and then his father when he was only eight years old. His older stepsiblings did not care for him, and he began working as a mechanic at a car repair shop until he was eighteen supporting himself. Upon reaching the legal age, his father's lawyer informed him that the car repair shop that he had been working at as a laborer, along with many acres of pistachio farms, were left for him by his father. My grandfather donated the pistachio farms to the hard-working people who had worked at the farms for many years and only kept the car repair shop for himself.

When he was in his early twenties, during the 1940s, many people were converting to the Bahá'í Faith in his hometown. Among them was his older stepbrother. My grandfather had heard many rumors about the Bahá'ís such as them being ritually "Unclean" and that their morals were against the Islamic Faith. My grandfather even interfered with his stepbrother's burial ceremony to make sure he was not buried in the Bahá'í cemetery and was buried in the Islamic cemetery according to Islamic burial rituals. After his interactions with the Baháʼís on a trip from Rafsanjan to Shiraz[11], he became curious as to what their religion was like, read their books, and even spied on their gatherings, and eventually converted to the Baháʼí Faith himself.

Although my maternal grandmother's grandfather had become a Baháʼí and was married to a Muslim woman who did not believe in the Baháʼí Faith. Years after their marriage, they were not able to have children, and in the 1800s, the women who did not bear children were fruitless because the man was never to be blamed or labeled as fruitless. He walked from Iran to Iraq, to visit Baha'u'llah, the Prophet of the Baháʼí Faith, who was exiled to this place by Naser al-Din Shah Qajar[12], the king of Iran at the time. My great-great-grandfather's wife, being a Muslim, had told him to ask the Baháʼí Faith's Prophet for a child, and if they conceived, she would believe that Baha'u'llah is the true manifestation of God and will also become a Baháʼí.

During his visit in Iraq, he was tempted to ask for a child, but due to being shy and realizing the insignificance of his request, he did not. On the last day of his visit, pilgrimage, he received a hand-written tablet from Baha'u'llah that said, "You will have a son; name him Gholam[13] Abbas." It was so unexpected for him to receive such a letter from his Prophet who had read his heart.

Thrilled and hopeful, he went back to his wife and told her the story, but she did not believe him. Soon after his return, his wife bore a child, it was a boy, and they named him Gholam Abbas. Even though her wish had come true, she never converted to the Baháʼí Faith. Their only son was my grandmother's father, and my grandmother was his first child.

---

11 The capital of the province of Fars.
12 Naser al-Din Shah Qajar was the Shah of Persia from 1848 to 1896 when he was assassinated.
13 Servant

Three years after my maternal grandfather became a Bahá'í, during the late 1940s, he was at a devotional event at the Bahá'í temple in his hometown. A young woman went on the stage of the temple to chant a prayer, and my grandfather fell in love with her voice. After the prayer, he turned to the person sitting right next to him and asked if they knew who she was, and said that he only saw half of her face from where he was sitting, and that he wanted to see the other half before proposing to her family. He was told sarcastically that both halves looked the same and he should propose to the girl's family.

The woman chanting the prayer at the temple was my grandmother. He approached my grandmother's father, Gholam Abbas, and proposed to him for his daughter's hand at their house, but his proposal was rejected. Before he left the house, my grandmother's mother saw him and asked him to wait. She then told her husband, "I have seen this man in my dream, and in my dream, I gave him something very valuable." My grandmother's mother convinced her husband to agree to the union, and my grandparents got engaged.

They were engaged for three months, as it is the tradition in the Bahá'í Faith, and they only saw each other a few times before the wedding day. They never spoke to each other prior to the wedding day, because in early 1900s in Iran, girls and boys were not allowed to interact before marriage. During his short visits to my grandmother's house throughout the three months of engagement, he had fallen in love with my grandmother's hair and had asked my great-grandmother to ask my grandmother to refrain from cutting her hair and to leave it long for the wedding. My grandmother always said that the love between her and her husband was an after-marriage love, with complete respect, and it was all she had asked for. She told us that my grandfather was beaten with chains by his hometown Muslims extremists many times because he had converted to the Bahá'í Faith and he had scars on his body. She loved him deeply and always spoke highly of him.

My mother had a hard childhood as she grew up with a lot of discipline. She was her parents' second child, their right hand, and always assisted with the house chores. Unlike my father, my mother did not get to experience cabarets and dance clubs since she lived in a much smaller, religious, superstitious, and closed-minded city. She left for Kurdistan[14], when she turned nineteen to become a social worker and teacher for children of low-income families. There she traveled to different villages helping people gain an education about cleaning, cooking, and personal hygiene and healthcare. My mother had a hard time getting into medical school because she was a Bahá'í, a religious minority, even though it was before the 1979 revolution and the systematic suppression of religious minorities. My mother, once selected as the most beautiful and accomplished single woman in her city, was rejected from medical school, due to her beliefs.

Years later, after she had married my father and they had their first child, she received a scholarship from the Shah's government to attend a nine-month training course in Europe and expand her knowledge in social services. She would then return to Iran to become an educator, coordinator, and developer of programs to improve society's safety and bring down unemployment among ex-prisoners and ex-addicts. As a social worker she had over 120 cases of people who came out of jail, rehab, or returned from the Iran-Iraq war and needed help finding themselves again and planning for a better future. She also helped people who had spent time in the foster care system who were without education or jobs, gain the necessary skills to improve their own living situation and get off social services.

---

14 Province of Iran that shares a border with Iraq.

THE SHEEP'S PROPOSAL

Traditionally, marriage in Iran is a union of two families. Based on old traditions, if a family liked a girl for their son, they would approach the girl's family and ask of their availability to visit their house and talk about "amre kheir," or "blessed subject," which is code for marriage proposal. If the girl's family is sure they do not want to consider the union between families, they would not agree to the visit out of respect for everyone's dignity. If the girl's family is interested or unsure of the possibility of the union, a visit is arranged for the families. The visit is a very formal gathering with well-known rituals.

The family of the boy has to bring a nice flower arrangement and pastry for the girl's family. The girl's family prepares and serves fresh tea, fruits, and pastry. Usually, the more senior and wiser members of both families attend the visit, which could include grandparents, uncles, or aunts. The parents of the girl and boy have to attend, unless they are deceased or physically unable to, in which case an older aunt or uncle will take their place. Normally, no children or teenagers are present, as this is seen as an event for the more mature family members. Sometimes the older siblings of the girl and boy attend as well, but it is understood to invite fewer people.

During this gathering a discussion of possible marriage is heard. Most of the people who attend this visit are people who will support this marriage and make decisions for the boy's and girl's future, since younger people normally depend on their families for a better financial future.

After the attendees are done with small talk and have had some delicious and aromatic Persian tea, the boy's family starts the marriage conversation with, "Okay, let's get to the actual subject." This is code that everyone should begin more serious talks about the marriage and see if the union could happen between the families.

If the girl and the boy have not seen each other before this visit, they would meet for the first time to discuss their future goals, dreams, and expectations. There seems to be a perception in the West that almost all the marriages in the Middle East are arranged, but in fact the arranged marriage tradition has almost died out in Iran and I, personally, do not know anyone that has had an arranged marriage other than my grandparents. Arranged marriages were common before the 1950s, and the boys and girls of today's generation meet, fall in love, and then have the formal proposal gathering out of respect for the traditions of the elders of the family.

Normally, the girl does not join the meeting during the proposal unless she has been called in by her family. This is when she serves the tray of tea one-by-one around the room, as everyone is sitting around the famous Persian rugs, which witness every family event throughout their expected lifetime. The girl wears her best modest outfit that displays her natural beauty as she enters the room. She begins by first offering tea to the boy's family, starting with the oldest member in the family; the boy is always served last. The boy would have this short moment to look at the girl, as he picks up his tea, to be sure that she is the one he wants to marry. By the end of the visit, if the families are open to this marriage, the boy and girl will talk in private, if they need to. If the families like each other or accept the marriage, they eat the sweet pastry, that the boy's family has brought. This act, seals the deal and is known as "sweetening the mouth." It is meant to be an acceptance of the marriage and their mouths will be speaking of sweet and pleasant words from that day on.

After both families settle on the engagement and wedding dates, they get together to start preparing and shopping. Traditionally the bride, the groom, and their mothers and sisters tag along for jewelry and dress shopping. There are certain streets and neighborhoods in every town in Iran dedicated to wedding clothing and jewelry stores. The bride and groom will buy matching wedding rings and save them for the wedding day. They begin their engagement by focusing on the engagement party if there is one and leave the wedding shopping for later. The bride's family buys the suit and tie for the groom, and the groom's family will buy the wedding dress for the bride. The groom's family will also buy the bride a set of jewelry, and the bride's family buys the groom a watch. These gifts are exchanged on the wedding day.

I personally have not seen other cultures or laws that would require blood and drug tests prior to the wedding, but in Iran it is a key requirement to ensure both parties are aware of contagious diseases such as HIV and any genetic complications that may occur during conceiving a child. It is merely done to benefit the couple. The sealed drug test results will be discussed by the marriage officiator with the couple, to ensure that the couple is aware of any drug addiction prior to the wedding. Iran also requires a pregnancy test prior to a divorce to ensure the possible unborn child has a known father, since women must not have children outside of the boundary of marriage.

Sometimes women in Iran and other countries feel as if they are sheeps auctioned at the proposal ceremony. They have no control over their future, and they know that they must obey their parents to satisfy them and possibly have a better future. Most of the time during the sheep proposal, money and status are more important than love, humanity, and education. The sheep proposal culture is almost dead in bigger cities in today's Iran, but my sisters around the world, especially in the Middle East's uneducated and poor families, are still sold by their parents as an object to men, in exchange for money, drugs, and more.

THEY MET

My parents met when my father was serving the last months of prescriptive two-year military service in Ferdowsi, Kerman.[15] In early the 1970s, just a few years before the revolution, my mother was stationed at the military base to educate the Ferdowsi village people on basic sanitary laws and more. My father had been transferred to an office at the same military base after intentionally breaking his own leg to shorten his service time and receive a transfer out of the field.

My father, young and energetic, was immediately attracted to my confident, independent, and beautiful mother and told her shortly after they met that he would one day marry her. My mother refused his assertion and replied he would never have her. Because my mother was raised in a Bahá'í family that was systematically repressed by the government, she did not want to marry a Muslim and be forced to abstain from practicing her Faith. She felt that marrying a Muslim husband would not bring the promise of freedom of religion; she was also concerned that her children would become confused as well.

My father was so entranced that he visited my mother's father to ask for permission to be married. My grandfather did not approve and declined the request immediately. Several men had approached my mother's family around this time to propose, including very wealthy and influential families from her hometown, but my mother had turned them all

---

15 Province in Iran on southeast of Iran, close to Pakistan.

down because they were Muslim and she wanted to practice her Faith without shame and secrecy.

My father was persistent. He traveled between Tehran and Kerman week after week to get permission from his mother and from my mother's parents. His mother was not thrilled about him marrying into a religious minority family, and she also thought he was too young to take on that responsibility. My father did not have a job at the time and had young siblings to support since his father was deceased. There was a very small income from my grandfather's pension, and my grandmother had no job or proper support other than my father, her eldest son.

An important note here is that Muslims traditionally are sensitive about family members marrying non-Muslims. If one marries a non-Muslim, which is otherwise forbidden, there must be a conversion to the Faith. Families will turn their backs on their children or siblings if this law is broken. In my mother's case, her situation took a sinister twist as some of the clergy members in town encouraged my father to work around this law by marrying Muslim wives on the side to compensate for the fact that my mother was not a Muslim, as if it were a righteous deed to have secret marriages on the side and cheat. At the time my mother had no knowledge of the women my father was dating in Tehran, or of his past.

My mother, unaware of my father's situation in Tehran, was so flattered by my father's insistence and passion that she decided to marry him despite their parents' wishes. After forty-five days of constant back and forth, their parents agreed to the marriage. My mother's father was disappointed in my mother's choice because he knew she could do better, and this young boy was not the right match for my strong, independent, and determined mother.

It did not take long to sense a foreshadowing of the incompatible marriage full of empty promises and gestures. My father's half-sister offered to sew my mother's wedding dress as she was a talented seamstress.

When my aunt failed to complete the dress, or to inform my mother ahead of time to buy another white dress, my mother ended up wearing a green dress on her wedding day.

My father had promised he would accept that my mother had different religious beliefs and would not interfere with her desire to practice her religion freely. This quickly changed after their union. He prevented her from attending any Bahá'í events. Because the Bahá'í Faith prioritizes marital health over its formal practice, my mother gave up attending events and clung on to her beliefs in her heart and through her actions.

Shortly after the wedding, my father returned to his military station at Ferdowsi to complete his service, and they did not honeymoon for this reason. My mother was then forced to stay at her father's home so my father could leave town, saying he would travel to Tehran to check on his mom and siblings. He did not want her to join him in Tehran to visit his family, and she still had yet to see his family's living situation.

This was the first insult of many for which my mother regrets not divorcing him. He literally left her in another town, not welcoming her along even as the weeks turned into months, and he would travel back and forth from Tehran to Kerman as he pleased. To keep consistent, as this was his only positive trait at this time, he broke his promise to relocate to Kerman and help at my grandfather's mechanic shop.

Two months after their marriage, my mother became pregnant with my oldest brother. Now pregnant, she had no choice but to follow her husband to Tehran. She was shocked when she learned that my father had been lying about virtually everything. He did not have a job, nor did he live in his own house. He was living under poor conditions with his mother and all six of his siblings in a small house.

Soon after my brother was born, my mother left her job in Ferdowsi because my father told her to move to Tehran permanently. Moving into my paternal grandmother's house was not easy. They were a relatively poor family living in a one-story house with two rooms and a basement. Seven children, my grandmother, and now my mother and my oldest brother were all living together. The kitchen, commode, and shower were separated from the house, each occupying its own corner of the front yard, and the cold winters could be extremely difficult under those circumstances. The home was not well-insulated, adding to the discomfort; my mom humorously remembers that the only floor insulator was a rug that was thinned due to its age, still witnessing the life of its owner on its last, stretched breath. A small pool was also located in the middle of the front yard, reminding my uncles and aunt of the day their father attempted to cut my father's head off out of anger and alcohol intoxication. During the frozen winters, my grandmother had to break the ice in the pool to wash dishes and clothes. This probably did not help prevent the arthritis and joint pain that she experienced throughout her life and about which she complained until the day she passed.

My paternal grandmother would make food for everyone with whatever she could afford, which was not much. Based on what my mother remembers, my grandmother would make soup for everyone, on more than one occasion, using a single chicken leg. My mother had found a job in Tehran as a social worker and would help the family, financially and socially, as much as she could.

One of my father's relatives had helped my father find a job at the government-funded Geospatial Engineering department shortly before my brother's birth. This job required frequent cross-country travel to collect soil and mineral samples for analysis. He would use this information to create maps showing the distribution of soil and minerals for use by miners and geologists. He traveled a lot, and his job must have been interesting since he was gone most of the time. Thinking back to my childhood, it was a relief when he traveled because when he was home, we lived under constant fear and threat.

He would travel for several days at a time surveying land that was of interest to the government and industry. He was treated very well on his travels, as the people of the small towns and villages he would visit were very generous to government employees. He was often allowed to stay in the home of the village mare, sort of like a mayor, who owned the nicest lands and properties in the village, with amazing views and amenities. The people in the village would treat him and his co-workers like royalty, cook for them and offer them freshly sacrificed animals. His team was given a driver and a cook who traveled with them and prepared all of their meals. I think he liked that lifestyle, with his friends and far away from his children, his wife, and the responsibility that goes along with them. Sometimes I wonder how many times he cheated on my mom when he was away on the road. It angers me to think that maybe one of those nights when we were in our cold apartment, doing our homework without the help of electricity, as my mom prepared food using an oil lamp, he was in the warm arms of some younger woman.

My mom lived with her in-laws for a couple of years, and then she moved with my dad and my oldest brother to a small apartment using the money she had saved. They probably would have never left my grandmother's crowded home if it had been only up to my dad. He did not seem as committed as my mother was to building a life with his new family. He did not care about improving his position at work or owning a property; he wanted to stay in one place and never move up. I do not have this perspective simply for the sake of taking my mother's side, but this is also my impression of him. I remember as a child that my mom would work hard and save her money to buy new things for the house and improve the quality of life for all of us. My dad often asked why I would always take my mom's side, and I replied that his side does not have anything good on it. I have no doubt that my mother pushed for her small family to move into their own apartment, and it was not initiated by my father.

My parents were the opposite of each other in almost every way. My mother liked to sleep under a heavy blanket, and my father under a thin bedsheet year-round. My mother liked her tea light, he, dark and strong. My mother liked to wear nice outfits, and my father never cared about his clothing. Throughout their marriage, she bought his clothing and dressed him for parties and social events. My father hated wearing new clothes and would always wear worn shirts and pants to seemingly impress that he was the son of a Dervish and did not care for the material life. My mother often told him that she was embarrassed by his choice of clothing, but I believe he did this to tease her, hurt her feelings, and get her attention.

BORN A MINORITY

My oldest brother is thirteen years older than me and took care of me a lot when I was a child. When my parents visited an office to obtain the birth certificate for their newborn son, it was without a consensus of his name. As they sat down at the table and continued to argue over the name, the employee sitting across the table scribbled something down on the certificate and congratulated my parents. As they looked at him bewildered, he informed them he chose their son's name while they were arguing.

My oldest brother was hyperactive as a young child and constantly in trouble with the school administration. My mother was often called into school to meet with the principal because of some new trouble that he caused. A couple of years after his birth, my mother was given a government scholarship to attend nine months of training in Europe with several other Iranians. The scholarship was created by the Shah to train committed students and help them start a program when they returned to Iran to serve underprivileged citizens. All expenses were paid by the government, including her own apartment at no extra cost because she was married with a family. It was a great opportunity for the family, as my mother could complete her program and the family could travel and experience life in three different European countries for nine months.

My mother left for Rome with my father's promise that he would soon join her. When my mother arrived in Rome and called my father, he told her that he was not going to join her. She pleaded for him to change his mind, but he insisted that neither he nor my oldest brother would be joining her while she was away. They fought about this situation for three months, but he did not make the trip.

Instead of joining her in Europe, my father took my brother to the province of Khuzestan, which borders Iraq, so his sister could help look after my brother. By this time, my mother knew that she would be alone for the remainder of her trip, and knowing my father's abusive behavior toward my brother, she returned to Iran after only three months of training. I have read the postcards that my mother sent home to my father and later saved, and it is clear that she loved her family and had missed her son. I still do not know why my father refused to join my mother after he said he would. It seems to me that he avoided the things that made him feel challenged. I believe my father was always afraid of being away from his country, and I think he feared leaving his comfort zone.

My oldest brother grew up fascinated with books and took great pleasure in reading. He used to have an amazing collection of classical philosophy and history, many of which were deemed illegal under the law of the Islamic Republic of Iran. Sometimes he would share these with me and encourage me to read these thick books about God, creation, and philosophy, which were hard to understand for a child my age. He was also great at writing short, deep passages about love or existence.

My second brother is nine years older than me, and he was also born right before the 1979 revolution. True to form, my parents argued about the name of my second brother before and after he was born. My father insisted on his own nickname, which was started by his aunt. My mother warned him that she would call my brother and introduce him to everyone by a name that would rhyme with my oldest brother's name. My father, continuing to be stubborn, went to the government office alone and returned home with a birth certificate that read his long-known nickname. Nobody has ever referred to my brother by his legal name to this day, and my brother actually changed his legal name later on to the one my mother had chosen.

My mother was still working, now with two young kids, and would leave for work early in the morning and return around the same time as my father in the evenings. My second brother was quiet up until he was in grade school, when he became interested in acting and performing. He loved to perform different types of dance, from breakdancing to Persian traditional, and everything in between. He became the life of any party, and family gatherings were not as fun without him. He was a character and was great at imitating just about anybody. As a teenager he signed up for acting classes, and my mother encouraged him and did her best to financially support his acting career.

My third and youngest brother is four years older than me. We look a lot alike and were often asked as children if we were twins. He was constantly destroying or building electronics growing up and got into trouble several times for destroying our brand-new TV or radios. He had an engineer's desire to understand the workings of everything and wanted to open every piece of electronic equipment he could get his hands on. His toys began as simple bulbs and batteries when he was young but grew more complex and expensive as he grew older. There was no argument as for his name since by then my parents had learned their lesson.

I shared a bedroom, for most of my childhood, with my youngest brother. Since I did not have a sister to play with, I decided to tag along and assist him with his destructive projects. My mom regularly warned me about the consequences of assisting him. Often before leaving the house for an errand, she would say, "Now listen, Donya, do not get involved in his projects. I do not want to come home and see that you two broke something again."

I would promise to stay away from him and not assist with his plans. Sometimes I heeded her warnings, but after playing with my dolls for a bit and becoming bored, I would check to see what he was up to. He was usually investigating the electronics. If something went wrong and my parents found out, I would bear the brunt of the punishment because I was "the assistant." To this day I am not sure why he was allowed to get away with his destruction. Even in a family as modern and educated as ours, which always had the latest and greatest technology, I, as a girl, was treated differently than the boys in the house.

My most vivid memory of mischief with my youngest brother began when he abruptly woke me up in the middle of the night. He whispered for me to walk with him to the hallway stairs immediately outside of our apartment's front door. With both hands, he passed me a piece of wood and instructed me to hit him if I saw him shaking. I had no idea what he meant or what to expect, but I was nonetheless prepared to hit him with the wood on cue. He had his own small table between our apartment's level and the access to the roof that reminded me of a research center.

In preparation to obey his request, I held up the wood high in case he would need to be struck hard if he began to shake. He gave me a scared look and told me to lower the wood a bit, that I did not need to break his bones and it was okay to be gentle. He also asked that I avoid his head. He was working on building an electronic device and did not know which wires would shock him. He was afraid that if he connected the wrong wire, he would get electrocuted and he wanted me to hit him with the piece of wood if he was being electrocuted to break the current path. In the middle of the night, with no adults present, I stood there at full attention as he connected a few wires. I was wide awake, scared, and unsure of the consequences of electrocution.

After he connected a few wires, he stopped moving. I asked, in a scared and shaky tone, "Do I hit you now?" and he quickly replied, "No, not yet." A few seconds later he connected two more wires. I was so nervous that I could not contain myself. I shouted, "Do I hit you now?" He turned around and saw me standing above his head, holding the wood like a baseball bat ready to hit him hard. He quickly stood up, took the stick from my hands, and told me to go to bed. He asked me not to tell anyone what he was doing out there, that was one of our secrets. Had my parents known he was playing with high-voltage and dangerous electronics; they would have killed him before the electricity could get to him.

I had something in common with all of my brothers. I admired and wanted to be like my brothers, even in the smallest ways. I would dance with one, read philosophy with one, and play with high-voltage electronics with another. I wanted to prove that I belonged and was cool enough to hang out with, mostly because they were preoccupied with their own interests and did not want to hang out with me. When it came to their sister, they expressed their love and attention in the form of protection, whereas I just needed their love and attention.

Many times, growing up, I wished I was a boy. I wished that one night I would go to bed as a useless girl and wake up as an empowered boy. This way I could blend in at home and feel more secure in society. This would solve the problem of my mother expressing worries about my future throughout my entire childhood. I would no longer be blamed or questioned for staying out after school or talking on the phone with the opposite sex. No one would check the phone after I hung up to see who I was talking to, so they could bother and bully me.

As a boy I would be able to walk around without wearing a hijab and even ride a bicycle freely. I would no longer care if someone bumped into my chest while walking on the street because I would not have young, painful breasts to protect from stray elbows. No one would question my decisions or forbid me from going out to play with my friends. If I were a boy, I could laugh freely and out loud without any judgment. I could choose my own partner and not feel judged for expressing my love and needs. As a girl growing up in Iran, existence was exhausting with the endless worries, shame, and fears; at times it felt like we were born as minorities.

BEAUTIFUL
AND UNTOUCHED

The Iran Iraq War started on September 22, 1980, just one year after the Islamic Revolution was complete and the Shah of Iran had left the country. Iran was vulnerable at that time as the new government regime had just executed the majority of military officials and generals from the previous government. Those military personnel who were not executed fled the country to America or Europe as political refugees. Iran had essentially no military, weapons, established governing body, or any sort of constitution. Western countries during that time were not sympathetic to the new Islamic Republic of Iran, especially because of the hostage crisis in 1979 in the American embassy located in Tehran.

Iraq seized this opportunity by attacking Iran with the intent of taking over the country. We were told that America and England backed the Iraqi government and supplied them with weapons and war equipment. On the other hand, no country would supply military supplies to Iran. Without a military or supplies, the majority of the Iranians who fought in the war were under-equipped volunteer soldiers, many of whom were teenagers and youths, as young as ten years of age.

My father had taken my oldest brother to work with him on the day that Iraq attacked Tehran. My father was standing in his office hallway, drinking tea with co-workers when he heard a door loudly shut. He quickly looked over and saw that his office door had been closed. He walked over, opened the door, and scolded my brother for closing the door so hard. My brother denied touching anything, and before my father could continue his reprimanding, the door by itself slammed even harder, and the glass pane of his office shattered.

Iraq had begun bombing Iran by targeting the commercial Mehrabad International Airport, which was a few miles from my father's office. The airplanes and airports were targeted first to prevent aerial retaliation and defense. The bombing stopped after the airport was destroyed, and many innocent civilians were either wounded or dead.

The volunteer Iranian soldiers received on-the-job training to use guns and protect their country. There was no time for drills or rehearsals. At times, during the eight-year war, Iraq progressed across Iran's border provinces, especially Khuzestan, but eight years in to the war, Iran had reclaimed their own cities and established their borders. Over 1 million Iranian volunteers and nearly 500,000 Iraqi soldiers had died during the dragged-out eight-year war. I did not know a single person, while growing up, who had not lost a loved one to the war. In addition, people also lost their homes and jobs. Cities that had been destroyed had to be rebuilt.

The countless sick and injured soldiers were forced to seek medical attention in a country without medical supplies, and that was under economic sanctions. Despite religious or political preferences, everyone went to war to sacrifice for their country. The 1980s in Iran had been full of extreme calamity and transition. People were ready to recover from the war, but they did not have a familiar country to which they would return, as the new government had seized power only shortly before the Iraqi attacks had began and they had yet to establish basic laws.

Chemical bombs were dropped on Iranians for years, and as far as we were told by the Iranian regime, Iran did not use them in return. To this day, people are suffering from the side effects of those cruel attacks. We were told by the Iranian regime that Germany supplied Iraq with the chemical bombs. The soldiers that were contaminated by the chemical bombs suffered enormously from the horrible side effects. Ironically, both Iranian and Iraqi soldiers went to Germany to seek medical attention after the war ended. Germany supplied the disease and cured it. Great business.

My father and his physically able brothers served in the war as volunteers. One of his brothers had a walking disability and stayed back to take care of their mother. My youngest uncle was the dearest of all the brothers, and many girls wanted to marry him. He turned eighteen just in time for the mandatory draft. Just a few months after I was born, he came home from the war to visit family. My mother says I wet myself as he was holding me for a family picture, and he had laughed about being in uniform and getting peed on.

My mother loved him like a son because he was only five years old when my parents got married and moved into my grandmother's house. He grew up alongside my oldest brother. He was only nineteen years old when he was killed in the war; my grandmother mourned for years over his death, and he was later posthumously honored by the government as a martyr. His death had a big impact on my childhood, as I have many memories of yearly visits to the martyr cemetery, Behesht Zahra, just outside of Tehran. This was always a day of sadness as all of my family members cried and mourned over his grave.

He was a well-known nurse in his neighborhood and the doctors had asked my youngest uncle to stay back and help them in the clinic instead of going to the war but instead he went to the war to fight for his country. His fellow soldiers said that he had gone out of the bunker to perform his daily chores, and there a missile had exploded near him; some parts of the exploded missile got embedded in the abdomen. His internals were completely injured, but his beautiful face remained untouched. They brought his dead body to Tehran; the military tradition was to bring him to his house, so his family could say goodbye to him before he was buried. He was the only soldier from my grandmother's small neighborhood who had died in the war.

The entire family and neighborhood with all of us kids were in my grandmother's front yard when they brought my uncle's lifeless body home. Of course, I was too young to understand the horrifying situation, but my mother says that my grandmother was extremely devastated, and she mourned so much over her youngest son departing from this world. To see him one last time, my grandmother had even opened the white cotton sheets that my young uncle was wrapped in. His beautiful face was untouched but cold and colorless.

My youngest uncle was in love with his half-cousin, and they wanted to get married after he came back from the war. He did not come back to marry her; he came back and married the cold soil in the cemetery. Months after my youngest uncle was buried, my grandmother suggested that her niece get married to my fourth uncle. They accepted, and she married my uncle, but I think she is still in love with my youngest uncle because to this day, she still dreams about him, he gives her messages from the next world, and she tells us about it with great passion.

Iran's government promised many things to the Iranian soldiers who fought in the war, but many did not even receive medical and financial treatment and are still suffering the aftermath with both physical and emotional side effects. Although the war had been fought, the fallout was far from over. The government used the war as an opportunity to spread propaganda of national pride by funding TV shows about hero soldiers who made the ultimate sacrifice for their country. Movies were shown glorifying battles and referring to those unfortunate enough to be killed in action as martyrs.

These war movies were released for years with the intent of creating anger toward Iraqis, but even I, as a child, knew that there was suffering on both sides. I did not enjoy watching the war movies because I knew that the Iraqi soldiers did not fight out of personal hatred toward Iranians. This was an order given by their government. There were virtually no movies released during my childhood that encouraged happiness and excitement or gave hope to the people who lived in cities destroyed during the war. There was no happy music played on the radio either, besides during the Friday morning show, *Good Morning Friday*. The fact that the government was investing in media and not the wounded soldiers or their families did not escape many, nor did it lead to popular support.

I was born at 10:30 PM on a hot summer night in 1987 during the Iran Iraq War. In Persian, *Donya* means life, existence, earth, or the world. Many different languages and cultures throughout the Middle East and Eurasia use this word, but it is not a typical name. Because of the meaning of my name, I thought growing up that I was born to change the world. I felt like a revolutionary leader whose duty was to make the world a better place. Often, I feel like I was wrong.

When I remember these feelings of power over the world, I recall a story my mother often told me as a child. A young man wanted to change the world and after many years realized that he should have just focused on his birth country. Therefore, he focused on changing his country and after many years realizes he should have only tried to make his own city a better place to live. This continues until he realized that he should have focused his efforts on making his family's life better by simply focusing on making himself a better person. I have always carried this story with me but have yet to give up on the idea of having a bigger, international impact. I truly believe this and try to practice changing myself for the better and becoming the change I want to see.

I do not think my mother was very happy when she became pregnant with me. I know that she told my father that he must take care of me forever, because she did not want more kids and had intended to have tubal ligation after my second brother was born. In Iran, the husband's permission is required in order for a doctor to perform this surgery, and my father would not sign the paperwork. He did not sign the paperwork after my second brother was born, nor my third brother, or me. He said he was willing to sign for the procedure to be completed immediately after both my third brother and I were delivered but changed his mind when my mother was unconscious in the delivery room. I do not know why he wanted so many kids in the middle of a revolution, war, and food and supply scarcity. Maybe he felt lonely and wanted more people who would potentially love him.

My mother was overwhelmed when she learned she was pregnant with me because of the living situation in Iran. At that point she had lost her well-paying job due to her religion, and my father was barely making enough for the family of five. He also had to look out for his mother and siblings who were growing up and in need of support while they were starting their own families. Life was difficult for everyone at that time due to rationing and scarcity of the essentials. Being well-off was not enough to live a comfortable life. She was also worried that I was a girl and would be growing up in a society that did not concern itself with respecting its women. My birth seemed like a burden at the time.

Although my mother was technically a stay-at-home wife during those years, she was hardly around the house. She would obtain or sell rice, sugar, and cooking oil coupons, issued by the government, so she could buy other household essentials. My brothers were busy with their friends, and I was not old enough or cool enough to hang out with them. I spent most of my childhood alone, playing with my inexpensive Barbie dolls, hand sewing them formal, lavish dresses. Before I learned how to write, I would tell stories to my mom and she would write them in a small notebook, and I drew illustrations of my stories on the opposite page to her beautiful handwriting. After I was able to write on my own, when I was a young teenager, I created poetry and stories fantasizing about my future.

Love poetry was not allowed in our household and that was my sole poetry subject. I would hide my writings from my family because I did not want to be made fun of and I did not think they would understand my stories. In our house, if someone would find my love stories, then I would have had to explain who I was in love with and why I was writing about him.

I would watch TV if my brothers would let me have the remote control, which was rare as I was the youngest and a girl. Atari[16] came out when I was a child and was very expensive. My mom found a way to afford it since all of my brothers wanted it. I did not really like to play most of the games, but I did like the duck hunting game. I mostly enjoyed watching my brothers play, and it would give me a chance to sit next to them and we would all hang out.

When I was in elementary school, my mother bought the family a computer, which soon became my youngest brother's toy and property. Most upper-class and some middle-class households had a computer, and they used to treat it with a lot of care. I only used the computer to play card games or watch Aqua music videos or the Aladdin cartoon in the beginning. Then I learned how to create an email address, go to chat rooms, and even purchase a program called EJ to make some music with it. The house was the boys' world and I just lived in it, trying to blend in as much as I could every day.

I did not have many forms of entertainment. I either watched cartoons on TV or the one cartoon I owned, *Cinderella*, on VHS tape. I was in love with Cinderella. She was beautiful and she married a prince who did not like that? Cinderella was recorded on a single VHS tape, preceded by a recording of a Charlie Chaplin movie. This meant that I had to beg my brothers to rewind the VHS tape so I could watch *Cinderella* and had to sit through the Charlie Chaplin movie every time I wanted to watch

---

16 home video game console famous in the 1980s

Cinderella. In the Charlie Chaplin movie, he would fall in love with a young, beautiful, and blind flower girl. It was a beautiful story; the love was so pure that even a five-year-old child could feel its honesty. Even still, I could not help but prefer the beautifully Persian-dubbed *Cinderella*.

We treasured the times that my mother would bake cake. She loved to bake and eat the cake right as it was pulled hot out of the oven. My brothers and I would help her, but we would fight over the batter left behind in the plastic mixing bowl. This felt like an event for us, and we all looked forward to the times that my mother had the time, money, and supplies to bake a cake. We were not poor, but we were living in a society after revolution and war. We had to save, learn to live with the minimum, and be thankful for what we had. I learned not to ask for anything, and when I had it, I appreciated it and made it last.

My mother did her best to keep us happy and make us feel like we had everything we needed, especially when my father was gone on work trips. She would do her best to make sure we were happy and did not feel his absence.

My father would bring all sorts of edibles and decorative souvenirs from his trips. If he would travel to the northern part of the country, he would bring back hazelnuts, walnuts, or almonds, sometimes even fresh with the outer skin and shell. He always brought huge amounts of each nut home, and my mom and I would spend hours peeling and deshelling them. We had so much at times that we would give them to neighbors and family. Olives also grow well in northern Iran, and sometimes my father would bring them home to marinate and mix with his famous recipe of pomegranate and walnut paste. My father was a very creative cook, and almost everyone enjoyed his food.

I was frightened on other occasions when he would bring home small alcohol jars of preserved animals and insects. I vividly remember the jars of snakes, scorpions, and one giant red bee that he showed off in the middle of our house, and the porcupine spikes that we had placed in the vase. I never touched any of those jars because I was very scared they would come alive and get out of the jar.

PERSONAL HEAVEN

Growing up in Iran was fun for us. We had simple lives with low expectations and were happy with the few things we had. I miss my childhood every day and wish I could go back and experience every bit of it again. We used to live on the fourth floor in an apartment off of a cross-section of a major street, Sattar Khan[17] and Baqir Khan[18], which was in a middle-class part of the town and was considered an established location.

I miss my childhood home. It was big and bright inside, and I remember it as comforting. My mother bought that apartment without telling my father. He did not want to invest in anything, and since my mother's salary was higher than his at the time, before the revolution when she still had a job, she bought the apartment. She applied for a loan and bought the apartment and did not tell him for a while. When she finally broke the news, he told her that he did not like the idea of owning a home. I am not sure why he was so scared, and I wonder if he just was trying to avoid change and anything new. My mother could have bought a house in northern Tehran, which was a wealthier neighborhood with a cooler climate, for the same price, but she knew my father did not want to live in the well-to-do areas since he was from southern Tehran and felt resentment toward the rich.

---

17 Sattar Khan is the name of a pivotal figure in the Iranian Constitutional Revolution, not the Islamic Revolution, and is considered a national hero. The Constitutional Revolution of Iran took place between 1905 and 1911 and led to the establishment of a parliament in Persia. This was during the rule of the Qajar Dynasty.
18 Baqir Khan is another key figure in the Persian Constitutional Revolution.

Our apartment was built by a family named Zandi and was located in a four-story building, each floor except the first had two units. There were eighty-six steps to our apartment on the fourth floor, and if we would fall asleep in the car after a gathering my parents would have to carry us all the way up. In my small world, those steps were large, and it was a pain to go up and down the stairs.

I am not sure why our apartment building was zoned as residential because it was off of a major street and most of the buildings in that area were in commercial use. We did not mind the noisy streets because none of the bedroom windows faced the street. Our living room on the fourth floor had a wonderful view of the busy Sattar Khan Street, but I would have rather lived in a house with a yard so I could play with the other neighborhood children for hours.

Our apartment had three bedrooms and a huge living room that could have fit 100 people in it; at least that's how I felt when I was a kid. The apartment was designed as a loop that would connect the small living room to the large living room and dining room, and then kitchen and hallways with doors that opened to bedrooms, and finally connecting back to the small living room, where the front door was located. Some days, I would ride my bicycle inside the house in the loop because no one had the time to take me outside in the nearby alley to ride my bicycle. Our laundry machine, located in the kitchen, had a scar on it and it sort of looked like a giraffe's body to me, so every time I made a full circle through the house, I felt adventurous, as if I was at the zoo.

Our building was very established and well-built, made with the most expensive building materials around at that time. The whole neighborhood knew that the builder, Mr. Zandi, used the best materials available and put in extra days and weeks to ensure that the building would be reliable and valuable in long term. Everyone in the neighborhood spoke highly of Mr. Zandi and said his goal was to build an apartment to serve its owners for generations.

The front of our apartment faced the street, and the back of the apartment faced a very small backyard on the first floor. From our apartment's balcony, I could see balconies and rooftops around us. We had a close relationship with our neighbors, and I considered their daughters as my own sisters; we would play at each other's houses as often as possible. When my mother would not allow us to play together, I would ask for permission to play by myself on the balcony. This allowed me to lean over our balcony and interact with the neighbor's daughters.

Our apartment was about two thousand four hundred square feet in size. Pollution from the busy streets below would find its way into our home above, so my mother covered the furniture in the formal living area with white sheets to keep it clean even though we lived on the highest floor of the building.

The first-floor unit was owned by a sweet, older couple, who were related to Mr. Zandi, the builder of the building. Now that they are gone, I wish I could go back and just sit next to them and get to know them. I was a child and did not want to hang out with older people, but now that I am older, I wish I could go back in time and sit by the old neighbors and listen carefully to their untold stories. I felt loved in their presence and remember the delicious sweets they would offer me each time I was their guest. They also babysat me when my mom was running errands.

They did not have any children of their own because Mrs. Zandi could not bear a child. It was common in older days for a man to divorce his wife and re-marry under these circumstances, and it is even permissible under Islamic law for a husband to keep his first wife and marry another woman in order to have a child. When the couple learned that they could not have children, Mr. Zandi never spoke of the subject again, even though his wife told him she understood if he wanted to have a child with someone else. This was true love. They lived together until the very end, and never spoke ill of one another.

My mom used to help them in different ways, such as cooking, shopping, cleaning, or even giving Mrs. Zandi a bath, since they were older and did not have children to run errands for them. They did not have many visitors since they did not have children, grandchildren and most likely their distant families had no time to attend to them. I can remember myself in their house, running around their brown, neatly kept mid-century furniture. I want to grow old like them and leave behind pleasant memories for a little girl, who can in turn remember me and the memories shared.

Every time that we would go over to Mrs. Zandi's house to help or visit, I would ask for permission to go to their backyard. Although the small yard was supposed to be of use for everyone in the building, they were the only tenants with access to the yard. I dreamed of living in a house with a large backyard where I could grow fruit trees and herbs. I was so small, and the seven hundred-square-feet yard seemed so large and so full of potential. Mr. Zandi took care of the backyard on a daily basis, watered the trees and planted flowers. It was so refreshing to walk through the yard on the stone pathway that probably Mr. Zandi had laid down years before I was born and forget we were in the middle of busy and polluted Tehran. Cool shade from the tall old trees made me feel I was in my own personal heaven. I used to think that if I died and went to heaven, I would be sent down to Mr. Zandi's backyard.

My mother told me a story about our Mr. Zandi's relatives, which I remember vividly. A young girl in their family was a member of Mujahedin-e khalq. The Mujahedin were active before and after the 1979 revolution in an attempt to overthrow both the Shah-led and the Islamic Republic government. The girl was an active member of protests and participated in planning terror attacks with other members of the group.

One day, she received a phone call from her best friend, also a member of Mujahedin. Her friend asked to meet at a new location to talk in secret about their next project. Mr. Zandi's family member showed up at the meeting location and was captured by the Revolutionary Guards[19]. Her friend was already dead by this time. The Revolutionary Guards were known for capturing members of Mujahedin-e khalq one at a time, obtaining the locations of their safe houses, and infiltrating by sending undercover guards to get more information on the projects. It was rumored that each member of the Mujahedin carried a cyanide capsule at all times and swallowed it if they were caught to avoid giving up information through physical torture.

The young girl had been missing for several days, and her family was extremely worried. They were completely unaware that she was a member of the Mujahedin-e khalq. They had reported their daughter's disappearance to the police and had not heard back. Several days later a man called their home and put the girl on the phone to tell her parents that she loved them and to ask for their forgiveness. The man took the phone from her and instructed the parents to stay home, and he would bring their daughter home later that day. Nobody showed up, and several hours later the

---

19 The Islamic Revolutionary Guard Corps (IRGC) - Army of Guardians of the Islamic Revolution or Sepâh for short - is a branch of the Iranian Armed Forces, by order of Ayatollah Ruhollah Khomeini.

anonymous man called back and instructed the parents to meet him outside of the city to pick up their daughter.

Once they arrived at the designated location, a man showed up alone. He told the parents that their daughter was buried somewhere on that land, which was used as a mass cemetery. He pointed to a grave site, where new ground movement was visible, and told them, "Your daughter is buried somewhere around there." The family was devastated that their young and beautiful daughter was tortured and raped for days before finally being killed. All girls captured by the Revolutionary Guard were raped because by Islam's definition, a virgin girl goes to heaven and they wanted to make sure that she was dishonored before death so she would end up in hell. My mother had heard that many youths who had joined the Mujahedin had been killed and buried in unknown locations in the middle of the night without anyone seeing or knowing.

Once Mr. Zandi had become very ill, my mom stopped by their house almost every day to help them out. My mother swore that one of those days when she was at their house helping out, he was in a bad shape, struggling with each breath, lying on the bed, he stopped breathing as my mom and Mrs. Zandi were sitting beside his bed. When Mrs. Zandi realized that her husband was no longer breathing, or maybe even dead, she screamed, "Do not leave me alone, Zandi!" and a second later he started breathing again. Apparently, that happened three times and each scream of "Do not leave me alone, Zandi!" brought him back to life. She loved her husband very much; he was her only family and friend, and she could not imagine her life without him. Mrs. Zandi died shortly after Mr. Zandi passed away because after his death all she thought about was joining him.

The Iran Iraq War ended when I was two years old, and nobody had a stable economic situation. Everyone had to save money and be extremely careful of their expenses. My mother had lost her job due to her religion at this time and my father, according to him, was not making a lot of money.

One day, my mother had taken me to the grocery store near our apartment, and I had pointed to expensive chocolate bars and asked her to buy one for me. It was an expensive snack, and she could not afford it. I insisted and nagged out loud in the middle of the store, making a scene. She tried to ignore me as I embarrassed her in front of the store owner. The store owner was kind and offered the chocolate bar to my mother as a gift, but she did not accept it and told him that I should learn not to ask for things in the store. I continued to cry my eyes out and stomp my feet asking for the chocolate bar. My mom finished her shopping and asked me to stop crying and follow her home. I refused and instead sat on the floor of the store, crying even harder. My mom threatened to leave me at the store alone if I did not get up and go home with her. Of course, I challenged her and stayed on the floor, crying. She walked out and waited for me on the sidewalk. She became tired of me embarrassing her in our neighborhood and walked toward the house. I knew the way back home, and I followed behind her, still crying and stomping my feet as I took each step. At some point my mom could no longer bear the embarrassment, and walked ahead into the apartment building, leaving the heavy front door open for me. She waited for me in the stairs, and when I finally showed up I was still crying and moaning, "Mommy, mommy"

Our neighbor, Mrs. Zandi, heard me crying and opened her front door and called me into her house. My mother knew that I was safe in her house and went upstairs, leaving the front door of our fourth-floor apartment open for me. I explained to Mrs. Zandi about the chocolate bar, and she offered me a bowl full of candy that she always kept inside her warm and cozy house and near the front door. I ate some, then grabbed a few more to take home using the skirt of my dress as a basket. After a while my mom came by the door to check on me and found me sitting on the stairs by the apartment, holding my dress skirt in my hands. When I heard her voice, I slowly stood up and told her that I did not want candy anymore.

My mom asked me to promise her that I would no longer embarrass her in public, and then she let me in the house. I learned my lesson to never ask for expensive items or make a scene in the neighborhood.

The neighbor on the second floor had two daughters and had moved in shortly after I was born. The neighbor's girls were both older than me, one by one year and the other by two. The father of the family owned an auto parts shop, and his wife stayed at home. Due to a rare genetic disease, the father had trouble walking, dragging his toes on the floor as he moved. Unfortunately, the two beautiful girls inherited this disease from their father and some of the school kids would make fun of them because of the way they walked. I fought with my classmates and told them not to make fun. I loved them like sisters. Their father had developed very strong arms and had very firm handshakes since his legs were not as functional. I used to ask myself why they had two kids when they knew there was a strong chance the children would inherit the same problem. They had a third daughter years later who did not have the same problem as her two older sisters.

Across the hall from the two girls on the second floor, right above the Zandi's apartment, lived a single woman in her late thirties, around the same age as my mother. She was an employee of the TV station and did not have any children. She was never married, and her last name was Zand. Ms. Zand was very blunt and outgoing for a woman of her age and social status. She was a bit too friendly with the men in our neighborhood and would wear inappropriate clothing. She smoked cigarettes, sometimes even with my father, in a society where women who smoked were considered loose. My mother would care for Ms. Zand's elderly mother at times, and I remember when her mother died of health complications, we all mourned together because she had been a part of our lives.

One time my mother went to Ms. Zand's house and saw my dad in her living room, the two of them alone, just hanging out. I think that Ms.

Zand liked that my dad was a flirt and antagonized my father's sense of cheating, and I do not think I can forgive her for playing with my mother's emotions. My mother had "the talk" with my father and Ms. Zand a few times and told them that their behavior was inappropriate. I never understood how Ms. Zand could flirt with our father and still look at us children in the eye.

There were two units on the third floor. One was owned by a family of four. The father was a government employee, and the mother was a teacher. They had two daughters that were a couple of years apart, around the same age as my two older brothers. The father of the family was a very religious man who would not even look a woman in the eye as he conversed with her. He would go to the mosque across the street several times per day for obligatory prayers. He even had a light brown, round mark in the middle of his forehead, about the size of a quarter, which was an indication of his long and intense prayers and prostrations[20] at the mosque. They were from the northwest part of the country, and had the same dialect as my father's mother, Azeri. It was hard for me to understand what they were talking about at times since they had a thick Azeri accent. Their daughters were very beautiful and were not as religious as their parents. Sometimes I stayed at their house after school or when my mother left the apartment to run an errand.

The apartment on the third floor across the hall from the Azeri family was owned by a man who actually never lived in his apartment, Mr. Amir Ghasemi. His apartment was always rented out, and the tenants changed every so often. I think it was interesting that for almost twenty years, over six families lived in that apartment. Mr. Amir Ghasemi had some walking issues, and he used a cane. When he was too ill to come to the building, his son took care of most of the rental agreements and

---

20 Traditionally among Shias, which is a major sect of Islam, the forehead is pressed on a dried clay during prostration.

maintenance. Mr. Amir Ghasemi never took off his special shoes when he walked on our Persian rugs during the quarterly building meetings. This upset my mom, but she never mentioned a word because she knew that he needed to wear them to walk evenly. There were a lot of families that rented Mr. Amir Ghasemi's apartments, and we befriended them. One family had a few sons, the youngest of whom had green eyes, which is not common in Iran, and who was a year younger than me. My mom used to give me a cup full of shelled, raw pistachios and yellow raisins and send me down to play with him. There was another family that had a little girl around the same age on the second floor. For a while a bucket, tied to a rope, would travel from the fourth, to the third, and then the second-floor balconies so we could all trade toys.

Another family that occupied Mr. Amir Ghasemi's apartment had three or four large, muscular boys who spent a lot of time at the gym. They became good friends with my brothers, and every time my brothers got into a fight with each other, my mom sent me downstairs to get the neighbor's sons to help break up the fight.

The neighbors who lived on the fourth floor across the hall from us had six children: three girls and three boys. They were around the same age as my oldest brother, and they all grew up to either become or marry doctors. They were from the northern part of Iran and were smart friendly people with kind attitudes. I have a lot of good memories from their house. We were invited to their children's weddings, and their grandchildren would come by years later so I could babysit them. I loved their whole family and have good memories from that neighbor.

Most of my friends lived across Sattar Khan Street, and I had to ask my parents or brothers to escort me to their neighborhood if I wanted to visit with them. I did not know anyone from school that lived on the same side of the street as we did. My parents did not have time to take me across whenever I wanted, so I would go whenever my mother had a chance or had something to do in that neighborhood.

A little girl was not allowed to walk on the street without an adult, especially on the side of or crossing a major street. There were many cases of kidnapping where children would be found dead somewhere in an alley or outside of the city. Many times, they were found to have been raped and their hearts or kidneys were cut out and sold on the black market. For this reason, most of my childhood was spent on the fourth floor of the apartment, isolated, playing on the balcony or in the room I shared with my youngest brother.

The best part of my childhood was when my youngest brother taught me how to ride a bicycle in the alley behind our building. He held the back of the bicycle and asked me to pedal and keep the handles straight. I was still very young and did not have to wear hijab. Since I was a skinny and short girl, no one could tell I was already ten years old.

The bicycle had healing powers for me because the act of cycling calmed me down and mentally took me to a happy place, where I was in control of my destination. Even though it was hard for a girl to ride her bicycle living in a Muslim country, I did not give it up. I kept my hijab in place and rode my bicycle on the back streets of Tehran, even though there was always the chance of getting caught by the volunteer moral police. I was always careful and would try to avoid busy streets, out of fear of getting arrested by the police. They would have confiscated my bicycle and arrested me for the sole reason of riding a bicycle on the street. Girls were not allowed to ride bicycles after they had reached puberty, about nine years old. Of course, boys could do whatever they wanted, and there were not many limitations. According to the government, a woman riding a bicycle was arousing to men, which is more insulting to a man than to a woman. The Islam that the Iranian government had made up placed no trust in men and had to put woman in a tight bubble, so the men did not misbehave.

ALADDIN GENERATION

Sometimes I inherited clothes from my older cousins. I did not mind what other people thought about me wearing used clothes, but I could tell that my mother was unhappy to see me wear hand-me-downs. We simply had to save money since our big family had one stream of income and after war economy was very unstable. Packages coming from Switzerland and America, where some of my maternal cousins lived, always had a heavenly aroma. It smelled like freedom, equality, and quality of life beyond everyone's imagination. We always thought that we had just received the best fabric. No other fabric from Iran would be as good as the one from America. Since the chocolate bar incident, I had learned not to ask for anything because I could not bear to see my mother's defeated reaction if we could not afford what I desired at the time. My brothers did not feel the same, therefore their wishes would be met.

Right after the revolution it was difficult for a mother raising four kids, three of whome were boys, with a man whose mind was not committed to the family. Raising us in that situation was a hard task, and I admire my mother's courage and determination. I talk about my mother more than my father, not because I do not care about him or feel he never did anything for us. I know that he loved us, but he never expressed his love for us. My mother did often and left no doubt.

My mother's oldest and youngest sisters had left the country shortly after the revolution. The religious police in Iran were persecuting all the

Bahá'ís in Iran, sending them to jail, and confiscating all of their possessions. The religious police seized all the property from my mother's oldest and youngest sisters, and their husbands were sentenced to prison for years.

My aunts and their family escaped the country, crossing the Pakistani border on the back of a donkey with $100 in their pockets. They lived in hard conditions for nearly two years, until they received their visas, one to move to America and the other to Switzerland. At this point, my mother had lost her father, and two of her sisters had moved out of the country. Everyone in my mother's family had lost their jobs and could not find work anywhere, despite their education, all due to their religion.

My generation, born in the 1980s, is known as the burnt generation. We did not have a Shah, but rather a new regime trying to establish itself with empty promises in the middle of a war fought by teenagers and volunteer soldiers. There were many days that we did not have food, water, electricity, gas, or a consistent school system, not to mention anything remotely fun. Most children my age did not have fathers or brothers to take care of them as they were lost during the war or revolution. There was virtually no government program to aid the families of the war martyrs or veterans. We were not showered with gifts for any graduations, achievements, or talents because our parents did not have a lot of saving, struggling to make ends meet, and besides that graduating from high school was the least we could do.

One day, soon after my third brother was born, my mother's supervisor asked her to either write down that she was a Muslim or she would lose her job. She did not want to lie about her religion or convert to Islam; therefore, she submitted her letter of resignation. Her supervisor knew that he would not be able to find another case worker with my mother's skills and drive, so he did not accept my mother's letter of resignation for two years after she had submitted it. My mother was one of many Bahá'ís who were let go or forced to resign from their jobs because of their religion.

The Islamic Republic of Iran put all Bahá'ís out of jobs and denied them access to higher education. Luckily, my father worked for the government or we would have struggled to have the necessary things to live as did many others. I considered our family to be middle class, and we felt fortunate considering the circumstances.

Even though my mother wanted to practice her religion, she had to prioritize the health of her marriage, therefore she stopped attending Bahá'í gatherings after the revolution. My father was against her or any of us children attending the Bahá'í gatherings. In order to make me ready for the unjust Islamic Republic of Iran, she even sent me to the mosque across the street every summer to learn how to read the Quran.

We, the 1980s generation, learned how to be considerate of others from early childhood and that not everyone could afford to have a nice pen, fancy notebook, or new shoes. We learned not to judge or bully others. My family could not afford everything that they wanted; we were struggling a lot, just like the others.

The 1980s generation grew up standing in long lines while holding onto the food supply coupons that each family would receive based on the number of people in their household. Sometimes my mother would sell the coupons to the men standing in front of the grocery stores, and she would use the money for something else. We would not use a lot of sugar in our household, so my mother would trade her sugar coupons for rice or just sell them for cash. Purchasing rationed sugar, rice, and some other items without a coupon would cost a lot of money, therefore there was a black market for the coupons.

One thing of which I am very proud is the Iranians' willingness to take and defend their rights. We were not handed our civil rights, but we take them when we see fit. Yet in our buses women are forced to sit in the back, behind men, and have fewer designated seats in the bus than men did. Even though more women used the bus, because it was not common for them to own a car, they were forced to stand in the back as the men sat in the front in comfort and had plenty of empty seats. I remember standing in the back of the bus due to lack of seating for women, staring at men sitting in their comfortable seats facing the back of the bus, spreading their legs wide open, to let their private parts cool as they enjoyed the view of tired, suppressed women forced to be covered in black hijab and endure the heat of the summer.

I grew up in a country where no one believed in lines or respecting other people's personal space in public. Many times, I witnessed my mother shout at the government employees to get her coupons on time or to get an appointment with an important figure to have her legal documents signed. It was hard to get anything done in Iran since the government employees were not interested in any work that would not benefit themselves one way or the other. One either had to bribe one's way through, or plan on spending the next few years trying to get approvals on legal documents.

Post-war life in Iran was difficult. Electricity would disconnect without any notice, and we never knew when service would return. My mother or father had to buy propane capsules and carry them to the fourth floor, our apartment, so my mother could cook food for us. When there was no gas available, my mother would use the Aladdin[21]. My mother would bring it to the middle bedroom and turn it on to keep us warm in the cold winters. She would use the heat to warm the room and cook soup, turnips, or beets as snacks or sometimes even dinner. The smell of cooking soup or

---

21 Aladdin was a brand of oil lamp commonly used for heating in the 1980s

turnips were better than actually eating them. Sometimes we would gather around and use the dim light from the Aladdin to complete our homework.

We were told to use the daylight to complete our homework and studying because at night we never knew if we would have electricity. Some nights we would just fall asleep next to the warm Aladdin in the middle of the room. The heat source brought my family together during the winters, and I loved every time my mother fired up the Aladdin and brought the family in the small middle room. To this day, if I can travel back in time for one day, I would go to one of the nights when we lost electricity, my mother was cooking turnips for the family that had gathered in the small middle room, using the Aladdin. No electricity, no cell phones, no worldly distractions, as my brothers sat around the room and made small talk. Most importantly, that was before all the bad things started to happen in our family.

Our apartment building was also equipped with a radiator. Of course, living on the fourth floor the radiator water was not as warm and our apartment would take a long time to heat up. Sometimes we would just gather next to the radiator with a thick blanket and pillow and fall asleep. I remember many times I fell asleep next to the radiator while doing homework or studying for an upcoming test.

As kids we would get invited to birthday parties, which were segregated by gender. After the revolution, girls and boys would attend separate schools, but kindergarten was a mix of boys and girls. I understand that ideally students would be more focused on schoolwork instead of the opposite sex, but in practice, teenagers would become obsessed with the opposite sex and think they were a completely different species. This was not healthy. Female students all wore uniforms all the way up to college, and male students up until they reached middle school, where they could then wear casual clothing. The benefit of wearing a uniform was that we knew what we had to wear every day and it would minimize the amount of time spent getting ready or shopping for new outfits. It also prevented jealousy or shame among the teenage girls in school, since poor and rich, all wore the same uniform.

Compulsory education in Iran was full of misinformation and deceit. To this day, I am still learning that many things we were taught were inaccurate. We were cut off from the other nations and isolated, without any internet, but this horrible situation and misrepresentation of the world does not compare to North Korea's situation.

The non-Islamic Persian history was cut so short that it seemed insignificant compared to the recent revolutionary history. The ratio seemed to be one book of Persian history for every several books just about the 1979 revolution and how Khomeini came to the Iranians' rescue, or as we know it, came to power. I was convinced that I knew everything about the recent revolution because books would not lie but as it turns out, the writers of almost all of our books were revolutionary successors working for Khomeini. After the revolution, all textbooks were changed to portray the new revolution as the best thing that happened to Iran in a long time.

It was not until recent years that I learned that Khomeini's paternal family had migrated from India, which is something that was never discussed in textbooks. I believe that his mother was from Iran and he lost his father, who was from India, just a few months after his birth so he was raised by his mother and aunt. He did not grow up in a stable, normal, family and yet we were forced to scream at the top of our lungs every day, singing songs and pledging our allegiance to the supreme leader of Iran, a man with daddy issues.

The overall history that we were taught in school is pretty worthless in terms of understanding Iran's history, let alone the world's. We were simply fed lies about the current Iranian regime, how horrible the Shah was, and how much better it was without him. There was a big emphasis on the history of the Islamic wars between Prophet Muhammad, Ali and his sons, the Khalifs and non-believers. We had to memorize the names of wars, where they took place, and who won the battles and how. No one ever explained why the wars were initiated and how they could have been avoided so hundreds of men and women did not have to die or be traumatized just because there was a new Prophet on earth. Plus, knowing all of Islam's war history never came handy in situations such as lack of electricity or food scarcity. No one ever magically gave us electricity because we recited the Quran or knew the Islamic wars inside and out.

Being a woman, growing up in Iran, it was hard to navigate through the society, plan for the future, and be positive and hopeful when there was no mention of women or their accomplishments in history. No one empowered women or praised them for their deeds. Women were considered evil beings that lured men into making bad decisions. In Islam, only women who were fighting for Islam were mentioned and praised, such as the Prophet Muhammad's wife and daughter. Women were not discussed as much as were the men and their place in the society. Men held a special place in society and religion since they were portrayed as the more complete sex. Even in my paternal family, since my brothers were the three men out of the five male grandchildren, who would carry the last name for the next generation, they were praised and encouraged over the women in the family. No one judged the men for their bad decisions or behavior, but no matter how much education women had, they could not measure up to the men because they would never be as useful as men were.

Our family was used to having conversations about the Shah at family and friend's dinner parties. My mother was disappointed in the decision that Iranians made to remove the Shah, though my father was very happy. After the Shah left, many religious minorities were forced to sit at home, leave their jobs or get fired, flee their country, or worst of all executed. It is absolutely heart-breaking when you are forced to leave your own country for your safety, just because of your beliefs, but the Muslims were either unaware of the consequences that minorities had faced after the revolution or did not care because it did not impact them.

In the 1980s and '90s in Iran, people did not have much to do for entertainment. They either watched sad stories on TV or hung out at each other's houses to avoid getting into trouble in public for silly reasons such as lack of hijab or on some occasions even laughing out loud. Many weekends we would get together with family or friends and just hang out in our homes. Women would sit together, to gossip, cook, bake, knit warm clothes for the kids, or sew the bedsheets and pillow covers. Men would sit together, drink tea, smoke cigarettes, and play cards or backgammon. Men would often get loud and trash talk one another during the games, and women would mostly cater tea and pastry for their husbands, as that was a sign of a loyal and committed wife.

My dad knew a lot of card tricks and would entertain our guests with those tricks, or by reading their fortunes. It is very normal for Iranians to drink Turkish coffee and ask someone who is experienced to read their fortune using the patterns shaped by the residuals of coffee in the cup. My father was actually very good at fortune-telling, and many things that he said to people later came true. He never read my fortune. I wonder if he knew the things that were about to happen to his own family.

BLACK-AND-WHITE CHUBBY TV

I was close to death multiple times. One time right after I was born, I had a high fever and my paarents took me to the hospital; they did not even admit me to the emergency department because they said I was most likely going to die. After my parents screamed and fought with the nurses, they finally admitted me to the hospital and saved my life. Another time I almost fell from the fourth-floor balcony. I was only two years old; someone must have left the balcony door open, and I had gone to the balcony and climbed to the other side of the balcony's railing. Once my mother saw me, she called for my father to come and grab me because she thought she did not have the courage to grab me without scaring me into falling down. One time during a minor surgery, as I was under anesthesia, my heart had stopped beating and the doctors wanted to pronounce me dead. After all of that, I believe I had to stay alive for some reason.

The nights when I would have a fever, my mom would take me to the one and only bathroom we had and put my feet in a red plastic container filled with cool water. She would feed me chilled watermelon to bring down my fever, and I would spit out the thick, black watermelon seeds in the red plastic bucket and would play with them as though they were fishes in a pond. My poor mother was probably exhausted, taking care of four children all by herself. I am sure my father took us to the doctor and cared for us too, but I do not have a memory of him doing so.

I felt guilty when I would get sick because my mother had so much to take care of around the house, let alone take care of her sick daughter. She took me to dental clinics starting at a very young age. We could not afford private dentists, so she took me to the inexpensive public clinic where dental students would practice in the presence of a more senior dentist. I remember days when we would get on the public bus and go to the dentist. Sometimes my mother would buy me crackers after the appointment was finished, since they were tasty and soft to chew on. We usually waited for what seemed like forever to be seen, as it was first-come, first-served, and I hated the smell in that large clinic. My mother did everything she possibly could for the four of us, and I do not know where she got the energy to deal with all of the personal, marital, and social problems.

The fall after I had turned six years old my father took me with him to work and told me I would be spending time with other kids around my age. His office had always offered free daycare and kindergarten for the employees' children but for some reason he had not mentioned this to my mother when my brothers were younger. Therefore, they never attended any daycare. When my mother heard from my father's co-worker's wife about the free kindergarten just as I had just turned six, she was furious that my father had never told her about this free service, and she told him that he had to take me to work with him every day.

I was very scared of being left alone at the kindergarten the first day and asked my dad to stay with me. I felt betrayed as if my mother was trying to get back at my father and that was why she sent me to kindergarten. My father said he would not leave me alone and would sit nearby until I was done playing with the other kids; of course, he just fooled me and left after a while without saying goodbye. I was distracted by the other kids making balls out of old newspaper and shooting them in a basketball hoop. I cried a lot that day and wanted to go after my dad. The daycare employees held me and forced me to stay there all day. My father picked me up after work. I was very unhappy about being left alone, abandoned, without him visiting throughout the day. How could I ever trust him again?

I attended kindergarten for a year and found many good friends who I remember very well. Sometimes I wonder if they remember me or ever think of me. I had a classmate, Amir, who used to bully me all the time. I remember his face very clearly. I wonder if he ever feels bad or even remembers the things he did to me when we were kids. I also had another classmate, Yashar, who was a sweetheart and took care of me at the daycare. Every afternoon we were all forced to take a nap. I still do not know why we were forced to sleep in the middle of the day; it just made me more tired. Maybe the teachers had to take a break from us and rest too. One afternoon during nap time Yashar held my hand and asked if I would marry him when we grew up. That is the first marriage proposal I can remember. I know a lot of kids do these things and say when they grow up, they will marry one another. I had said yes.

When I finished kindergarten, we had a celebration that our parents attended. They played live music, and we sang the songs we had learned throughout the year. The music program was led by a man who would come to our kindergarten every week and play keyboard and sing for us. We learned his songs and practiced at home while listening to the audio cassette recorded by him. I still remember some of the songs he taught us. One was about how the police were awake at night, keeping us safe while we were asleep. I would sing this song to every policeman I ran into as a child, and it made all of them very happy that a child loved them.

Kindergarten graduation was the last time I saw Yashar. As I was growing up, I never asked about him, but when I started high school, I asked my father several times to request the daycare to find him for me. I went to the daycare once when I was a teenager, in high school, by myself to look for the files; but they could not find our class list, too much time had passed by and they had disposed of the files. All I needed was his father's name, since he worked in the same company as my father did, and then I could find him. I was not looking for him to cash in on his marriage proposal, I just wanted to see him and see if he remembered me. Maybe he still thinks about the day he proposed to me. Maybe he is married now and tells his daughter or son the story of his first proposal during naptime in kindergarten.

My father drove on the back roads to work every morning to avoid traffic. I would sit in the back, and sometimes he would give rides to people waiting for taxis, to make extra cash. Most of the time he would give a ride to my kindergarten teacher. She was tall and beautiful and very friendly with my father, and she never paid for rides. My father would talk to her and laugh out loud while driving her to work. I told my mother that dad was such a generous man, giving free rides to my friendly kindergarten teacher. They had a major fight over that, and although I did not understand why then, I do now.

Sometimes, for major Islamic events, my mom and I would go to the mosque across the street. She did not have a temple to go to for practicing her religion since the Islamic Republic regime had demolished the Bahá'í temples after gaining power. I liked going to the mosque because I would get to see my friends who lived in the same neighborhood. During the offered summer classes at the mosque, I could hang out with my friends. Obviously, all of these classes were gender segregated as we were being prepared for the unequal future.

Sometimes there would be Islamic events to celebrate the birth or death of an Imam. During this time, many would make a pact with God that if they were granted a wish, they would donate food or money to the mosque or to those in need. For example, if they had a sick relative, they would make a pact with God that if this person recovered, they would sacrifice a sheep and give away the meat to the poor or donate some money to some cause. Sometimes we were fed at the mosque on different holidays, and I enjoyed that very much. The most famous and easy type of donation in exchange for a granted wish was to donate one's time to give away Ajil Moshkel Gosha, a mix of nuts, raisins, and chickpeas, that would be wrapped in fancy lace fabric and distributed to other members of the mosque.

I dreaded having to go to the mosque for someone's death memorial. Muslims would cry and mourn so much that it was traumatizing. Unfortunately, many of my paternal family members passed away when I was a young teenager, and I have many of these memories. I truly disliked the mourning and annoying preachers at the mosque because they would make the women sit separate from the men and treat women as if they had to serve the men. Plus, no one was listening to the preacher anyway. Men and women were there to eat the sacrificed food and take some home to freeze for future meals. I soon learned that hungry men have no ear for the preacher.

Nobody at the mosque knew that my mother was not Muslim, and it could have been a complete disaster if they found out. They would probably cut off our heads right in front of the mosque, or order the mosque to be bleached, since Bahá'í's were considered unclean. At home my father would nag and disapprove of my mom for saying her prayers in her own bedroom. Sometimes, when I was with my mother's family members around the time of a Bahá'í celebration, they would take me to their gatherings. They would most often picnic in a valley or forest where they would not be seen by Muslims. My father would not have approved of me going to Bahá'í events, and this was kept as a secret.

As a child I learned that Persian rugs are more than their famed beauty and quality. They were the center of many activities. I learned to use the flowers on the rug as a garden for dolls and the lines along the edges of the rug as streets for the mini cars. In the summers, I would cover the balcony with some cotton bed sheets with the help of my youngest brother, and I would bring a small rug and pretend our shelter was our little house. I would invite the rest of the family for dinner and was in charge of making the rice for the family dinner and lighting the balcony tent with some light bulbs resembling Christmas light decorations. I would find pillows for everyone to sit comfortably as they snacked on the fruits and food my youngest brother and I had prepared. Out of all the memories I have, I have not forgotten this one because it brought our big family physically close together. I knew they would not stay for long and would want to leave my childish game as soon as possible. These short moments that probably meant little to them, meant the world to me.

I loved plants and was always on a mission to grow something, but our small and long balcony, located on the fourth floor, could not support much vegetation. No plants besides the gigantic cactus that my father had, or his Sansevieria[22], would grow on our balcony. He had at least thirty Sansevieria pots, and every year he would replace the soil. He usually asked me to help him with this process as he waited until the weather was not too cold for the Sansevieria roots to be exposed. I now understand how much joy he got from growing these plants, and he sure passed that joy and passion for growing plants to me. I noticed that every year in the spring they would bloom tiny flowers and their flowers would give out a sweet, honey-like paste that attracted small ants into the house. I know how it tasted because I had tried tasting it myself.

My mother forced me to take a nap every afternoon if I was not at school. I was good at keeping quiet when people were asleep, but she wanted me to actually sleep, which was very difficult. I thought it was unfair to be forced to sleep in the afternoons, but now that I am older, I know she wanted me to sleep to keep me out of trouble. She was afraid I would touch the gas stove or get involved with my youngest brother and

---

22 Snake plant

his mostly destructive quests. I always found some activity to do that did not make noise but mostly just observed my brother, who also refused to take naps, from under the blanket, instead of participating in his afternoon plans. Boys did not have to do what they were told, but girls were expected to obey their parents, regardless of what they thought. It was a way to train our brains to take orders from an early age so that when we would get married, we would take orders from our husbands, which would guarantee a happy future.

We had a large and heavy, black-and-white TV when I was in kindergarten. It did not have a remote control, so we had to turn it on or off, adjust the volume, and change the channels using the knobs next to the screen. There were only two television channels at that time, so we mostly adjusted the volume when it was on. When I was in elementary school, my mother, her sister, my cousins and I went to Kish[23] to buy a color TV with a larger screen and a remote control.

At the time, Kish was a port for Chinese and other foreign products and Iranians would go there to purchase foreign branded goods. We mostly looked for American or German products because we thought they had the best quality, but China was a big exporter to Iran. The color TV was soon opened and inspected by my younger brother, because he was curious to know the difference between the skinny, new, color TV with a battery-operated remote control, versus the old chubby, black-and-white TV. He waited until my mother was out of the house one day and just the two of us were at home. My mother was not pleased when she came home and saw TV parts scattered across the floor. We were both in trouble, though I did not help him.

My mother was good at making financial decisions and never counted on the money my father brought home. She wanted to stay an

---

23 An island in the Persian Gulf

independent woman and could not get used to staying home after she lost her job. I think her desire to work and feel equal to my father was one of her weaknesses, yet so powerful. She was always looking for better deals to save money, but instead she should have let my father feel the need for more income to support the big family he helped create. She was always updating the furniture and buying better and newer technology for the house with her own money that she had saved up.

We never asked our dad for help or talked to him about our needs. He did not have a gentle attitude, and we did not want to start a fight. We would always go to my mother for help with everything. If we needed money, school supplies, or homework assistance we would ask my mother. My father would usually act so upset and disappointed, and he would start comparing us with other kids in the family or circle of friends that our joy and creativity were extinguished. In his opinion we had no talent and needed to catch up to his sister's and brother's children. He did not understand that we each were unique in our own way.

As a child, I did not receive much guidance from my parents. My father was always gone, tired, or busy with his work, and my mother was always worried about saving money and feeding us healthy food. My brothers were usually busy with their friends and short-term goals. I often sewed cute little Barbie outfits that were never noticed at home until my mother's friend, Shahin, complimented me on my sewing skills. Shahin was a talented and experienced seamstress herself. I wrote short stories and poetry often but did not receive encouragement; instead, I was made fun of every time I said I wanted to become a writer. Writing was not considered a job in Iran at the time, and I believe people around the world still do not consider it a decent job. I felt that I had the artistic talent, but no one's help or support in channeling my talent the right path to succeed. My parents' generation were mostly in survival mode, month to month; artistic talents were not much appreciated.

JINN DETECTIVE

The fall after I turned seven years old, it was time to begin elementary school. I was not happy about being away from home and my mother. I had the experience of being away from home while in kindergarten and was not ready to do this all over again. On a positive note, elementary school was only a half-day, unlike kindergarten, and we were not forced to take naps or brush our teeth after lunch. I had a brand-new, colorful backpack and a navy-blue uniform that consisted of long pants and an oversized button-up shirt, which looked like a lab coat with large buttons, which covered my body up to below my knees. I wore this uniform every day with a white head scarf that would cover my hair, neck, shoulders, and even some parts of my chin. We had to cover our hair with a hijab and pretend it was fashionable.

I felt important for the first couple of months when I was wearing a head scarf, as I felt that I was becoming an important member of society or contributing to some sort of goodness by wearing the hijab. That feeling wore off before long, and it became annoying to be forced to wear my hijab and leave it on, even in the all-girls school. Under Islamic law girls are not obligated to wear a hijab before the age of nine, yet we were forced to begin at age seven, upon the start of elementary school, which felt very inconsistent and unfair. The interesting part was that as soon as we would leave the premises of elementary school, we would all push our hijabs back and let our hair loose.

Every year before the first day of school, which also began on the first day of fall, my father wrapped my textbooks and notebooks with thick and ugly clear plastic wrapping and sewed them to my book covers. He was concerned that our books would come apart throughout the school year and we would lose some pages. He did not care that I was bullied by some of my classmates because of how hideous my books looked. There was only one way, and it was his way.

Our elementary school had two shifts, one in the morning and one in the afternoon. I was part of the morning shift throughout elementary school, which began at 7:45 in the morning, six days per week. We were taught three subjects each day and were given two fifteen-minute recesses in between the classes. We followed the curriculum very strictly throughout the entire school year. There were no orientations or fun activities during the first day or week of school that I remember. Every day we finished at 12:40 in the afternoon, and there was no after-school program. We did not do any homework at school and had to bring our books to and from school every day. During elementary school, we would have a different teacher each year and that one teacher would teach all subjects except the sports class. We only had one session throughout the week that was dedicated to sports, and we usually practiced basketball, volleyball, or we ran around the very small yard.

It never occurred to me that we were separated from boys nor did it ever bother me. I believe we focused more on schoolwork without having boys as distractions. Sometimes if the classroom was too hot, we would push our scarves off of our heads to rest on our neck and shoulder. The breeze from outside, or from the ceiling fans would cool us off. We never completely removed our head scarves in case the only man working at our school passed by in the hallway or came to the classroom for maintenance unannounced, which never happened. We also had to cover our hair just in case a classmate's father came to the school, which is bizarre now that I think about it. They had daughters that went to school with us, why would they care about my hair? How sick was it to think that my hair would arouse my classmate's father?

Elementary school boys wore shorter lab coat-like uniforms with matching long pants, and they had male and female teachers. All of the girls-only school staff were female, other than the one man who would take care of the school maintenance work. We were not offered health or sex education classes that taught us about boys during the twelve years of elementary, middle, and high school, nor was this an acceptable topic to talk about at home or school, so that just left the journey to and from school for this subject among ourselves. In our minds, boys were from a different planet, a separate species, getting involved with whom was forbidden, and we were brainwashed to avoid them as if we were dodging bullets in a video game.

We would always walk to school or get a ride from a parent. Sometimes my mother walked with me, other times I walked alone. I believe for the first one or two years of school, my mother walked with me back and forth every day. I feel guilty that she spent so much time and effort to escort me back and forth to school, but there was no school bus. Neither the school nor government would allow students to ride their bicycles to and from school. There was no bike rack to park bicycles, and riding a bicycle was an unacceptable act for a girl anyway. I still find it extremely odd that a seemingly harmless and normal act such as a child riding a bicycle was sexualized, as if all Muslim men were uncontrollable child molesters.

As children growing up in Iran, we were exposed to religion, mostly Islam, constantly. Teachers and staff would scare us of Jinn, or evil spirits, to the point of having nightmares. They would tell us that a Jinn looks like a human and exists and walks amongst us, but we did not know who they were. They looked human, but their feet resembled sheep or goat hooves, and some of them had tails as well. They would tell us Islamic tales about a

Jinn that would bear a message or a lesson, but the message would get lost between all the frightening details they made sure to emphasize.

I had many nightmares about Jinn, and I could not even go to the bathroom in the middle of the night because we were told that Jinns dance in the bathrooms during the night. Many times, I dreamt of a Jinn following me around, given away by its goat-like feet, but I was never strong enough to defeat it. This was unfair, to be exposed to this nonsensical superstition. We knew that the stories were fake, but we were still intimidated because there were many sources that confirmed their existence, from teachers, to classmates, and even the Quran. I often stared at people's feet to check if they were human feet or hooves. I paid close attention to their shoes and tried to estimate the size of their feet inside of their shoes. I started with my own family members, then friends, and then neighbors. My friends and I would speculate about the physical characteristics of these Jinn and argue about their existence, aims, and behavior patterns. I felt that I was developing into quite a Jinn detective, if that had only been a real career, I would have been very well-practiced.

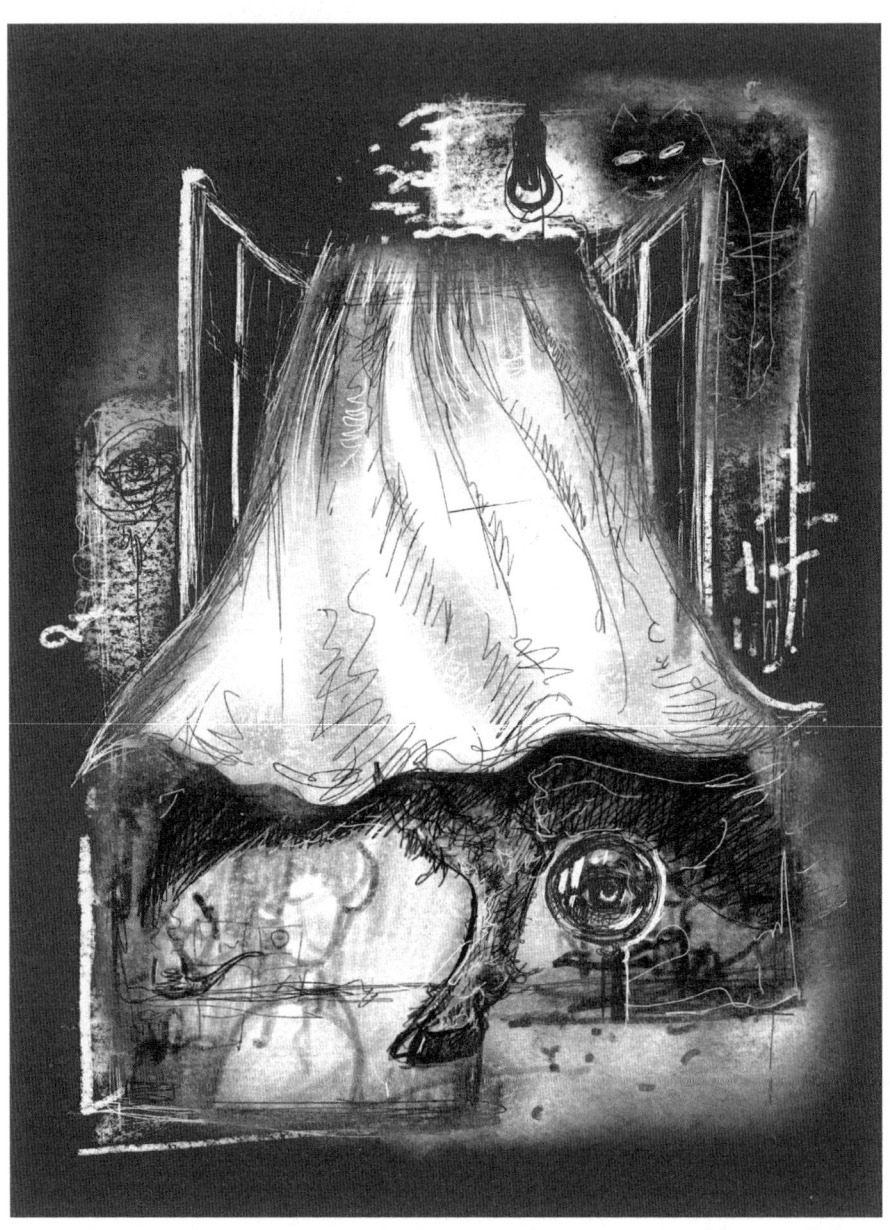

Our teachers were very strict, to the point that we were not allowed to use the restroom without their permission and were never allowed to eat food or chew gum in the classroom. They scared us and warned us of the consequences of skipping our daily obligatory prayers or of eating during the fasting month. They taught us that God's angels would ask us questions during our first night spent in our burial tombs. The questions to be asked would be whether or not we read all of the obligatory prayers, five times a day, fasted for the entire month of Ramadan[24], respected our parents, teachers, and elders, and if we lied or harmed any living thing. They raised us in fear, and it was not a healthy, spiritual, pleasing relationship, nor did it help us build a healthy connection between us and God.

All that fear and all those threats did not encourage us to pray, fast, or be good for the sake of God or humanity. If anything, we were only motivated to avoid trouble and cruel tortures in hell after our deaths. I did not like that our intentions were misguided. We were afraid of hell because it was described as a terrifying and hot place where we would be tortured physically and emotionally, and would have to live in a state of starvation. Hell was a place where the devil would pour molten lava in your mouth if you had lied, or poke your eyes with searing-hot rods if you had looked at things you should not have looked at, such as pornographic pictures, videos, or men who were not your husband, brother, or father. Where was the healthy loving relationship between God and his creation? Where was the love of and closeness to God? We were motivated mostly by the fear of hell rather than by love for humanity and God, and were not allowed to question it or to discuss our own opinions.

There was nothing to encourage me to go to heaven. Heaven was filled with rivers of wine and unlimited food, which contradicted what we were allowed to have here on earth, according to Islam. I did not like

---

24 Ninth month of the Islamic calendar where Muslims fast during the entire month.

eating in general, therefore I did not have an interest in going to heaven where there was plenty of lavish food. Men were promised the seventy-two female virgins and an unlimited amount of sexual pleasure, but there was no pleasure promised to us women. It seemed like even in God's heaven, men and women would be treated differently. If Islam's God was sexist, why would I want to be close to him? There were all of these laws and rules for women and almost none for men. If a man would feel excited by me, I would go to hell, not him, as if I had the power to provoke his desires. If he would get aroused by my hair, they would hang me by my hair in hell, and if he was excited by the curves of my body, I would have to suffer eternal physical torture. There were almost no rules for men to keep their excitement under control, or to suppress their animal desires and purify their hearts and intentions. I had to cover my hair and body to protect my spot in heaven, the heaven clearly made to satisfy and adore men. I was sure that if there was a heaven, all of us women would have to serve men in it. There was no reward for being a good woman in this world or the next.

As the month of Ramadan would approach, the whole school would be decorated. Some days the decorations were black, since Ali, the first Imam of Shias, was killed during this month. The students, had to decorate the school for most of the religious and national holidays. The definition of holidays had changed after Shah left. Year-round we crafted decorations to be hung for Ramadan, Palestine Day, the anniversaries of the deaths or births of the Prophet Muhammad or the Shia Imams, Islamic Republic Day, the anniversary of the day that Khomeini entered Iran after the Shah left, the day that Khomeini died, and many more Islam- or revolution-related dates.

After the revolution the birthday of Imam Ali[25] was celebrated as Father's Day, and his wife Fatimah's birthday[26] was celebrated as Mother's

25 First Imam of the Shia Muslim Sect, and fourth and last caliph of Sunnis.
26 Prophet Muhammad's daughter from his wife Khadijah Bint Khuwaylid.

Day. For all of these holidays, I stood side-by side with my classmates in the schoolyard, and we would be forced to yell as loud as we could, "God is great," "death to Shah," "death to America," and "death to Israel." This ritual was very common and done on an almost daily basis. We had to listen to recorded readings of the Quran, or a volunteer schoolmate chanting verses of Quran aloud in front of everyone in the schoolyard. It was like we were being brainwashed to hate the Western countries, "the enemies of Islam", on a daily basis.

Children of the 1980s generation, had two lives, one was in school, pretending to hate America, Israel, and England, and the other one was at home, where we watched American movies and music videos using satellite TV. We were brought up to pretend one way and be the other way, separate our personal feelings from our social life and image. We were two-faced hypocrites, who would dance to NSYNC and J.Lo but scream death to America on a daily basis.

During Ramadan, the school cafeteria would not sell any food. We were not allowed to drink water or eat food in the school common areas. This rule was not as strict in elementary school as it was in middle school. Therefore, whether or not I wanted to fast that day, I had to go hungry at school and eat when I returned home. If our teachers knew we were fasting, they would show us love and attention. I wanted their attentiveness as well, but I could not bring myself to fast. I was very skinny already and could not handle a full day without any food.

One morning, in middle school, the principal asked me if I was fasting and I told her yes, only to break down and eat a snack later. I felt guilty and ashamed because we were taught, trained, to feel those emotions if we ever showed weakness. They made us feel guilty and small if we were not praying, covering all of our hair, or fasting. Everyone at school just gave us constant guilt trips to urge us to follow the rules of Islam, so they could show the government they were raising the children of Islam. The kids who followed the Islamic rules were undoubtedly favored over the rest.

Anything that was not Islam-related was considered inappropriate. Cartoons that were not demonstrating the pain that Prophet Muhammad and his followers felt were deemed inappropriate. They would plant depression and sadness in our young hearts. My generation prefers to listen to sad songs instead of happy songs, I think, because we grew up around constant mourning and sorrow in a depressing school system and society after the revolution and war. Even the one day per year when our class was taken to see a movie, it had a depressing ending. These were the years immediately after the war after all, and there was much to grieve for the loss of our volunteer soldiers and ruined cities. I thought that we spent too much time mourning, and too little time building a better future for ourselves.

In recognition of Ramadan, our school would host an Eftari, which is a gathering to break the fast at sunset. We all had to participate with our parents. Some parents, including my mother, were on the school's parent committee board and they helped with these types of events. Of course they suspected my mother was a religious minority, but they never tried to single her out since she was very helpful and respected all Islamic laws and holidays. She was the open-minded member of the board and had great ideas for the betterment of the school.

Each year our school organized a multi-course buffet meal for Eftari, which included fruits, dates, tea, and traditional Persian noodle soup[27], cheese and walnut wraps, and some sort of traditional Persian pastry[28] normally served during the month of fasting. As children, we were happy as this was a big, celebratory event. We would put together plays and songs for breaking the fast, and I always volunteered for event planning and writing the plays and programs. I had the opportunity to cast and direct a play and

27 Ash-e-Reshteh.
28 Zoolbia and Bamia.

was the emcee for one of the Ramadan events in middle school. That same play was enacted several times at the neighborhood mosque the following summer, and I was empowered by my accomplishment.

On the school walls, both inside and outside, quotes of Khomeini, Imam Ali, and Prophet Muhammad were artistically written. Most elementary schools have a famous quote by Khomeini, "My hope is in elementary scholars." I do not know why he ever said that and what he meant! What did we the elementary scholars ever have to do with politics? Maybe he wanted to make future soldiers out of us and brainwash us to be his followers by projecting his hope on us at an early age.

In our house no one ever talked about politics. My mother, even though she had lost her job because of this new regime, talked positively about Khomeini all the time. She had disliked Khomeini for a very long time, but she had a vision on the day he died. The vision was of Khomeini walking toward her when she was standing in the kitchen. From that point forward, on the anniversary of Khomeini's death, my mother made Ash-e-Reshteh[29] and distributed it to the neighbors in his memory. She had made peace with him and maybe even forgave him for the damage he had done to the country and to her life.

We were taught in school that "America and England cannot do a damn thing" because we are protected by a higher force, Islam. We were taught a song that sang, "America, America, damn your trickery, the blood of our youth is dripping from your fist." We were brainwashed that everything negative happens because America and England are behind evil plans and want to take over our country and brainwash our youth with Westernization ideas such as rock and heavy metal music AKA evil music, freedom of religion or expression, art, any sort of equality, drugs and alcohol, and last but not least, sexualizing women. I personally agree with the

---

29 Persian rice noodle soup traditionally made when someone has made a pact with God.

last one, but Islam also did the same thing by promising men seventy-two virgins in heaven.

They made us believe that America and Israel are the two major enemies of Islam, Iran, and the world. They insisted that the injustices to the poor of the world or even to us in Iran, were because of the politics of the United States, the United Kingdom, and Israel. In their words, America was sucking the life out of other countries, "America, the world-eating country."

I was not aware firsthand of anything that America or Israel had done to us. Where could I verify their crimes? We were taught that America was taking all the opportunities from us and that we should yell "death to America" as loud as possible so they can hear us. They wanted us to take pride in hating other countries. In other words, we were encouraged to grow hate in our hearts for an entire nation. This was in contradiction to the teachings of Islam, the Quran, or Christianity, such as be nice to your neighbors and friends, and turn the other cheek if you were figuratively slapped in the face by an enemy. Teachers would sharply reprimand us if we raised controversial questions to them or classmates regarding Islam, the Islamic Republic of Iran, or the Prophet Muhammad in school.

Sometimes during the school day, our teacher would make us all go down in a big room and pray together. The room was called the "prayer room" and it was long and rectangular with some old, worn-out Persian rugs on the floor. We were told to wash our face, arms, and feet, a ritual before the obligatory prayer, then remove our shoes, and stand in several rows behind each other, and God would give us extra points because He loves those who sacrifice and standing in the back rows was a sacrifice. I always stood in the very back because I wanted as many points as possible.

I would start the year with one or two uniforms. Sometimes I would inherit uniforms from girls who had graduated a year or two earlier than me. If I outgrew the uniform during the school year, my mother sewed some fabric to the waist of my pants to extend the legs so I could get through the year without buying another expensive uniform. The head scarf was never comfortable and would tangle my long, straight, soft, dark brown hair. It was also very hot during the spring or summer if we attended extra classes offered by the school, mosque, or other institutions.

During the school year I could not do anything fun. I either had to be eating, sleeping, or studying, according to my mother's rule. I looked forward to summer because then I would bring out my dolls and play with them. It was tricky to play with my dolls and other toys as my mother did not want me to break them and I had to be extra cautious. After I started school and made friends I wanted to go to their homes and play, which again, I could not do because I did not have anybody to escort me to their house and I was not allowed to go anywhere by myself.

We only had one television, so being the youngest in the house and a girl, I was not allowed to choose channels. If I wanted to watch a VHS tape and nobody was there to play it for me, I was out of luck because I was not allowed to touch the VHS player by myself. I did like reading because it seemed pointless to read in the summer after spending the entire school year doing the same. Plus, in our house we were not encouraged to read books and expand our Farsi language or knowledge of Persian culture and poetry. My oldest brother tried to get me to read books, but I was not really interested in philosophy and religion. In my defense, I was in elementary school.

During the school year my mom would force me to do my brothers' chores in addition to my own because they were studying and needed more support than me. She would tell me that they would help me do my chores in the summer. It was not fair that I had to do everything at all times and not complain. I was the baby, and nobody had patience for me, nor cared about my needs. I was mentally trained to take orders and complete tasks; sometimes I felt like Cinderella. My mother treated her boys more importantly than me and gave them more attention. I needed someone to ask me if I was okay because I was not, I very much felt neglected during my childhood. I felt rejected by society as a girl, like I did not have much purpose, and was around only to please and serve men. We were encouraged to work and learn household chores so that one day we would make good housewives. This was during a time when society was changing, and women were trying to take on other more leading roles and responsibilities.

I will never forget my first day of elementary school. I had no idea who all the other kids were or where they came from. Even though I had gone to kindergarten, I had not gone to the park or the alley near to our house to play with other kids in the neighborhood. On the day of first grade registration, I made a friend, let us call her Tera. In the middle of the registration hall, through an ocean of kids and parents, we saw each other. We talked, who knows what about, and I vividly remember her face and that we wanted to be friends with each other. Sometimes I wonder what would have happened if we had not met each other or become friends. We would both have had very different lives. She was a good-hearted person who would always smile and share her school supplies and toys with me.

Tera and I ended up in the same first-grade class. I did not sit next to her during first grade. Instead I was assigned to sit next to Fatimah. My mom kept a secret about Fatimah for almost twenty years. I never knew she was adopted until I was in my twenties. Now I know why she was the only child, and her parents were so much older than my parents. She was shorter than me and had a dark complexion and hair. Her family owned a corner store that sold fruits and vegetables, and we would shop from them from time to time. Their house was located directly above her father's store and was on the path to school.

Every morning after I would walk to the newspaper stand and buy a *Hamshahri* newspaper for fifty Toman, to only read one short section of it on my way to school, I would cross the street using the overpass, and see

Fatimah through her bedroom window looking out and waiting for me. By the time I had crossed the overpass, she would be outside and standing in front of her apartment's front door, ready to walk to school with me. We had so much fun walking and talking on our way to and from school every day. We wished the walk would be longer so we could talk more. Tera would meet us on the way as we passed by her apartment. I wish I could go back to those days and carve those moments deeper into my memory, but some memories are still very vivid.

Soon after the school year began, I would go to either Fatimah's or Tera's house after school without informing my mother. She would get worried and call Tera's and Fatimah's homes looking for me, and after I returned home she would punish me by putting black pepper in my mouth and holding my mouth shut until my nose was burning. I stopped going to Tera's and Fatimah's house without her permission after a few times of tasting the Persian, raw and spicy black pepper powder. My mother was concerned about me and not pleased because not only did I not inform her beforehand and that was considered rude, but crossing a major street to get home was required and she was worried that I was run over by a car as I had the habit of not using the overpass and instead just crossed the major street of Sattar Khan on my own.

I did not share a class with Tera in second grade, so we met every recess and shared snacks. Sometimes she would show me her paintings or beautiful handwriting. I do not remember the subject of our recess conversations, but I am sure I did not tell her that my family was constantly fighting at home.

We soon became acquainted with two other classmates and ended up expanding into a circle of four friends who have kept in touch regularly since then. We met each other during every recess to spend time together, hung out after school, and when we were out for the summer, we met at each other's houses or participated in events at the mosque. It was easier for them to hang out with one another as I still needed an adult to escort me across Sattar Khan Street and into a different neighborhood I usually felt rushed when I was able to hang out with them.

I was a child yet found myself in many fights in elementary school. Classmates often made fun of my last name, and I would start by asking them to stop it, but the fights would get physical and turn into pulling each other's hijab off, and then pulling each other's hair. Thankfully I had thick hair. Ms. Ismayili, who lived at the school with her family of three and her husband were in charge of maintenance and the small food store in the yard, would sew the hijab back for me and tell me to not let the bullies bother me.

The school staff knew me by name, and fifteen years later when I walked into the same elementary school, Mr. and Ms. Ismayili remembered me and they reminisced about the head scarf events. Mr. Ismayili said I had not changed one bit and he would never forget me. I still dream about that school. I feel like I left my soul in it, and though it has changed throughout the years, I still love it. My mind still lives in the yard, the classrooms, and the cold winters of Tehran with no working heaters in our crowded and small classrooms. I met my best friends in that school. They grew to become strong, independent women and mothers of the future generation. We bonded for life and stuck together through thick and thin. Some nights when I close my eyes, I can imagine myself lying on the floor of the schoolyard, looking at the cloudy sky of Tehran. I want to fill my heart with the yard, the tilted asphalt floor, and the faded colors on the yard walls. We learned how to read and write, how to love and share in that school. We learned how friendships can last forever if you treat them right, and how to not judge one another based on income, looks, or weaknesses.

I had a friend in elementary school who was tall with a large facial bone structure. She was pretty but never tried to look feminine. She kept her hair short throughout the years, her uniform sleeves rolled up and always wore bulky shoes. She walked and talked like a boy. It was cool to have a friend so tall and muscular to protect us on the way home. One year her family moved to a new neighborhood, and she stopped attending our school. As the years passed and we continued on through school. We fell silent at the mention of her name because we had lost touch. Some tried to call, but she did not answer or return messages. One day, several years later, one of our classmates claimed to have seen her on the street wearing men's clothing and no hijab. Thinking back, she never talked about her crushes on the boys in the neighborhood, though we did not think anything of it because she never told us she was attracted to girls and even if she did, we would not know much about it due to lack of education. I asked around years after graduating high school, and my friends told me that she never dresses like nor considers herself a girl. I am just sad that she had to hide her true self from us for years. I loved her regardless of her sexual orientation and would not have thought any different than what I think now; I was a minority too and could have understood her pain of being different from the rest.

I was taught to respect all humankind, no matter what kind of financial status or physical appearance they may have. I tried to enlarge the circle of friends I had even though I was different from most of the other girls. I chewed my nails due to anxiety and did not wear the best shoes or carry the fanciest school bags. I did not have all the stickers and school supplies that others did but did not feel like I needed them to be successful. Most of my friends' parents were in their late twenties or early thirties, and my parents were in their forties. I had the cheapest notebooks that functioned just as well as the more expensive fancy notebooks that had a colorful hard cover displaying Disney cartoon characters. I did not want my mother to buy me more expensive school supplies that would make me look cool in front of my friends. I had learned my lesson when she left me on the street while I yelled "I want the chocolate bar!" I was clumsy and would lose school supplies on a weekly basis; therefore, my mother would punch a hole through the erasers, run a piece of yarn through it and hang it around my neck, but I would still manage to lose them.

At home, I was alert that we were financially cautious, and we did not receive rewards in return for house chores, as it was considered part of our responsibility. I saw that it was financially difficult for my mother to get us through the month and did not dare ask for an allowance. Occasionally, she gave us money and I would splurge on "Love Is" brand gum, which also included stickers that I would trade at school with my friends, or a fat, delicious chocolate ice cream cone from the little corner store near school on my way home. I still dream about that chocolate ice cream cone and can taste the sweetness of it in my mouth.

Another reason my mother would not give us money to buy snacks at school was because she did not approve of the chips and cheese puffs sold at the kiosk. She had a very clean, healthy diet herself and had seen remarkable results, and did not want us eating unhealthy snacks. My mom used to pack delicious and simple snacks for us that I never ate because I was rarely hungry. I did not eat much as a child, which probably did not help me grow out of being so skinny and short.

I knew that if I showed up at home after school, and my mom would see that I still had the snacks she gave me that morning in my bag, she would be angry, therefore I gave all of my snacks to Tera to finish them for me. I would skip breakfast and lunch and would eat very small dinners. While attending elementary school, during the winters, my mother made me a bread, butter, and sugar sandwich, which again, I gave to Tera. When my mother found out I used to give my snacks to Tera twenty years after the fact, she was mad. Eating has always been a major point of emphasis in my culture, especially in my family, as food is a sign of love and they seriously get mad at you when you do not eat.

There were street vendors selling random items such as unhealthy snacks or even colored chicks, which would only live a couple of weeks. Random vendors would mostly stand right outside of the school gate and yell out their product name and try to get our attention. It was tempting to buy from them, but if you did not have money, like me, you did not have that problem. There was a small store that sold amazing looking pens, pencils, and fancy notebooks. I could only afford to look at them and not more. My schoolmates and I would gaze at their products through the window, almost every day after school.

I remember when I was in elementary school, I was fascinated by Tera. She was very sweet to me, and her family used to live on the second floor of a small apartment building with her younger brother who used to sneak up on us at times. She was pretty, polite, clean, neat, and she always earned awesome grades. I was none of those. I had horrible handwriting, I was dreadful at painting, I was not organized, and I would always forget the due dates for homework. I was always in a rush to get the homework done on time, and most of my teachers would tell me, "Great answers, but take your time writing." I did not care or pay attention to school as much and mostly went to school to be with my friends, and to escape from home and its dramas. Tera was patient with me and helped me study. She never looked down on me for my low grades.

I was well-known in school, and everyone wanted to be my friend. I was polite and trusted by everyone. I did not have a lot of support at home, but Tera was the oldest child in her family and her mother would stay home and take care of the two kids. This was unlike my mother, who had four kids and three of those kids were rambunctious boys, and who was at least sixteen years older than Tera's mother, and was not entirely a stay-at-home type.

Tera and I had expanded our circle of friends to Setare and Roxana. I felt jealous every time she hung out with the other girls more than me, but they all lived on the other side of Sattar Khan Street. I did not have many close friends and did not want the only one who showed me care and attention to be attracted to others. Over the course of the years, Tera's family moved to a bigger house but stayed in the same general area.

Tera would not come to my house as often. Her family did not let her, because I had three older brothers and ethically that was not a norm, even though my brothers would view her as a little sister. Morally and religiously, it was inappropriate for Tera to come to our house, therefore if I wanted to hang out with her, I had to go to her house. But someone always had to escort me to anywhere I wanted to go. My brothers were trained by the society to disregard me as a human who had feelings and to shield me from some imaginary and potential dangers. On the other hand, my brothers always had their friends hang out at our house. My mom wanted us to be home and in front of her, since she was so protective and worried about the things we could have been exposed to in the real world. Therefore, she would tell my brothers to bring their friends over and she would cook and provide refreshments for them. That is why I would hang out with my brothers or sometimes even with their friends more than my own female friends. I do not know how we lived with all these socially made-up rules, stuck in a box of shame.

Most of the brothers and sisters in Iran had a love and hate relationship. It was not their fault. It was the school's and society's fault, teaching men that they are superior to women, and that they need to control and protect women. This behavior was even encouraged on television through shows and feature films. Women did not need to be controlled; they needed to be loved by their families and to feel respected and wanted.

At home my mother would just ask me to give up my right and do not argue with my brothers. She was convinced that I would have a doomed future in this society, under the new regime, if I wanted to be a tough and feisty woman like she was. It seemed like God was not fair and neither was my mother. She was never on my side and would try to de-escalate the situations by asking me to submit and obey. In private she would tell me that she did it for my own good. I do not know what exactly she meant by "you will realize in the future." As if she was training me to be okay with getting disrespected or disregarded, but she always said that we do not know where this society is taking us, and I need to adapt to the Islamic-inspired rules to survive in Iran.

My mother did not have the time to take me to my friends' house as she was always busy taking care of the house or planning meals so we would survive the day-to-day life. Eating out was not a normal or common practice at the time. Eating out meant one was rich and/or was celebrating a milestone. My father never escorted me to my friends' house either. He had more important things to do. Sometimes when my mother's siblings and their children would come to Tehran for vacation, they would take all of us kids to the only amusement park right outside of the Tehran city limits. Kids were not the center of attention; our generation did not matter. Adults had more important things to worry about than taking us to parks or friends' homes for play dates. It was about survival, not emotional intelligence or growth.

My mother's mentality was that I did not need to spend time with my friends when I had half a day to spend with them at school, but in my defense, we were in class and were not allowed to talk to one another unless it was recess, and even then, we only had enough time to use the restroom or eat a snack and run back to class. There was no time to play nor was there a playground on the plain asphalt floor of the schoolyard. She would allow me a quickly visit to Tera's home whenever she visited her friend, Shahin, who lived close to Tera's new house.

Sometimes my brothers would show up to my school unannounced to pick me up and take me home. They probably wanted to shelter me from the boys who would come and hang out by our school to check us out after school was out. They would know of the other boys' intention since they had the same intention just a few years back. My brother's escort did not make me feel loved or secure. It made me feel followed and controlled, especially because they did not show up with a smile or offered to carrying my heavy school bag home. My brothers would show up by the school gate and treat me as though I had done something wrong or provoked the boys to show up at our school. It was not our fault that the hungry young boys would show up at the school gate. They were curious, just like we were.

During the elementary period, we would have exams throughout the nine months of school, but the grades did not count. The school only counted the final exam grades and that would determine if we had passed our classes or not. If we would fail even one course, we had to re-take the test at the end of the summer, and if we would fail the course again, we had to repeat that whole year and could not move on to the next grade. Before final exams, school would give each one of us a sheet of paper that had the date and time for each final exam. Exams were held during a two-week period, back-to-back, and there were no classes in between.

If it was an easy, light course, the school would give us one day to study for it, but if it was a heavy course, like Math, they would give us two or sometimes three days to practice for it. I did not have much help or support from my family during the final exams and had to pull through and pass my courses on my own. Spring and all the flower blossoms made me sleepy, and as soon as I would open my books to study, I would fall asleep. It was hard to focus because we were so close to summer and I could not wait for the last test, so I could come home, take out my Barbies and some fabric to design new clothes for them.

During the third year of elementary school, when girls turned nine years old, they would have a celebration named "Jashne Taklif," which means celebration of puberty, irrespective of whether they have attained puberty or not. This ceremony celebrates the mark in a girl's age that she is ready for more womanly duties in her life, such as marriage, overseeing a household, and even bearing children. If you do not tell the school your religion, they just assume you are Muslim and force you to participate in all Islamic events.

When I turned nine years old, I was barely fifty pounds and definitely not ready to be married or even trusted with a pocketknife or matches, let alone becoming a mother. None of my classmates felt mature at age nine, but according to the Islamic laws, women matured faster than men did. I am not sure about 1,400 years ago, but the girls of my generation were definitely not ready to take on more responsibilities, cook, clean, or make significant decisions or have babies. We were playing with our dolls up to high school; we were not going to make good mothers.

I had to participate in the celebration of puberty event because it was the biggest event for girls during the entire five years of elementary school. My mother asked her best friend, Shahin, to sew me the prettiest hijab, so I could wear it at the celebration. From that moment, by Islamic laws, the girls has to wear a full hijab and read the obligatory prayers five times a day. From that day on, school staff occasionally would ask us to go to the school's prayer room and pray. They had taught us the prayers, and we had memorized them in Arabic.

My mom was asked to go to my school only once throughout the entire thirteen years that I attended school. She was embarrassed when they asked her if we were financially stable and could afford breakfasts. School never fed us anything, as they did before Shah left or is the practice in other countries. We had to eat our breakfast at home before we went to school or take our own snacks. My mother told the school staff that she could afford breakfast and as a matter of fact she begged me to eat food every day, but I always told her that I was not hungry. She was upset when I went home that day. She said she was embarrassed in front of the school staff and I needed to eat so I did not look so skinny and give others the impression of having a poor family.

School staff used to bother us during the school year for different reasons. The worst feeling was when I would get to school in the morning, and no one was in the yard. That meant all students were in the class and most likely teachers were in the classrooms. They would not allow us to enter the classroom if we were late. They would ask for our parents and interrogate us to find out why we were late. Ninety percent of the time the reason for being late was that we had overslept. They would torture us emotionally, and then when they were done watching us cry and apologize, begging for forgiveness, they would allow us to go to class.

Principals and other employees were responsible for digging into your personal life, books, and school bags to find evidence against you, to prove you were a bad Muslim. I would try to be on time, so I would not get questioned. We were not even able to use the restroom and we were never allowed to eat while class was in session. Recess was for eating and going to the bathroom, and I had teachers that did not care if you were passing out from hunger or about to wet your pants, they just would not allow you to leave the classroom. It was some kind of mental sickness and a power fight. They were less strict in elementary school than middle or high school, but still, instead of building a meaningful relationship with the students they would scare us. If we had a problem, we would not dare tell the principal or teachers.

At school we would sit at these long benches, which had a desk attached to it. We could rest our school bag in a little opening under the desk. Usually, two to three students could share one bench and that is how we learned to share. Our bodies would be touching, and sometimes it was hard to take notes or focus on the course because there would be three of us sharing a small bench. But that was the opportunity we had to learn, and we adapted ourselves to it. Because we were sitting so close to one another, we had to separate ourselves and our exam sheets during the exam times using a school bag. If there were three people sharing a bench, two would be separated by a school bag in between them at the table and the other one would go down on the floor, between the other two people sitting on the bench, and use the bench seating area as a desk to write on. They never trusted us, and I am pretty sure if they did, we would have cheated.

Soccer is a religion in Iran, and people take it very seriously. The 1998 FIFA World Cup was hosted by France and one of the important qualification matches for Iranians was between Iran and Australia. I was in elementary school, and the game was in the middle of the school day. The entire school staff wanted to watch the game, and so did we. If we would beat or even get an even score with Australia, we would have a great chance at making it to the World Cup. The teachers invited all of us to go to the prayer room that had a small TV and asked us to take our shoes off and be quiet. How could we be quiet? Australia had scored two, and we had scored only one. Iran's national soccer team had to score at least one more goal to qualify for the World Cup that year. The staff was impatient with us because we were loud and they were getting ready to send us home. When Iran scored the second goal, we all began to scream and were completely out of control. That was the only hope and type of entertainment we had as a nation, after the 1979 revolution.

For the second goal, there was a one on one with the Australian goalie where he fell on the ground and the ball just rolled in the basket. That day we got sent home early, and as we rushed out of school and said good-bye to one another, people were coming out of their homes and expressing happiness. I ran all the way home and witnessed all the cars honking and playing upbeat music loudly. My brothers were so happy on that unforgettable day. We all went out on the street until two in the morning and danced among the neighbors. During the same World Cup, Iran was matched to play against the US soccer team, and we were afraid the Islamic

Republic of Iran government was going to ban this game and demand the Iran soccer team to back off from the game and assume that game as a loss. The government just knew that they cannot mess with the soccer games, and that would cause chaos in the country. After the revolution the government had canceled many Olympic matches, even chess, with American or Israeli players and had refused to play with those countries for political and religious reasons and accepting the loss. So many Iranian athletes had to put their careers on hold or give up their dreams because of politics. Soon many of them left Iran and sought citizenship in other countries where they could play freely under a new nationality.

The greatest part of the school year was the end of it, because the day that we would take the last final exam, all students would be on the street cheering. We would take pictures with one another and tear our books and notebooks apart as we promised each other to always stay in touch. I had a ritual on the last day of final exams. I would wait for the night after the final test, and my paternal cousin, Assal, would come to our house. We tore our books and burnt them on the balcony in an old, empty metal pot as we planned our summer. I will never forget how much I hated Math, mostly because my father would force it on me. I would always start tearing and burning the Math books and notebooks first before moving to other subjects. I have this image stuck in my head of sunset in Tehran, while books burned. It is a safe memory, ending nine months of school like a pregnant woman giving birth and watching the beginning of three months of the hot summers of Tehran.

Summers were fun for me. I was worried all summer that it would end and would count every day of it, thinking it would slow down the time if I counted. My mother would sign me up for classes at the mosque across the street. Tera, Fatimah, Roxana, and Setare would come to classes at the mosque too. The mosque would offer Quran reading classes usually in the evenings and some computer classes during the day. Some days they had classes that would teach you how to make decorative fruits or flowers from variety of fabrics, or a specific dough that would solidify within hours. I took computer classes, decorative flower making classes, and always Quran reading. My mother wanted me to know Quran and learn Arabic, but the only Arabic thing that I was ever interested in were the belly dancing songs. She wanted me to be the best at chanting Quran, which I was at some point in school, and that just lasted until they found out my mother was a religious minority. I could only sign up for some classes, not all of them, and mostly my mother would get to choose them for me. She wanted me to be busy for the summer and learn something too, which was great, but I felt like I was in school again and had to make sure I performed my best. All I wanted to do was to write stories or design dresses for my Barbies, which was looked down upon in our household.

Summers would have been more exciting and eventful if my father would allow us to visit my aunt, my mother's younger sister. When I was around ten years old, my mother's sister moved to a city called Karaj, close to Tehran, and we had the opportunity to spend time with them every once in a while. My father would not easily give permission to visit my aunt's house because he thought every time we went there we attended the Bahá'í children classes or other events. I did attend them several times when I went to stay with my cousins in Karaj, and my dad was very scared of us being around my mother's family and exposed to the Bahá'í Faith.

I do not know what he was trying to protect us from; all they did in those gatherings was to pray and socialize. In the children's classes, kids learned how to share and be polite to one another and I remember my cousins used to play music and chant prayers. The children's class coordinator taught us patience, self-respect, truthfulness, and love for all of humankind with impartiality. They taught us powerful songs to chant, and I even remember a few to this day. I am not sure what my father was afraid of; there was nothing scary or out of the ordinary that we did at my aunt's house or at the other Bahá'í gatherings. He was scared we would convert to the Bahá'í Faith or stop attending the Islamic events. He may not know, but he helped us turn to the Bahá'í Faith by not being a decent Muslim.

My aunt, who lived in Karaj, lived in my mother's hometown for a long time after she was fired from her job as an early childhood development teacher and her husband had lost his job, both due to their beliefs. Because we lived in Tehran, the only relatives nearby were the members of my father's family. None of my mother's relatives lived in Tehran. Sometimes my maternal aunt would come to Tehran by bus, on Thursday after my cousins would get out of school, and they would sleep over. Weekends were very short being only one day, Friday, so they would leave on Friday afternoons and we had to squeeze all the fun in less than twenty-four hours, and complete our homework for the following school day, or sometimes for the rest of the week as well.

The ride from Karaj was a short one to two-hour ride; it was only twenty-five Toman per person, at the time. Sometimes my mom and I would get on the bus and visit them for a day or two. If there was a long weekend due to some kind of holiday, we would stay over at their house. There were a lot of gardens and farmers markets around that area, which we loved to visit to pick fruits, and shop. I remember that if my mom wanted to go and see her sister, my father would either start a fight or bring up some lame excuse to prevent us from visiting them.

I remember once my mom bought me new black, flat, velvet shoes with a red bow on them. We wanted to go visit my aunt in Karaj, and I wore my new shoes, because I wanted to show them off to my cousin. As soon as my mom and I were about to leave the apartment to go catch the bus, my father said, "You cannot go," grabbed my wrist, and started a fight in the stairways of our apartment. I do not even know what he was yelling about as he held my hand and would not let me leave with my mom. At that point of my life, I did not care about their fights, or the subject of their fights, I just wanted to go, leave that house, and just be away from all that chaos for a little while. I wanted to see my cousins, show off my new shoes, and play in their yard, the yard I did not have at our apartment. I wanted to spend some time watering their flowers and fruit trees, and just sitting under their grapevine.

That day my father told my mother, "Go if you want to, but Donya is staying." He was using me to manipulate my mom and see if my mom would stay because of me.

My mom walked down the stairs, tearing up, and she said, "Donya, go inside. I will be back soon." I always thought it was mean of her to do that to me, to leave me with my father, and walk away. But now that I am grown, I understand. I know it tore her heart out of her chest, but she probably realized that if she had given in to his manipulations, she would have lost control over the little freedom that she had left as religious minority married to a Muslim.

She left without me. Maybe if I were her, I would do the same, but I remember I cried so much that day. I do not know if I was more upset because I could not show off my new black velvet shoes to my cousin or because my mom left me with the beast. He had this big mustache, which did scare me, but it supposedly was the symbol of manhood and power. I did not even want him to kiss me because his mustache would poke my face every time; it was rough on my face just like his attitude on my soul. I do not know what I did that day exactly, but days like that I would cry myself to sleep. Or talk to my Barbies and make up love stories with happy endings.

I would serve the men in the house like a maid when my mother was not home. If anyone needed anything from the kitchen or their room, they would call me to get it for them. I was scared of being alone with my father. He did not talk to me unless he wanted to order me around and get me to do things for him. As a girl, my brain was trained to respond to orders given out by men. In the beginning, doing things for them around the house felt to me like a kind gesture, but after a while it became more like an expectation and if I would refuse to complete their chores or attend to their needs in any way, there would be a fight and I was called disrespectful.

I do not have many memories of my father visiting my mother's hometown, but I remember him driving us there. He would drive a non-stop eleven hours on the craziest roads of Iran, through the desert. Iran has one of the highest rates of fatal road accidents. If we wanted to get on his last nerve, we would ask him to pull over so we could use the restroom. He would ask us to hold our urge to visit the bathroom for the next city gas station because he had already passed some cars and trucks and felt ahead of the game and did not want to fall behind. He would roll down the driver's window just about enough to puff out the smoke from his consumed Winston cigarette, and if we complained about the secondhand smoke, he argued that the smoke traveling through the cracked driver's window was visibly pushed out of the car and was not coming inside the car.

I remember we often took the train from Tehran to Rafsanjan, which would take approximately fourteen hours. We would get on the train in the evening, and by early in the morning we would reach Rafsanjan. I remember my mother would always bring some bread, canned Tuna, and fresh lime to have for dinner while traveling by train. We would share the small room on the train with strangers, whom we always befriended within the first hour of the trip. We would talk with them the whole time we were on the train to Rafsanjan or Tehran. They would place the women together on the train so they would not feel awkward sharing a room with strange men during their trip. Once we were in Rafsanjan, we would take a taxi to my grandmother's house. It was amazing to get there in the morning, since the mornings were much cooler in the desert. I knew my grandmother would have breakfast ready, and she would keep the house quiet for us to take a nap afterward. She would always buy me fresh Kermani faloodeh[30] because it was my favorite form of dessert, which I enjoyed as breakfast.

30 A noodle- / starch-based dessert from the province of Kerman.

HORMONES, BATHROOMS, AND CHALK BOARDS

Elementary school was over, and even though I would miss my friends, I was happy to start middle school. No one wanted to be treated or seen as a child, and by moving on to middle school I would be able to show I had grown up. In middle school, I started caring about my looks more and would make sure my gel-styled bangs would peek out of my hijab. I wanted to look more decent for the boys who would stand outside of our middle school gate and were so hungry for the attention of the opposite sex. Our middle school was just a few streets farther from our elementary school, and most of my elementary school classmates attended the same middle school, unless their families moved away.

I remember in the second year of middle school, Roxana, one of us four friends, migrated to England. We were all very sad that she was moving away and did not understand the reason why. She was the most beautiful girl in our group, and she was so elegant and charming. She still is. One of the last nights that she was in Iran, we all gathered at her house and had dinner together and took pictures to capture the last moments. Roxana left, and our small group got even smaller, but we never forgot her. She would come back to Iran almost every summer, and we would plan to visit with her.

There was a morning shift and an afternoon shift in middle school, and for the first year of middle school, I attended the afternoon shift. I would go to school around noon and get out around 5pm, and then I would watch some cartoon on TV, maybe take a nap, and mostly leave my homework for the next mornings. Whether I was in the morning or afternoon shift, I was always in the same class as Tera, except for one year. It was in middle school that I realized that one of my elementary school classmates also had one parent who was Bahá'í. It became our little secret, and I felt so unique and important that both of us were different from the rest of the school.

I remember we all looked forward to walking home from middle school every day as we passed by the boys standing outside of our school gate, who would be waiting for us to come out, so they could say something charming to us that made us giggle as we walked away. I always felt comfortable and confident answering them back, after all I grew up with three older brothers and I knew what kind of girl they liked. They wanted a confident girl who would listen to their needs and dreams and act like she cared.

I had to rush home after school and would get in trouble if I would have changed the path to or from school. My mom and brothers continued to come by the school and pick me up unannounced. It was an uncomfortable age; I was experiencing hormones and changes in my body, and there was a lot happening in my family that I was never consulted or informed about. I felt like I was always being watched by God, my brothers, and even neighbors when a boy would try to talk to me. It was exhausting, and I often felt ashamed to be a woman or have urges and feelings. It felt like more of a curse than a blessing to be a woman in that society.

I was as attracted to boys as they were to me, and I wanted the attention of the opposite sex as much as they wanted it. If I would get involved with any male, it would mean embarrassment for the family in the neighborhood as well as distraction for me; therefore, I would keep my head down in the neighborhood and would not give an excuse to my brothers to start a fight and take my limited rights away.

During the first year of the three-year middle school, we started learning Arabic, and the second year we started the English course. The importance of the Arabic class was more emphasized than English because by learning Arabic we would be able to understand the Quran, the language of the Prophet. Arabic is one of the hardest languages to learn, and I did not learn much in seven years of attending Arabic courses. There were many Arabic words that were similar to Farsi due to the Arab/Islam invasion hundreds of years ago, when Arabs forced Persians to replace their alphabet with the Arabic alphabet. I enjoyed learning English because it would help me to translate the American songs and movies I enjoyed, and I always earned much better grades in English than in Arabic courses.

At home, I never spoke about my grades, good or bad, and instead I would tell my mom that I was, again, in charge of planning school events, which meant to plan the events to portray Islam and the Islamic Republic of Iran as the savior. I just enjoyed being in charge and a part of the team. I did not care what event it was and what it was representing.

At school and especially during event planning, creativity was frowned upon. If one was wearing the hijab head to toe, she was liked more by the school staff. But if one would dress like me, different, outside of the box, and free, one was not liked. I enjoyed pushing the boundaries at home, school, and society. For me, school was not a place to study, it was the place to change people's minds and explore new ideas. I went to school to stay away from home, to see my friends, and satisfy the need to know more about some school topics, such as physics and English, but I felt out of place. There were some teachers and principals who gave me the wings to fly, but most of the school staff and principal, who would be dressed in full hijab, as the regime approved, and were directed to brainwash us and cut our creative wings.

Innovation was forbidden in our society, unless it was aligned with the Islamic Republic of Iran's version of Islam. They did not care about the Persian culture or ancient rituals. The theme after the 1979 revolution was the state of mourning for the Imams and hate for the Western countries because they were considered sinful. Yet the children of the 1980s generation, copied Western music on CD's and passed it around at school. We talked about the latest NSYNC and Backstreet Boys' music videos and did not let the new government take that from us by keeping it a secret. There would be consequences if the school staff figured out we even recited non-Islamic music, the evil music which ruins lives and promotes bad behavior. We were definitely in our own little world, isolated from the rest of the globe. We would have celebrity crushes on the goalie or the soccer players of Iran or Italy. We would read every interview and collect every magazine that had a picture of the famous Iranian and non-Iranian soccer players and other actors, and singers, such as Brad Pitt or Enrique Iglesias.

Being a very active member of school, I became a candidate for the school's student president. This was a new idea, to incorporate the students' needs in school by having the student president as the bridge between students and school staff to communicate new ideas and implement the appropriate plans. I was very well known in our middle school but did not have good grades, and the staff knew my mother was a religious minority.

The student president would be able to meet with the school principal and staff and ask them to make improvements to rules, regulations, or the quality of student life during the six days per week, and five hours per day of the school week. The first thing I wanted to fix was the school bathrooms that were not appropriate. Some of the metal doors would not close properly due to being old and a few had signs of oxidization on the bottom edges. The bathrooms were located outside of the buildings, in the corner of the schoolyard, and in cold winters it was very uncomfortable to use the bathrooms. I personally felt as if my private parts would freeze every time I had to use the bathroom in the winter due to lack of adequate.

I wanted us to have white boards for each class so we did not have to be exposed to the chalk residuals. We would suffer from dry skin and our uniforms would get chalk on them on the days we had used the board; we had to wash, dry, and iron them for the next day. Since most of us had only purchased one single uniform for the entire school year, or sometimes years, it was hard to wash and dry the same uniform every day. showing up to school with a dirty uniform would get you questioned by the principal.

Even though I had a great chance of winning the election, they chose another schoolmate who had better grades and normally wore the full hijab. That year, the quality of our life at school, again, did not improve and neither the bathrooms nor the chalk boards were fixed. When I reached high school, I finally had the opportunity to serve on the school board, and made my classmates' wish to take a trip to a different state come true.

QUESTIONS ARE A SIN

In middle school, religious pressure did not get any softer. We were older now and expected to behave more religiously. Schools were training the future brainwashed Islamic Army. School principals would question a single hair if it was showing outside of the hijab or they would scare us with questions like, "How are you going to answer to God and the Prophets in the next world?"

Religious classes were getting more intense, and they were feeding us more superstition than before. I was full of questions, and thought school was a safe place where I could get answers. I had to ask, whether it was a Math class or a religious class, I always had questions and I would always come up with creative ways of solving problems in the class. Most of my teachers knew I was full of energy and that I had good intentions by asking questions. I was not the smartest kid in the class, but I sure had creativity and drive.

One day in middle school, during the religious class, my teacher was lecturing us on the importance of reciting the obligatory prayer five times a day. Now that we had passed the puberty, nine, we had to act as adults and recite the prayers five times per day. This teacher was short and heavy, and as always, wearing her full black hijab, even in a class that was filled only with young girls, and no man ever entered. She emphasized that it was important for us to recite the prayers in Arabic and make sure we pronounced the Arabic words correctly. I was full of questions about the obligatory prayer and wanted to fully understand the reason behind the things she was saying. I raised my arm, tall and firm, a gesture meaning I had a question to ask.

Our religious teacher allowed me to speak by nodding her head yes and pointing towards me quickly with the hand that was free from holding her hijab. I asked, "Do we have to say the obligatory prayer in Arabic? Can we say it in Farsi?"

She replied, "Yes, you have to say it in Arabic, and you have to say it with correct pronunciation, or your prayers will not be accepted."

Her response did not really answer my question or satisfy my thirst for reason. I asked, "But why do we have to say it Arabic when we do not even know what we are saying to God? What is the point of praying five times a day when we do not even know what we are praying for?" Plus, in my head was the question of why we were expected to recite the obligatory prayer at age nine, third grade, when we were actually taught Arabic in sixth grade. The whole thing did not make sense and, as always, I was a curious young girl who did not fully understand the consequences.

My religious teacher, a middle-aged woman who had never thought outside of the box, did not like my questions at all. She felt challenged and maybe uncomfortable that she had to now answer to the entire class and not just me. She came close to my desk and leaned over, very close to my face. I was sharing the very front bench with Tera that year. She was sitting on my right, closer to the wall. My teacher said, "I know you are trying to poison the class with your questions. I will make sure the principal knows and that you are not going to pass this course to move on to the next year."

I was shocked. I had no bad intentions in heart by asking questions. I just wanted to know what was the point of praying when we did not even know what we were saying or to whom we were saying it? Islam's God was very strict, and I just did not want to disappoint him. I was a young, curious child, and I can think of many ways she could have answered my question in a peaceful way without attacking me in front of my classmates or threatening to have me expelled. Maybe she had never thought about the answer to my question, because no one had ever asked such questions. Maybe she was struggling to make sense of this as much as I was.

Soon after that event my mother went to the school to explain that I just asked a question, that my question did not mean anything, and that it was completely unintentional and unplanned. She apologized to the religious teacher and the principal and promised them that I would keep my questions to myself from now on. Therefore, instead of going to school to learn more, I had to go to school to control my questions and curiosity. My mother asked me to quit asking religious questions or they would expel me from school. The school staff knew my mother was not Muslim. I am not sure if they knew she was a Bahá'í, but they knew she was a religious minority. She knew that if I ever chose to become a Bahá'í, I would not be able to go to university or have a decent job in my own country; therefore, she wanted me to get as much education as possible. For Bahá'ís that meant a high school diploma. My father would have blamed it on my mom if I would get expelled.

In general, school was not a place to be creative or act different from other students. It was a place to listen to your teachers and behave. If you had any creative questions, you were told to shut it down and to never bring it up again. I had a lot of questions about religion, history, astronomy, life, and existence, and that is why I was the only black sheep in the class and would be kicked out of the sessions more frequently than any of my classmates.

My father was always working and traveling, and my mother had to take care of our schooling and manage the money in a way that she would not be short throughout the month. Sometimes she invested in some financial opportunities to make extra money. I often wished I was not born so my mother did not have to pay for my expenses too. It was a hard time to have multiple kids, but it was encouraged by the Islamic Republic of Iran to have more children. They were thinking about their future Islamic Army.

More often than not, my mother and I had to stand in long lines at the local grocery store to see if there was a bottle of milk left by the time it was our turn. We would travel by bus to the center of the city to buy fresh herbs and meat, where they would be less expensive than in local stores. There was a store just a hundred meters away from our apartment, the one at which I had demanded a chocolate bar; it was truly convenient to shop from there since it was so close to us. But the owner would sell the products at a much higher rate than the stores closer to the center of the city. I never understood why, but people kept on shopping from the local store owner without complaining about his high and unfair prices. I know that my mother had told him that he needed to be fair and we did not shop from him because he was greedy. Of course, the store owner did not like what she told him, but he always respected my mother for telling the truth and not letting him go on thinking we were all unaware of his intentions and did not know that he was abusing his customers for the sole reason of location and convenience.

The country could not provide for all after the revolution and the war. Sometimes we could not find food items such as milk, cheese, rice, or even tea. There were black markets for everything, even medication. Therefore, our mothers came up with smart comments like, "Too much cheese will make you stupid," and we believed them. We ate less cheese, or none at all. I remember one day my oldest brother's college classmate came to visit him from a city in the northern part of Iran. He slept over and, in the morning, he joined us for breakfast. I remember that he rubbed a chunk of butter on his bread and then he put a big piece of cheese on top of it and ate it.

My jaw dropped. I was holding a small piece of bread in my hand, and I still had not put anything on it. I turned towards my mom. She was just as shocked as I was, but she just smiled and winked at me so that I would not make any comments, and she looked away. We had all learned to eat less or be considerate of others when it came to food. Sometimes we were too considerate and would not eat the things that were in the fridge, and they would go bad and we had to throw them away.

We spent hours cleaning the herbs that we had purchased from the center of the city. Most of the herbs that we would bring home had a lot of mud or dirt attached to them, and that would add to the weight of the herbs we had to buy. My mother would make sure she did not pay for mud instead of herbs; therefore, she would argue with the men selling herbs to her. I hated cleaning herbs. The mud would get underneath my nails, and I would get grossed out. It was labor-intensive to clean all those herbs. We sat in the middle of the kitchen or living room, and after we were done cutting their ends and separating the good ones from the bad we had to wash them well, cut them, sauté some of them, and package them to be stored in the freezer for future use. It would make it easier to make food if we had some ingredients, such as herbs or sometimes beans already prepared in the freezer.

We would also buy fresh sweet peas and lima beans that were sold in their skin, and we had to open the skins, bring out the beans or peas, and wash, sometimes cook, and package them to store in the freezer for future use. Most of these items were seasonal, and therefore we had to purchase them in their season to have for the rest of the year. This was a better and cheaper way of getting legumes.

Most of the time we would make our own yogurt, pickles, and sometimes even cheese. I learned a lot, helping my mom at home. It was not fair to be the only one in the house to help my mom, but I was the only daughter and socially the women were obligated to help, not the men.

Sometimes we would get together with neighbors or family members and make an event out of cleaning herbs or legumes, juicing immature grapes, limes, or even cooking tomato paste. This was a way to socialize and get things done at the same time. I now understand where I get my multi-tasking skills from.

My father would not give my mom enough money to pay for our daily needs, and my mom had to be creative with ways to save money. If something was on sale or cheaper than normal, that was what we would have for dinner. She was not used to asking for money from my father. She was proud and was still trying to have her dignity even after she lost her job. She had always worked and had made her own money since she was eighteen, and it was hard for her to extend her hand to my dad for money. She always implied that she did not need him or his money to succeed, and she was right, she did not, but too much pride was not helping our family either. I believe he never liked her independence, or pride, or that she stood on her own two feet to show him that she was capable of handling this life without him. Men want to feel needed, and she never made him feel needed and when she did, he ignored her needs.

Other than being a mother of four, my mother was the president of the building we lived in. Everyone trusted her and respected her opinion in the neighborhood. My mother was given a set of keys to all units. She was open to others' opinions and would try her best to improve the entire community, and not just our own apartment building.

To make more money out of what we had, my mother decided to build another apartment out of our apartment on the fourth floor. Our apartment was so large that it could be split into two decent-size apartments.

It was an incredible idea, but she had to get construction permits from the city and permission from all the neighbors in the building. She went back and forth to the city hall to get permissions from the city for not just our apartment unit, but all the other units in the building to have the capability of splitting the formal living area, which was connected to the formal dining area into another apartment unit. There would be two front doors next to each other, and one would open to a new eight hundred and sixty square feet apartment with two bedrooms, open kitchen, and large living area and new bathroom and shower. My mother would use the other side of the house and turn her bedroom into a living area for the family, knock down half of the kitchen wall, opening the kitchen to the new living room. She would keep the other two bedrooms and the one bathroom and shower that we originally had.

My father did not like the idea of course. Again, he would disagree with everything. As a matter of fact, he had a nickname in the house, "Mr. Bad Attitude" and last name "Born to Disagree." I believe he even disagreed when he liked something, or he just disagreed to stay consistent. My father told my mom that he had no savings, and he could not pay her for this construction. She had gone through a lot of trouble, back and forth, almost every day of the week for months to the city administration, and from one office to the next to get the permits approved. It had taken her months, and she had given a lot of pistachios as gifts to the government employees to convince the city and then the neighbors to give her permission to split her house into two apartments, only to find out that my father would not pay for it.

My mother is from the greatest pistachio-exporting city in Iran, Rafsanjan, and she always had a lot of pistachios in the house. She could get the best pistachios for cheap and gift them to people. She used the pistachios to speed up some of the construction permit approvals from the city. In Iran, neither the city nor the general government employees will do work unless their wheel has been greased. A bag of fresh and delicious pistachios, of high exporting quality, was very valuable twenty-five years ago.

My mom wanted to prove to my father that she was independent and did not need her man to step in when she was in financial need. She borrowed money from her brother and mother and hired a contractor. She came up with the construction plan herself and started the construction. Her long-term plan was to rent out the new and smaller apartment and have some extra monthly income, or to sell it and loan the money to someone and get the monthly interest as extra income.

During the construction phase, I would come to a house full of dust and mud. My father was not happy, and I think he was gone on work trips for most of it anyway. Construction only took a few months, and the result was amazing. My mother's plan had worked, and the fact that other neighbors could benefit from the fruits of my mother's efforts and now had the option of splitting their large apartments into two decent sized ones, made them happy.

Soon the new house became a new cave for my brothers. They would bring their friends and hang out at the new apartment. A family consisting of a mother with two young daughters moved in. We spent many nights with them, getting to know each other, and the mother was talented and patient enough to teach me how to sew.

After a couple of years my mom sold the house next door because our second-floor neighbor, Ms. Zand, wanted to sell her house for a very reasonable price. With the money she got from the sale of the new apartment and after borrowing some more from her brother, my mother managed to buy the house on the second floor. We moved to the second floor shortly after, and my mother rented the larger apartment to a family with three children.

After a few years of being forced to live in a small apartment, we were excited to finally move to a three-bedroom, two living room apartment. This time I shared a bedroom with my oldest brother and my parents had their bedroom and privacy back again.

My father was gone on his works trips most of the times, and when he was back home, he never offered a constructive solution to the problems my mother was dealing with; therefore, my mother refrained from most of the subjects that would cause conflicts in the house. We all did.

Around the same time, one of my cousins who lived in Karaj had moved to Turkey, so he could move to America as a religious refugee. He was very close to my brothers, and it broke everyone's heart when he moved away. He had no future in Iran, after being mistreated while serving his mandatory two-year military service, and then not able to attend any universities or get a job due to his religion.

Soon after he left, my mother's oldest brother decided to leave the country as well and move his family to America as religious refugees. They sold everything and came to Tehran to catch their flight to Austria, and after staying in Austria for at least four months they would possibly move to America.

My uncle came to Tehran to send his wife and children to Austria, and then after a few months, he would join them. I spent time with my cousins knowing I may never ever see them again. They lived in a different state, but at least we were in the same country and I had the opportunity to visit them if I ever wanted to.

I felt like I was losing my family and most importantly maternal cousins, one at a time, and there would be a day when my family and I would be the last standing. I had lost two maternal aunts and their family before I was born to religious persecution and now, I was losing more.

A few months after my uncle's wife and his three children had moved to Austria, he sold his house and came to Tehran a few days prior to his flight to Austria. My aunt from Karaj and her daughters, as her son had already left the country, came to our house to say goodbye to my uncle. My youngest uncle and his daughter, along with my grandmother, also came to Tehran from Rafsanjan. They all fit in our house to spend the last few days with my uncle. We were all so sad that my uncle was leaving, but dancing around with our cousins on the night of his flight is a great memory to hold on to. We all took the last photos, and in the pictures my grandmother, mother, aunt, and uncles all have inflamed and red eyes due to excessive crying. We, grandchildren, sat on the floor as the adults sat on the couch to take the last picture.

In order to pay back her brother before he left the country, my mother sold the last apartment on the fourth floor. She had no other savings, and my father always said that he would not help her financially because he did not agree with her decisions. She did not want to owe anyone money, even though her brother did not need his money back. The apartment's value increased exponentially soon after, which is how I learned that when a husband and wife do not agree, there will always be financial losses encountered.

My aunt from Karaj and her husband were both educated people, but after the revolution, due to their religion, they had lost their jobs. Her husband had to work all week and only come home on the weekend, Fridays, to spend time with his family. Their son had moved to Turkey and had made it to America on a religious minority refugee visa. One man working was not going to support a family of four. They decided to move to America and join their son to keep the family together and gain the ability to provide for their family. I was extremely emotional when I learned they were moving to America. They were the last cousins from my mother's side, and I was very close to one of my cousins. We were like sisters and would share everything with each other. I would read my poetry and short passages to her, and she was always supportive of my writing and would encourage me to write more. I actually had an appetite to eat at their house and would eat every meal, maybe because my mother was not there to force feed me.

After everyone left, I was left with one maternal cousin, who lived in my mother's hometown with my youngest maternal uncle and grandmother. I would not get to see her often, unless we would go to visit them in the summer or during the New Year holidays in the spring. Every time one of my mother's family members, whether cousins or siblings, were leaving the country as religious refugees, they would sell their homes, pack their belongings, and come to Tehran weeks before leaving the country to spend the last days at our house. I remember my mother, known in the family and circle of friends as the rug expert, would go to Tehran's grand bazaar to help her family members buy handmade Persian rugs to take with them to America. Persian rugs were witnessing Persians leaving their homeland to be free.

My maternal family members, being a religious minority, were not able to find jobs, and their children had no future in a country that did not honor their rights as citizens and taxpayers. The government had seized their properties and bullied them until they had no choice but to leave. I believe the government did all of this to force the Bahá'ís to leave the country.

There was not much to do after almost all of my mother's maternal family left. I did not have my aunt in Karaj anymore, so I was stuck at home on the weekends as well. Friday nights were movie nights, but after the film, my father would order us to go to our rooms to work on homework or get ready for Saturday, the first day of school. Most of the time, the credits of the film on Friday night meant "start of a fight." My mother was not a fan of this situation, but we did not have much choice but to stay out of sight when my father was around.

My father was good at Math. Well, I was in middle school and anyone can do that Math, but he was so proud of himself for knowing the ins and outs of algebra and geometry that he would tutor me and sometimes my friends, but he would judge me and belittle me if I did not know the answer to a Math problem. Maybe that is why I hated Math and was discouraged to learn it. He was not willing to explain anything twice, at least not to me. I would be sitting on the floor, next to him, and he would emotionally torture me until I cried, and then my mom would say, "Do not do this to the kids. Why cannot you be nice to them!" and he would start a fight with her because he did not want her to say those things in front of us. He often claimed she protected us a little too much.

I remember Tera, or sometimes my cousins, would come over to study Math and learn from him. I would try to stay out of my father's sight so he would not ask me to join them. He was so kind and patient with the other kids. He would call them "My dear" or "My sweet daughter," but he never treated me that way. My brothers would not put up with my father's belittling and loud voice. They were boys and could storm out of the room or even the house, even if they were seventeen, but not me.

When my father was gone on his work trips, my brothers and I would listen to Michael Jackson's music and try to mimic his dance moves until we were out of breath, or until my mom would come home and ask us to keep it down. I remember when we were kids, my brothers and I would always talk about the possibility of Michael Jackson coming to Iran for a concert. We always said we could not wait for this regime to change so Michael Jackson, Ricky Martin, Enrique Iglesias, or some other famous musicians, actors, actresses, and singers would come to Iran and perform. We would have given anything to go to a Madonna's concert or even see the Queen up close. We would always watch their music videos and would admire their art and passion and the fact that they would have the opportunity in the United States of America to achieve their goals. In Iran, which

I would like to call the center of agriculture, culture, poetry, science, religion, and love, we will not be able to achieve our dreams and goals under the regime of the Islamic Republic of Iran.

Art and creativity were highly frowned upon in society. If it was not Islam, revolution, or war-related, then it was not important enough to be developed or published. I never stopped writing poetry or short stories. As I moved on from elementary school to middle school, I got better and better at writing stories. No one knew at home, but my teachers knew. One day I wrote an essay about "Pencils." I was in a rush; right before I got to school, I had remembered that I had to write a passage for that day's class. Our Farsi teachers would call us to come and read our passages for the whole class. I was called to go and read the passage that day. I was scared and did not think highly of my writing, but I would probably get some credit for the fact that I had done the homework. I had horrible handwriting and was not very confident about my stories because I was never encouraged at home.

After I finished reading the passage, my teacher asked to see my notebook. I told her that I wrote it in a rush and did not have very good handwriting. She did not care about the handwriting and read the passage again, this time to herself. She asked me to re-write it for her in a better handwriting and bring it to class the next day. She said she liked it and she thought I had a chance in winning the city-wide competition in writing short passages. I told my mom, and she read the passage for the first time. She asked where I had gotten the idea for the passage. I explained to her my thought process, and she was amazed. I re-wrote the passage on nice paper and took it to school. All the school staff read my passage, and they submitted it for the city-wide competition. I found out later that I did not win anything, but I always remembered being recognized for my writing in middle school and that was a big encouragement for me to continue writing.

TV IN IRAN

As a family, we did not watch a lot of television. I remember we only had two channels, no satellites, only channels one and two until we moved to the second-floor apartment. They would have news and one or two TV shows, but most of the day they had a lot of Mullah's[31] who would give a lot of religious talks on TV and other programs. After eleven in the evening there were no more programs other than the news, which was on the hour, though I'm not sure if that was every hour. There would be repeats of the previously aired TV shows in the afternoons, for those who that missed the last episode, and if you missed both of those opportunities to catch up with the show, you just had to call a friend to get the details.

Iran's film industry had to start over after the revolution because all of the pre-revolution movies portrayed women in miniskirts, people drinking alcohol, engaging in sexual contact, playing music, dancing, and worse than all, loving one another. When I was very young, most of the TV shows that were allowed on television were about Islam or the recently ended Iran Iraq War. I remember that throughout my childhood we had no other option than to watch war movies portraying the different battles during the war. It was sad and boring, and as a child I was not really interested in watching people blow up each other up. I did not even understand the purpose of it anyways. Most of the things shown on television were sad, or would encourage society to stay in a sad state of mind.

---

31 A Muslim educated in the Islamic theory and laws.

There was *Oshin*, a Japanese serialized morning television drama, following the life of Oshin Tanokura. *Oshin,* for us Iranians, was a modestly dressed woman who was hard working and grew up facing many hardships. People were obsessed with *Oshin's* life. I would run home from school every day just to watch the five to ten minutes that TV would show her new episode. I was consumed with the Kimono, the Japanese culture, and the interesting and exotic food they ate in that TV show. That was the only opportunity when I had to connect with the world outside of Iran, not knowing the show was filmed at least ten years prior to the time it was aired in Iran.

I would try to make my own chopsticks and act as if I was in their world. I was obsessed with noodle-containing foods. Almost twenty years after watching *Oshin* as a child, the 1980s generation realized that *Oshin's* TV show was highly censored, and that the story of her life was very different. My generation felt betrayed because we were all lied to, but I give the regime the credit of doing an amazing job of fooling us. For example, some stories contained prostitution and brothel houses, and so much more of the story was censored. The Islamic Republic of Iran had managed to censor a Japanese show and feed it to us as if *Oshin* were the Virgin Mary.

Pre-revolution movies, which were highly illegal and forbidden, were available and watched by all adults and children at almost every house. It was common to find the tapes labeled as cartoons or wedding videos to throw off the secret police in case the house was raided. Our parents would watch them, and then tell us how great it used to be and how women wore miniskirts and men grew their hair out and had mustaches. Then we would ask who changed the regime if most people liked the miniskirts? Most of the time the answer to that question was simply a dirty, long stare.

If the police would find the pre-revolution videos in homes, they would take the tapes away and charge the owners with jail time and sometimes even hundreds of lashes for owning such unclean videos. Most people still owned and played music from singers before the revolution, or from singers who had left the country during the revolution and had gone to Los Angeles or other parts of the world to continue their careers. We all listened to the forbidden music on a daily basis. They were forbidden because the songs were about love, and made us feel like dancing. In Islam, anything that can change your mood from neutral to anything else is forbidden, whether it is music, alcoholic drinks, drugs, or love for the opposite sex.

Our household would still watch pre-revolutionary films, and dance to the latest Iranian songs exported by the Iranian singers in Los Angeles. For years we were not allowed to listen to music in our cars, and if we did, we had better turn it down or the moral police could stop us on the street and take us to jail for disturbing and provoking the public.

Both television and radio were owned and controlled by the government. On the radio the only music played was either the music about Khomeini and his successful revolution, about martyrs of the Iran Iraq War, or about the Holy Quran. There was no danceable or uplifting music on the radio or television, and all songs were sung by men. No woman was allowed to sing in private, in public, or on television or radio. There were harsh consequences for the ones who that did. For years there was not even a comedic movie shown on TV. It was years before the Iranian channels sponsored and produced comedy TV shows and actually brought laughter and hope into our homes, but that was only once or twice per week.

In the post-revolution films, people wore conservative clothing and absolutely no makeup. Televison shows were unique, carried a hidden message, and were less than thirty episodes. Women and men were not able, and are still not able, to touch one another in the films. In some cases, male actors would dress as women in the film and they would have more freedom to touch men.

Actresses would wear dark-colored, long head scarfs, long-sleeved loose shirts, and even pants underneath their long and oversized skirts to cover all body curves. The children of the 1980s generation, did not learn to show affection and love to siblings, or to future spouse, since in our homes our parents were not touching each other in front of us and neither did anyone in public nor on TV. It was a struggle for us to communicate love and affection to one another when there were no role models and love was not as fluid as we needed it to be.

When I was a teenager, feature movies began to show some hair and play some music. Actors and filmmakers had become very creative under the new conditions. They would not show the opposite sex touch one another and instead, for example, they would show a man reaching for the woman's hand and she would reach for his hand and the camera would show their touching hands in the moving water reflection. They had to play with the rules of Islam and encourage Islamic behavior through the tiny window of black-and-white television. They were not and are not yet allowed to show a man going to his bedroom with his wife, or to even show her taking off her hijab at home or even while she sleeps. They always show the woman going to her bedroom while the man sleeps on the couch, and we made jokes that they show men and women sleeping separately from each other but yet they have children, perhaps through pollination, and that just may be Islam's miracle.

There were many films in which the actors were married in real life, but they would not touch each other in the film. Many actors, directors, and singers left the country during or soon after the revolution, but some stayed and chose a life of poverty because they had to say goodbye to their acting careers, and no one would employ them under the new circumstances. Some who stayed in Iran chose to confess to the sinful movie scenes that they were involved in and ask for God's forgiveness in order to continue their acting and directing careers in Iran.

When I was a teenager, there was a new system that would allow us to access the Iranian TV channels that were initiated from America. Using a satellite dish, we were able to access these few channels, and they would be airing pre-revolution movies and a lot of happy and upbeat Iranian music performed by Iranian musicians that had mostly migrated to California after the revolution. All the artists and singers who had left the country after the revolution had a chance to restart their careers in America. Once the Iranian regime discovered that people were accessing the new satellite channels and even a lot of other Arabic, Turkish, and European channels, they would confiscate the satellite dishes unannounced, arrest the people who owned and installed them, and fine them or assign jail time to them. The Californian channels were pro-Shah. Most of the hosts were political refugees that had fled the country during the revolution and would encourage people to protest against the current regime, and of course the Iranian regime did not want people to have access to the outside world. As soon as we would hear the helicopters over our building, sent by the Islamic Republic of Iran to identify the locations and remove all satellite dishes across the country, we would rush to the roof to take down ours so we would not get in trouble.

I was not a fan of the idea of having another king, which is what the pro-Shah group in California was advocating. I wanted to live in a free country. Free from a king who would dictate, or a regime that was mixing religion and politics to the point that people hated both. I wanted a different regime, not the late king, and definitely not the current regime. I never understood why the Californian TV hosts wanted us, the young, to go out and protest so the son of the king could come back and rule over the country! They knew that if we went out to protest, more youths would die, or be captured and tortured. More mothers would have to live without their sons and daughters when they had just gone through a war and lost their husbands, brothers, and fathers.

Several years after Iranians outside of Iran started TV channels for Iranians across the world, Iran's government started channels for Iranians outside of Iran as well. They tried to portray Iran as a modern and laidback country by playing new, upbeat music produced in Iran. I loved getting on the satellite channels. I was able to watch upbeat Iranian and non-Iranian music videos, TV shows, and movies as if it were a window to the outside world.

Since Friday is the only day off in Iran, television aired more shows and other entertaining programs from Thursday afternoons through Friday evenings. The *Good Morning Friday* radio show would have jokes and news. My father loved to listen to that show every Friday morning, especially if we were driving to some place for a visit, and we would all listen to it in the car. He would turn the radio up and laugh each time the show host told a corny joke. I enjoyed that show as well, but not as much as my father did. On Thursday afternoons there was always show on TV, which was only shown once a week, and on Friday afternoons, they would telecast a feature film. It would mostly be war- and Islam-related movies, but sometimes it was a European or even an American film that was highly censored and dubbed in Farsi. Even the cartoons were about the Hadith[32] and Islamic rules and practices, which was not horrible, but cartoons are supposed to make the kids laugh while carrying an educational message. These Islamic cartoons were not funny at all.

I remember when they started Channel 3, shortly after we moved into the second-floor house. It was supposed to be a sport channel, which it was, and it still is, but they occasionally telecasted a few TV shows and feature films. Channels 1 or 2 would have cartoons around five in the afternoon, right before dinner when all the kids were home, perhaps had already taken a nap, and were done with their homework. The female host

---

32 In Islam Hadith refers to the record of the words, actions, the silent approval, of the Islamic Prophet Muhammad.

of a children's TV program would tell us to go sit away from the TV in order to protect our eyes and we did not want to disobey or upset her by sitting too close to the TV, so we would do as she said and would sit away from the TV to protect our eyes.

When I was a young teenager, if one of my brothers would be home, I would not dare touch the remote control. They always wanted to watch soccer on Channel 3, and I did not care for soccer at the time, when but when I grew up a little more and my oldest brother taught me the rules of soccer, I fell in love with the sport and would join them in watching the games on the weekends or when the FIFA World Cup, or Asian and European leagues were in process.

BEAT UP CANDLES

My mother would send me to summer classes, hoping I would learn Math or English and be prepared for the school year. I wished instead that she would take me to the park or just let me do some artistic activities at home to enjoy the summer off. I did not learn much during the summer attending summer classes anyway and always felt guilty that my mom paid for the classes, since I did not really pay attention to the material they were covering. At least there was still some time in the summer when I could get away and go to my paternal cousin's house in Tehran, since the only maternal cousin left was in a different state.

I remember one late summer I was staying at my cousin's house in Tehran for a few days. My uncle's wife was very talented, and she was interested in making fabric flowers and other sorts of decorations. She would make us delicious food, and we would play with each other in the house or in their backyard.

One not very special day, one of the last days of summer, we were all playing in my cousin's bedroom. When we got bored, we came running out to play in the living room. As I was passing by the TV room, I saw the TV showing some burning buildings. My uncle was sitting in front of the TV, in his colorful pajamas, on the floor. He was shocked and was not moving. He was just staring at the TV in disbelief. I stopped running around with my cousins and stared at the TV.

Soon my cousins joined me, and we all stood outside of the TV room, and just watched the burning buildings. It seemed like a movie scene, but soon I noticed it was not a movie, it was the news. My uncle seemed upset and disappointed at the scene, the way I feel sometimes with the way humanity is moving forward. At that exact moment, there was no sound of running children in the house anymore. We did not dare step inside of the room, my uncle was extremely upset to have kids running around and God forbid ask any questions. The only noise in the house was that of the reporter's voice on TV, saying that there are a lot of people trapped in these buildings, dying, as the buildings are collapsing.

There was no more playing for that night. Instead we all watched TV in silence. I was only thirteen years old and did not know what a terrorist attack meant. Who was the bad guy and who was the good guy? I just know that many Iranians, young and old, men and women, protested on the street that night and the nights to come and lit candles in the memory of the people who died in that tragic attack. Because of sympathizing with Americans, many Iranians were taken to jail and treated as if they were spies. I came to know years later that no one even knew Iranians mourned when 9/11 happened. Of course, we were sad that this horrible event happened to innocent men and women.

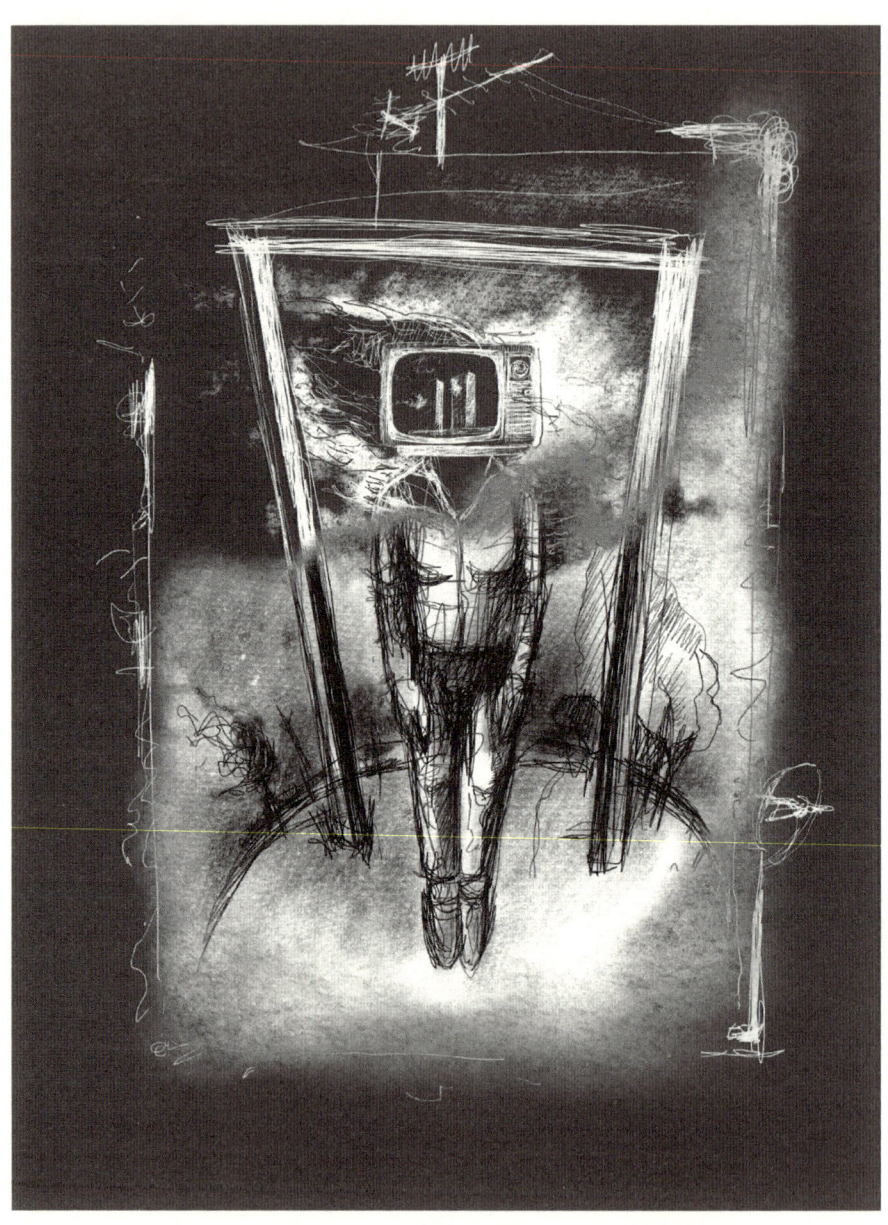

POPPY FLOWER

My mother always said, "Every time a bird lays an egg on our home's premises, someone dies in the family." As a child I thought it was a myth, but
when people started dying right after the birds laid an egg on our balcony,
I changed my mind. More interestingly, my mother would always dream
about the person's death exactly one week before they died.

When I was eleven or twelve, a month after the Persian New Year,
when my oldest paternal uncle, the one from my grandfather's first marriage, got very sick. Because my mother cared about him deeply, she insisted
that he and his wife come and stay at our house so she could care for him
until he felt better. My oldest uncle had five daughters; the youngest was a
year older than me. Only the first daughter had married, and the second
one was preparing for her marriage in the following next few weeks. My
mother and father took my uncle to his doctor appointments at the hospital very close to our apartment.

I remember him staying at our house, sleeping on the floor, on the
soft, delicate Persian rugs. We were still living in the fourth-floor apartment that was then divided in two, and there was not a lot of space for
everyone to feel like they had some privacy. I was learning how to play
the santoor[33] that year, mostly because my mother wanted me to learn

---

33 Santoor is a trapezoid-shaped hammered dulcimer, the instrument is generally made of
walnut and has 25 bridges. Each bridge has 4 strings, making for a total of 100 strings.

an Iranian traditional instrument. Almost all Bahá'ís knew how to play a musical instrument since it was highly recommended by the faith. I was not that interested in santoor, but I attended the classes for at least a year, just to please my mother. I could not do anything for my uncle's pain, but I could play the few songs I knew on the santoor, and his wife would sing the traditional songs from the northern part of Iran, which was where she was from.

Soon, my uncle's condition worsened; the doctors did not know what was wrong with him. I would see him miserable, in an unknown pain that he felt throughout his newly weakened body. He would ask me to walk on his back, as a back massage to ease his pain, and I tried to distract him by telling him jokes or playing the santoor.

One day, my mom walked into the room in which my uncle was resting, and she saw him taking off his pants. She had asked him to stop getting undressed without closing the door, but he had not cared and continued undressing in front of my mother as if he had not heard or understood her. He had started to perform unnecessary and inappropriate behavior, and he was unaware of his actions. He was transferred to the hospital for further testing and was admitted for care. From the first signs of his symptoms to the day he passed it only took three short weeks.

The day that my oldest uncle passed away, my cousin, Shaghayegh, Assal's oldest sister, was at our house. She had just arrived for a visit and was taking off her Hijab. Under her Hijab she was wearing a black blouse; that I remember very vividly. We were both in the middle bedroom, with the curtains open, and there was plenty of natural light coming into the room. As always, the tall glass doors that opened to the balcony were wide open and the light breeze softly blew the white lace curtains into the bedroom. My mom asked my cousin, "Why did you wear black?"

She told my mom, "For no reason."

My mom told her, "Do you not know it is bad luck for a young single girl to wear black?"

Shaghayegh started telling my mother that this is just a myth and there is nothing true about it, but they were interrupted by a phone call.

No one had cell phones yet, but we had a fancy, cordless, chunky white home phone. My mother walked to the kitchen to answer the phone, and she left Shaghayegh and me in the bedroom. I remember I was admiring her beauty and youth as she was fixing her curly black hair, which was messy due to wearing the Hijab. We heard my mom, saying, "What do you mean? Tell me the truth, what happened?" and then she screamed "No, oh God!"

Shaghayegh and I looked at one another, surprised for a few seconds, and then ran towards the kitchen. My mother was on the kitchen floor, crying. She said that my oldest uncle had just passed. We all started to cry and soon wondered about the myth "It is bad luck for a young single girl to wear black."

My oldest uncle was only fifty-two years old when he passed away, so young. After weeks of mourning, cooking Halva[34] and making a lot of walnut-stuffed dates[35], all of my cousins had become experts in taking care of their parents and the hosts visiting.

It was not even the next year when Shaghayegh's father, another paternal uncle, passed away. One day we got the phone call that he had a heart attack and that week we went to the hospital to visit him. I was not allowed in the ICU but saw him through the glass window of his room. He used to smoke a lot of cigarettes, and maybe that is why he had a heart attack. The day we visited him, my mom had made him shrimp and rice, because he loved my mom's cooking, and my mother hand-fed my uncle on

34 A pastry made of flour and Saffron, served at someone's memorials and/or funeral.
35 A dessert served at someone's memorial and/or funeral.

the hospital bed. I remember that my mother had purchased black leather fabric and had someone sew matching black leather Nowruz outfits for my brothers and me. Nowruz was less than a month away. She had not listened to her own myth of purchasing black fabric—it was bad luck to buy black fabric when no one was dead as well as for young single people to wear black. My mother had a dream about both of my uncles exactly one week prior to their passing.

I remember the day that someone called to say that Shaghayegh's father had passed. I was alone in the house with my oldest brother, and I got my period for the first time. My mom was at my uncle's house, and I had to call her to ask what I needed to do. My mother's myth was that I got my first period because I was very stressed that my uncle had passed. She told me where the pads were and how to use one over the phone. I was never actually trained on using the pads. There was no time to have those special first moments in our family.

Since my oldest uncle had already died, one of the other uncles had become his family's legal guardian. My younger uncle was the legal guardian for six single girls since, by then, two of his brothers had passed away and had left their wives and single daughters behind. It was a lot of responsibility. Since he would manage their financial affairs, and if any of the girls wanted to get married, he was legally bound to get involved to ensure they were making the right decision.

My cousin, Shaghayegh, had a disagreement with my younger uncle, her legal guardian, about marrying the man she loved. The man she loved did not have a lot of money and was from a large family. My father was not anyone's legal guardian, but he was present at the proposal ceremony, and neither my father nor my uncle agreed to the marriage. Shaghayegh was hurt, and tired of the uncles making decisions for her life. She was very young to get married, only twenty-one years old, and my father and my uncles wanted the best for her.

For the entire winter, Shaghayegh and her mother would come over to our house to discuss the marriage, and my father would say no, you do not have my permission. They did not need my father's permission anyway since he was not the legal guardian, but they needed his support to influence the other uncles. I did not know how intense the situation was at Shaghayegh's house, but I was a young teenager and happy that my young beautiful cousins were getting married and that we had an excuse to get together and dance.

Two years after Shaghayegh's father passed away, a few weeks before Nowruz, and two days after her father's second memorial, one of the five sisters of my oldest paternal uncle was getting engaged. That long, dark winter night, we all drove to my oldest uncle's house to participate in my cousin's engagement party. Everyone was going there to celebrate her engagement. No one knew that this was going to be a night to remember, not because it was an engagement party, but because it was going to be a wicked night.

We arrived on time, dressed up and prepared to dance and have a good time. Most women and children were in the only bedroom of that house, waiting for the male adults to have their talks about the future of the bride- and groom-to-be, and then announce the engagement.

We had to be quiet and polite; we could not be loud or walk into the living room, so we all stayed in the bedroom. Everything was fine, until we all got concerned because my cousin Shaghayegh and her family were late. Not everyone had cell phones those days, so my mother called my uncle out of the ceremony and asked him to call Shaghayegh's house. He called, and as he mumbled on the phone, his face turned pale. After his phone call was over, he rushed out of the room and gave no answers to us. When he pulled my father aside and whispered in his ear, the women got concerned but did not want to make a scene in front of the groom's family.

The word "hospital" came out of my father's and my uncle's secret conversations. Hearing that, a couple of the women that were in the bedroom passed out. We had been told to add gold jewelry to water to electrolyze the water to help people come back to consciousness, so we forced some of that twenty-four carat gold-infused water down their throats and they soon regained consciousness.

My uncles and father went to the front yard and smoked some cigarettes. There were phone conversations and worried faces. Some people left the party early to make it to the hospital even though it was still unclear who was at the hospital. The engagement ceremony was rushed to a happy conclusion, and there was some music playing in the background just to save face in front of the family of my cousin's future husband. At some point we found out that it was my cousin, Shaghayegh, who went to the hospital, but why was still unknown. A few minutes had passed when Assal, Shaghayegh's sister, was instructed to take a taxi to get to the engagement party. She told us that they took Shaghayegh to the hospital, but she was unclear about what had happened.

The engagement ceremony ended much earlier than we all expected. I did not care that we did not get to dance around and hang out more with family members. I just wanted Shaghayegh to be okay. No one rushed to the hospital after the ceremony. I remember my father smoking in silence on the ride back to the house, and he dropped Assal and me off at our house. Not many of us were staying or sleeping at our own house that night. The entire family and cousins were scattered around the city, spending the night at each other's house. My oldest brother bought us pizza and fries. He had never done that before; we never ate out, but he was trying to treat us to something nice. Later that night, as we all slept next to each other on the soft and delicate living room Persian rug, I heard from my brother's conversations with others that Shaghayegh was dead. I did not tell Assal that her sister was dead; I just told her that everything would be okay.

Right now, I am proud of the thirteen-year-old Donya for being so strong and not saying anything to Assal. I held Assal's hand all night and promised her that I would take care of her and she would never be alone, and I stayed true to my promise. I did not leave her side; I have always made sure she is included in all of my life events and is surrounded by happiness. The next day we were told to wear black before going to Assal's house. Her mother did not know Shaghayegh was dead, or maybe she knew and was in denial. They told her that she could not see Shaghayegh because she was very sick, and the hospital would not allow it. Assal's other sister was only nineteen years old, and she knew that Shaghayegh was dead.

It was almost noon, and Assal's mother was still crying and asking the men to drive her to the hospital so she could see her daughter. She would ask us, "Why are you all here? My daughter is alone at the hospital." My uncles were just smoking cigarettes in the yard, they did not know how to tell her that Shaghayegh was already at the morgue. Maybe they just did not have the guts to tell her. They were the men, but not man enough to tell a mother that her daughter was not coming home.

Finally, Assal's other sister, tired of her mother not knowing, walked over to her mother, who was sitting in the middle of the living room, on their beautiful Tabriz Persian rug, crying and hitting herself. She sat on her knees and said, "Mom, she is dead."

Her mom looked right through her and ignored what she just said, stood up, and started looking for her Hijab to leave the house. She said, "I can take a taxi and go to the hospital on my own. I want to see my daughter."

I remember this all very vividly, because my cousins and I were in the bedroom watching this turning point in our lives. I held Assal close to me. I knew it was going to get very scary very soon. She stared into my eyes, looking for an answer. I looked away but held her tighter in my arms, hiding the soon-to-fall tears that I had been holding back all night.

Shaghayegh's mother was being followed around the house by other women who were telling her to calm down. One more time Assal's, sister, now her only one, walked over to her mom and said, "Mom, sit down. Why do you want to go to the hospital? She is dead." There was a deadly silence in the house. There were many people, standing around the living room, staring at my cousin and her mother, but no one was crying yet.

After a few seconds of silence, her mom screamed so loud that I felt the vibration of her scream pass through my body. My head was pounding, my heart was beating hard, and anxiety had filled my veins. I was no longer able to hold back the tears. They fell from my face one after the other as if there was a faucet connected to my eyes. I was holding Assal so tight, not letting her see my tears as she had just learned that Shaghayegh was dead. Everyone began to cry out loud now. We had all been holding back our tears since the last night; we could not believe that she was not with us anymore. I wish I knew the last time I saw her; I would have taken a mental picture to have and to cherish now. My mother had a dream exactly one week before that horrible event. She had dreamt that Shaghayegh's father, who had died two years earlier, was burying his own daughter, Shaghayegh, inside my grandmother's house.

Assal was crying on my shoulders, and I told her that I promised to always be there for her. Her mom still did not believe the news. She screamed so much, and even attempted to leave the house and go to the hospital. By the end of that day, she had lost her voice and for several days she had to write on a piece of paper in order to communicate with. I remember all of this so clearly, because I always stood in the corner of the scene and watched. She would scream "My daughter! My virgin daughter! She wanted to get married. Why are my Shaghayegh's flower petals scattered?!" We were all dehydrated from crying so much. We were not eating. No one was attending to the kids or cared how we felt.

This was just the beginning of dark days in our family. For forty days, including the Persian New Year, we did not do anything but cry. More family members came to Tehran from other provinces to attend the memorials. We had many memorials for her in our homes, mosques, and at her grave site. We knew that her burial was going to be insanely horrifying, with all the potential screaming and crying, and the possibility of some people passing out at the burial site. I had seen the burial of my two uncles and was suspecting this one to be many times worse. Therefore, I kept Assal with me in their house and told her that she should not go to the burial. She wanted to, but I did not let her.

Years later she thanked me for that. The burial had been a disaster, with people crying, screaming, and passing out at her grave site. Assal spent almost all of that summer at our house. She lived fifteen minutes away from us, but I wanted to take care of her; therefore, I had her pack some clothes and come to stay with us. We would go to different summer classes together, and we became very close. I would distract her by talking about celebrity crushes, doing our nails, and watching American and Iranian movies. That summer, I was writing a love novel, and Assal was very encouraging to me and liked listening to my short stories because it distracted her from the loss of her sister.

It was such an emotional torture to be around my father's family after someone had passed, especially Shaghayegh's family, but it was nice to go to their house and keep their mind off of their loss. I was a natural comedian and would tell jokes to entertain and distract the family, at least until they went to bed, when they wondered how it could have been prevented, or how they could ever move on.

Shaghayegh's death changed the way we all looked at one another. She was gone, and we felt her empty seat at the gatherings. Shaghayegh means poppy flower. A red, short-lived flower with a black and yellow center. She changed our family with her death and to this date, no one has gotten over the tragedy of a life lost so young.

THE MAGICIAN

Our immediate family had a very close friendship with another family as we were growing up. My mother had met them when she was trying to find a rental apartment during the revolution, after she had given birth to my second brother. She had found a suitable apartment, owned by a wealthy man, but was short on the deposit. She told him that she knew that his rental rates were high, but she could not afford the rate at the time and since her newborn child was sick, that she had spent a lot of money on medical bills, and that she needed to find a shelter for her family.

The man, Ali, saw my sick brother in my mother's arms and told her, "You can move in anytime you want, and you pay as much as you can, sister." My mother soon moved into Ali's rental property, which was the level below Ali's apartment in the same building, and only paid as much as she could at the time. This is how they became great family friends for life. During the short year that my mother lived in their rental property, the noble man's wife gave birth to their fourth and last child, a girl. My mother moved out of their rental property once she bought the house in which I was born and raised, but they all kept in touch even though our homes were far from one another.

Ali's family was closer to us than our own family, and we would spend weekends and many summer nights together, juicing sour grapes, and cleaning and packing fava beans and herbs. Most of the time we would go to their house and sit on their large balcony around a mountain of beans and herbs. The large Persian rug covering the surface of the large balcony would accommodate all of the women as they completed their chores, while the men played backgammon, drank tea, and smoked hookah.[36] We would have dinner parties and sleepovers at each other's homes since our houses were far apart, and we never wanted to drive back to our homes in the middle of the night.

Even my uncles and aunts knew and respected Ali's family. In the winter we would pray for snow, so that schools would be canceled, and we could stay longer at their house. Ali would always say, "Kids will grow up, they will catch up with their schoolwork, but these are the nights to remember. So what if they miss a couple of days of school?" He was right, we grew up and missing a day or two of school made no difference, but those memories will live forever. We would spend at least one night of Ramadan at their house, since they were Muslim, and would have large gatherings for breaking the fast in the evening. More importantly, we were always there for each other through happiness and grief.

Ali and his wife, Ava, got engaged when she was only nine and he was nineteen years old. She always said that after they got engaged, he would come to her father's house and wanted to touch and kiss her, but she would run away to the neighbor's house through the narrow window of her bedroom. She said she had a skinny, short body and had not even had her first period yet when her family forced her to marry Ali. After the marriage she moved into her husband's house.

She had her first child right after she got her first period at age thirteen, at her husband's house, and found herself playing with life-size dolls instead of plastic dolls. She did not marry for love, but she loved her children, and she did not believe that a husband and wife had to marry for love. Her husband was a wealthy man until his fun times of smoking

---

36 A Persian water pipe used to smoke tobacco

opium turned into a habit and then into an ugly addiction. He lost most of his belongings, buildings, and lands, as well as his family's respect, because of his addiction.

One day, a few years after my mother and Ali's family became friends, Ava went to the hospital to accompany her pregnant sister during a checkup. While at the hospital she ran into Ali, and asked him what he was doing at the maternity ward. That is when she found out that he had cheated on her, married another woman several years before, and his second wife was now giving birth to their second child, another girl. Ava was shocked but did not have any way to leave the marriage. In the case of a divorce, she would have lost her children to Ali would have had to move back in with her parents, and would probably never be able to re-marry. She would be viewed as a burden by her family for the rest of her life.

She did not get a divorce. She did what almost every Iranian woman did at the time she made him divorce his second wife and leave his first daughter from the second marriage with his second wife. Sometimes the oldest daughter from the second marriage would go to live with Ava and her family. Both of the girls from the second wife were deeply hated by their stepsiblings.

The second daughter from his second wife is just a year or two older than me, and she would write poetry, which would get ripped and thrown away by the older half-sisters and -brothers. It was not her fault that she was born in this family. Her father had decided this future for her, and she could not have chosen her parents. Ava's kids even renamed her so that her name would rhyme with the other half-sisters' names. They would say his second wife had mental issues and she was completely aware that Ali already had a family when she married him. Having had two different lives, and having gone through an embarrassing divorce, his addiction to opium had ruined whatever was left of his reputation. He had lost all his power in the house as if a lion had lost his claws.

After that, Ava did not like Ali as much anymore. I grew up playing with the youngest daughter in the family and always thought to myself that Ava had some nerve to live with Ali and forgive him after what he had done. She also had to raise his love child, which must have been hard on her. Ava would order the young girl around and tell her to complete all of the household chores. After I grew up and saw what kind of freedoms and rights Iranian women have after divorce, I realized that she had made the best decision, staying with him for her children's sake.

Life was the same if not worse after we had moved to the second floor of the building. There had been some death in the family, and everyone was dis-oriented. We spent a lot of time with my father's remaining family members. My mother was always busy making sure we had enough food, and school supplies, and that our basic needs were met. We did not feel the absence of my father being gone on his "work" trips since my mother was always there if we needed her.

Our history is divided into two sections, Before Dividing the fourth-floor apartment into two smaller apartments (BD) and After Dividing the apartments (AD). Because of my love for participating in house chores to help my mother out, my mother had left the stepstool by the sink so I could stand on it and wash the dishes. One day, before my mom divided the house, my father was sitting in the hallway by the kitchen and he asked me a question that made my seven-year-old's blood boil. "What would you do if I marry another woman?" he asked, calmly, as if he had always wanted to ask me this question.

What kind of sick-minded father would ask his little, only, daughter this question? I had to give him an answer, a question like that needed a strong answer, or at least that was what I thought at that time. I told him, "I would kill her; I would put poison in her food and kill her and maybe I would poison you too." He often asked these hypothetical types of questions about him having another wife and would laugh at our answers as if our anger pleased him.

A while after we moved to the apartment on the second floor, my two older brothers moved out of the house and into an apartment close by to practice their independence. I finally got my own bedroom, which was between my youngest brother's bedroom and my parents' bedroom.

There were months when my father claimed that he had lost his birth certificate, but I am not sure if my mother believed my father's side of the story. It was the election year, and I was finishing the last year of middle school. At the time, Iranian people voted with their birth certificates, and the government stamped the last pages of their birth certificate to prove that they had voted. There was a rumor, spread by the government, that there would be some consequences if you did not vote in an election and were over eighteen years old. The consequences included a possible loan or job rejection. This was a way for the government to make sure everyone voted at every presidential election. Large numbers of participants were important to the government because it gave the impression that people were engaged in politics and, therefore, that they liked and supported the new regime.

The closest voting stand to our house was the mosque across the street. I was underage and was not able to vote, but that day my father voted. Since most of the important events in Persian culture happen in the kitchen, ironically, that day we were in the kitchen when he came back from voting. As he approached the kitchen, through the narrow hall that connected the TV room to the kitchen, I asked if he had voted. He replied, with pride, "Yes, of course." He said that to me because my mother was advised against voting in Iran, where one has to take a political side in order to cast a vote. As Bahá'ís, we are advised against taking a political side. He always took pride in participating in any political or religious event and he made sure he bragged about it to all of us to show that he was a strong supporter of the Islamic Republic of Iran's regime and what they stood for.

Quickly after his reply, I confronted him in front of my mother and asked how he was able to vote without his birth certificate. By then he had reached the kitchen and was standing by the wall, right next to the old yellow fridge. He had just walked into a trap. I was standing by the sink; my mother was busy sautéing something in the pan on the gas stove. She heard my comment, stopped cooking, and turned around, slowly, to follow the subject. I walked towards my dad, and as I reached in his button-up shirt's left pocket, I repeated my question, "How could someone vote without their birth certificate?" I emphasized the "how" as I pulled out the supposedly lost birth certificate out of his pocket.

My father was shocked, speechless, just like the rest of the family, and he froze. It was as if I just had pulled an alive rabbit from my father's pocket in front of everyone. I was the magician and for once I was seen. My mother quickly walked over to me and said, "How did you know that?"

I said, "Mom, how was he going to vote without this? It's just common sense."

My father was staring at me the entire time, in disbelief, and I know he felt betrayed by me, his only daughter. I could smell "busted" in the kitchen, or maybe it was what my mother was sautéing on the stove.

My mom snatched the birth certificate out of my hand and told my father that she was going to hold on to it, so he would not "lose" it again, which seemed more like a threat than a kind gesture. There was much bickering and arguing after that event that day, but my job was done and I walked away into my bedroom, listening to music to block their fighting noise.

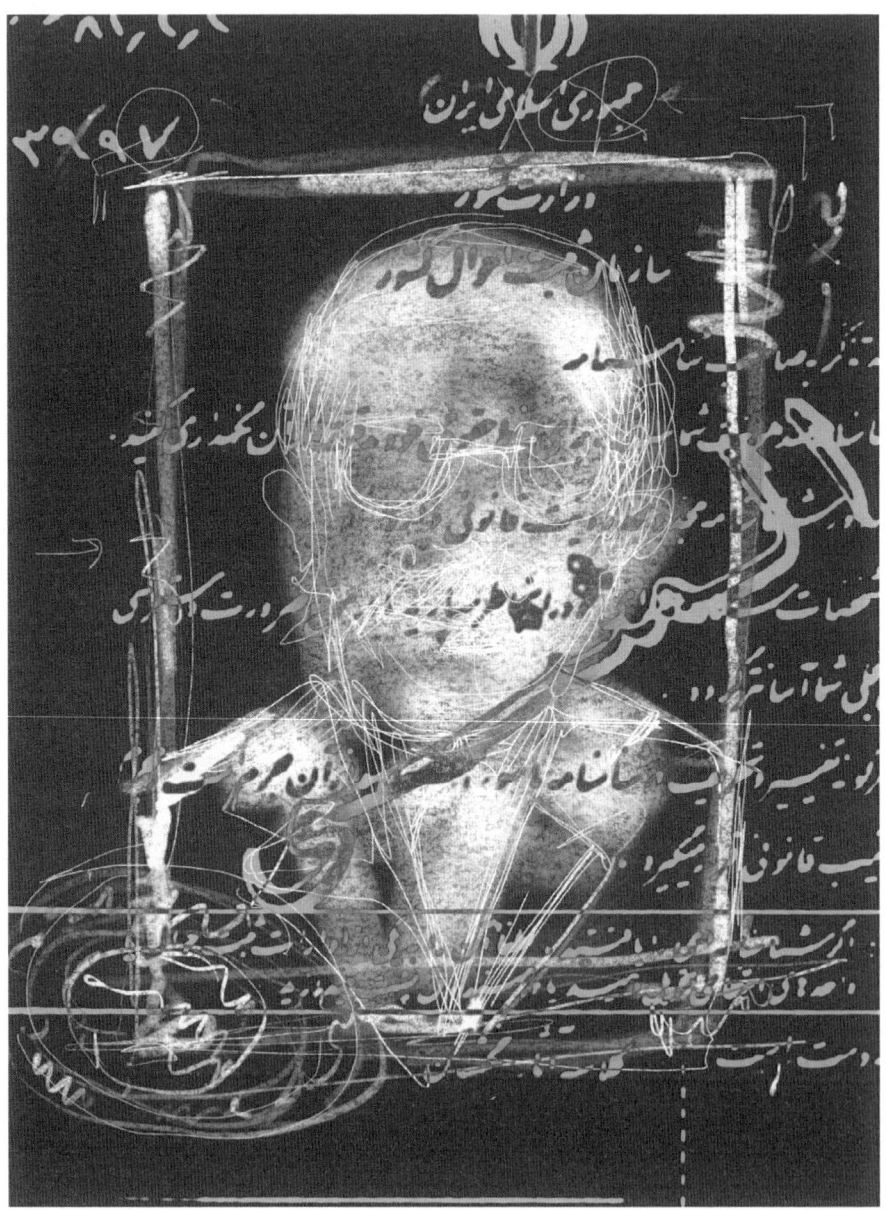

After this incident, on a school night I was in my bedroom with my door open when I heard our home phone ring. The phone call was answered after a few rings. I heard my parents' bedroom door close, which was odd. I heard my parents talking, and while I normally would not spy on their conversations, I was curious as to who had called and why my parents had closed the door. Did someone die again? They never talked to each other behind closed doors. My father did not believe in consultation he simply yelled. My mother thought people could improve their relationship by having civil conversations with one another, which never worked in our house. No one ever had the temper of being confronted or consulted. It was not necessarily bad news if people were yelling at each other, but it was definitely bad news if they were talking in low tones behind closed doors. Something horrible was about to happen if two people were talking quietly behind closed doors in our house. There must have been something going on, and I had to know it.

I walked quietly out of my room, taking soft steps. My parents' bedroom door was completely closed. They could see my shadow and discover my presence if I would stand by the bedroom door, or worse, if my brother were to walk out of his bedroom, he would find me spying on my parents. I went to the shower through the kitchen and stood behind the master bedroom's cracked door that opened to the shower. I could see the room through the cracked door. My father was sitting on the ground, and he was leaning on the bedroom wall shared with my bedroom and my mother was across from him, holding the phone to her ear, walking back and forth. I could not see her face, but she was uneasy and impatient. My father was holding his head in his hands. He smoked his already lit cigarette occasionally, but he was not enjoying it; he was just too nervous. The whole setting made me anxious and worried, but I was undercover, spying on my parents, and could not ask questions at the time.

My father had a flushed and fearful face. He would look up at my mother hesitantly. I cannot remember what exactly was being said on the phone, but I later found out there was a woman on the other side of the phone. The woman had called our house to tell my mom that she had married my father the day before. I do not understand why she had to call my mom and announce that. It is not as if it was an important moment of my mom's life and neither was she dying to know it. I did not see my mother's face, but I am sure it was fearful. I heard my mom's worried voice, trying to be polite and patient with the woman on the phone. I felt neither sad or pleasant. It felt as if I had been waiting for my father to mess things up for a long time.

HEADQUARTERS IN MY MOM'S BEDROOM

I was my parents' first child to find out about my father's betrayal, and I did not tell the others. The night of the phone call was a quiet night, and my parents did not raise their voices; they kept to themselves. I believe this was expected from my father since he often flirted with other women in public or private. The knowledge of what had happened made me feel like I had a big load on my shoulders to carry. I never told my mother or brothers about what I had overheard. I went to school the next day and told Tera about what had happened. She comforted me by telling me that things would work out in the end.

There was nothing I could do for my parents. I was just fourteen years old and had no power in the house or in society. Soon my mother told friends and family about my father's betrayal. She had to talk to someone and that was not going to be her teenage daughter or twenty-some-year-old sons. My father left the house and told us that he was staying at his mother's house for some time. As the news of my father's affair spread, my father was embarrassed, and it made his return from my grandmother's house even harder. My father would leave the house for days at a time, and then upon his return to the house, he would fight with my mom and leave again. I guess I wanted him gone anyway, so I did not care that he had cheated on my mom. Soon after, my brothers found out about the affair and the situation got uglier and the fights became physical.

Family members started asking me weird questions such as "Have you seen your father's second wife?" or "Oh, poor you, how do you feel now?" It seemed like we were living a documentary, and my parents were trying to make their marriage work on camera. Why would my mother want a lying, cheating man back in her life? She had put up with his lies all her life, and now it was time to move on. The interesting thing is that my father's brothers knew about him cheating on my mom and they often dropped hints to let my mother know that he was a cheater.

Before my father cheated on my mother, or more correctly, before we found out that my father was cheating on my mother, we witnessed the same thing happen to Ali and Ava's family. Because of Ali's affair, their children were not raised properly, and they suffered from emotional trauma for life. I thought that witnessing that horrible situation would have taught a lesson to all men, and would prevent or stop them from cheating on their families and would help them appreciate what they already had.

My father claimed that he stayed at his mother's house the days and nights that he was away. Everyone knew what that meant. He was not at his mother's house; he was at his second wife's house. We did not have a car to go check on him, and getting a taxi from our house to his mother's house was not cheap at all. Plus, if we would ever do that, he would start a major fight.

My father cheated the legal system to marry the second wife. He got a second birth certificate by lying to the government that he had lost his original birth certificate. The new birth certificate did not have my mother's name or any of our names on it, and he used it to marry his second wife, portraying himself as a single fifty-some-year-old man.

In Iran a man can have multiple wives, but he has to ask for his current wife's permission before marrying the new one. Of course, no woman, including my mother, would like to share her husband with another woman. He probably bribed someone to marry them in secret, which was a common thing to do among Muslim men who wanted multiple wives, then he immediately felt guilt and remorse and told my mother. Maybe he thought he could undo his mistake with a single apology. But it was too late, and my mother had already started to tell everyone.

I am glad she did not forgive him right away and was not okay with my father having two wives. We all knew it was not his first time cheating on her. Maybe he did not feel guilty about his actions and he was just immature enough to inform my mother by having his second wife call my mom. My father's second wife showed herself as a weak, lonely, nagging woman, and my father portrayed himself as her protector. In contrast my mother was strong in this situation. She did not want to present herself as a needy and weak woman she never was.

One of my brothers was the first one to break the unspoken rule of "never visiting my father's second wife's house". He probably got tired of the situation at our house and went to my father's second wife's house. I should say that our house was very accommodating to my brother's needs, where my mother provided him with anything he asked for, but maybe he wanted to see that side of the story for himself. Regardless of his intentions, I felt like he was a traitor, but now being the woman, I have become, I do not judge him. I did not have the desire to see my father with another woman, or to help him gain confidence in the biggest mistake of his life.

Soon after my father left the house and told us he was living with his mother, my father's older half-sister came to Tehran and stayed with us. She would not leave; she stayed at our house and talked to my mom for days about this newly developed situation. My aunt would talk on the phone and give the latest news of our house to other family members on a daily basis. Her husband had taken a second wife as well, and he had taken their three children to live in a border town just a few years before. She knew how painful it was for my mother, and she had started a family campaign against all men, and her headquarters was my mother's bedroom.

I never liked that my aunt was sharing more information with others than my mother liked to, but since my mother was in a vulnerable place and none of her sisters were around, she let her stay and be there for her. My mother and my aunt would plan new counterattacks every day to get back at my father. One day they would plan for me to be dropped off at my grandmother's house so my father was forced to stay at my grandmother's house and take care of me or take me to his new wife's house so she had to take care of me, expecting her to soon get tired of taking care of me and eventually leave him. Another day they would plan to write letters to the second wife's family members and expose the truth. Either way, we were all miserable, and the marriage laws of the Islamic Republic of Iran favored the men, not the women.

SHE-DEVIL

We have watched the famous *She Devil*[37] movie was watched many times in our house when we were kids, as it was one of the VHS tape movies we owned. My mother loved the movie because the main female lead role acted by Roseanne Barr was that of a strong one. She was a dedicated wife, who did all she possibly could for her husband, and he did not acknowledge her at all. She was not an amazing cook nor the prettiest, but it seemed like she was trying. He would have his love affairs and lie to his wife all the time. He would say he was working late, but he would be spending time at a lover's house. She would stay up all night worried about him, and take care of their children, who had no manners. Then one day she turned her life around. She burnt the house down so her husband would not have anything to go back to. She dropped the kids off at the lover's house, so her husband and his new lover would have to take care of them.

My mother would always say that if my father ever cheated on her, she would drop us off at his lover's house like Roseanne Barr did in *She Devil*. She always said that she would have absolutely not tolerated such acts and she would leave us with him, so he had to take care of us just like in the movie. She did not know that life was not a movie, and even if she used us to get back at my father, she would not be able to stand the torture to which we would have been subjected. The message that I got from the movie was to try and become a strong and determined woman. Women

---

37 Dark American comedy movie from 1989.

were not weak in American movies. They had choices and free will. I did not know my rights as a child, but I learned as I grew older that I would lose my choices and freedom to men.

Years later my mother told me how she had found out about my father's betrayal. One day in late summer my mother was getting ready to say goodbye to my father as he went on one of his famous work trips, when my father's driver told my mother, "Your husband is not an honest man." My father tried to stop his driver from revealing more things, but the driver told my mother, "Your husband is not who you think he is."

That day, after my father left for his work trip, my mother prayed to God to show her his true side, if he was hiding anything.

When my father came back from that trip, my mother was remodeling the bathroom in our apartment. She loved remodeling the house and had a talent for it. Apparently, my father did not like the changes to the bathroom, and they got into a fight over the bathroom floor tile and my father left the house. One of my brothers told my uncle that our father had gone to his mother's house. My mom had called, and my grandmother said that my father was around, but she never put him on the phone.

Finally, my mother went to my grandmother's house, but no one opened the door. She waited for him at the neighbor's house, across the alley, until they came home. Through the neighbor's window, my mom saw him arriving with his mother, and they both went inside the house. My grandmother's neighbor, who was a distant family member of my father, gave my mom a ride home and my mother did not tell my father that she had seen them. Later on, my mother found out that was the same day that he married the second wife.

Even though my father often claimed that the reason for his affair was the difference between religions, I do not believe it because he knew my mother was a Bahá'í when he had pursued and married her. My mother had not been practicing her religion for years because my father had forbidden it. We were all so young and needed both of our parents and we had lost them both, my father to another woman and my mother to revenge.

While I was growing up my father tried to lecture me on Islam. I told him that I was not Muslim, and that religion was not genetic. I had told him that the Islam he believed in did not catch my interest. Of course, he was demonstrating the wrong, less desirable Islam to us. In Islam, and all other religions, yelling at other people, beating up one's children, or cheating on one's wife are frowned upon. One does not pretend to pray; one actually does it. In Islam one does not just pray when one has had a fight over religion with his wife, one does it regardless of circumstances, five times a day, sincerely, and not in the middle of the house to show off. In Islam one gives to others and should be kind to everyone, especially to one's children and parents. I did not like the Islam my father practiced. His Islam was fake, corrupted, and confusing.

30,000 TOMAN

Family and friends were coming over to our house to show their support for us after my father's betrayal. My uncle's wives did not want to support my father and were against his decision because they did not want their own husbands to do such things. My father did not want to lose his mother or his brothers, and that is why he would ask his brothers and their families to go to his new house, which he shared with his second wife, to show their support. His brothers were vulnerable and fragile. They did not want to give up their relationship with their oldest brother, and they did not quite understand that by going over to my father's second house they were supporting his actions and turning their back on us.

Anyone who would go to my father's house would lose my respect. When my uncle's wives were forced to go over to my father's second home, they came to my mother, apologized for their actions, and asked my mom for her forgiveness. They said that their husbands forced them to go, and they did not even talk to the new wife during the house visit. Of course, we do not know what would have happened if the situation was reversed. Would they have forgiven my mother if she had gone to their husbands' second wives' houses?

Family and friends would come over to visit, and my mom would consult with them on what would be the next move to get revenge on my father. She knew the only things that would hurt my father was his loss of reputation and money. If he would lose parts of his income, he would lose his power over my mother. After years of my mother's sacrifice, living with the limited amount of money that my father always claimed to make, she had to start paying for everything by herself. She was not able to get a job as a religious minority and did not have much savings since she had invested so much in our home. My father was close to his retirement age with all the benefits and pension and had not paid any money for child support, bills, or alimony since he had left the house.

My mother sued my father to get money for alimony and child support. She even took me to the court one time, as it was required for me to be present at the court to show the need for child support. She said that this way we can teach my father that he has made a mistake, but I did it because child support was my right, and since I was his daughter, he was legally responsible for my financial needs.

I believe I was fifteen or sixteen years old when we went to the court. My mom dressed me in black colors, the color for the conservative hijab. She had some water with her, and the guards at the courthouse entrance security made her drink some of it to make sure it was not a flammable liquid. I believe that there were some cases of people burning each other or themselves in the courthouse if they were disappointed by the court's results.

The day we went to the court, I was very stressed out and scared of what was about to happen. It had been months since I had seen my father. He would just come to our house and fight with my mom, cause chaos, and leave. There were never any interactions with us, his own children. I waited as my mother went to complete some paperwork and came back to get me. I did not talk to anyone; I just sat in the middle of the first-floor lobby. I watched all these people fight with one another, mostly husbands and wives since this was a domestic court. I saw their fears, lost futures, and lost hopes. I knew that they had loved one another at some point and now they were in court asking for divorce, money, or their children's custody. Where did the love go? Why did their dreams not come true? Did they know this would happen from the beginning?

My mother came back for me, and took me to the court room, which was on the second floor of that large, round, white building. The courthouse was very close to the train station, far from where we lived. The court rooms were large enough to seat five people. I had always imagined a much larger room in my head, as that was what I had seen in movies. My mother had filed a lot of paperwork to get this court appointment. She knew I was bothered by going there, but she needed me to get back at my father and at least collect some money to pay for the house expenses. Maybe after all these years he would show some responsibility towards his kids. I was my parents' only child who was still under eighteen years old, and my father still had to pay for my needs.

We waited by the courtroom's door and minutes before we were called in, my father arrived and just looked at me from a distance. He stared me down, as if I had done something illegal, unethical, or God forbid, a sin. He did not come close; I did not approach him either.

My mother had taught me a few things to say in the court, and I had memorized them. Standing outside of the courtroom, waiting for our turn, felt like an eternity. I did not feel guilty for going to court against my father, asking for child support; I believed he needed to pay for me, one of his many mistakes. Why did my mother have to support us financially when my father gets to make a lot of money and spend it with his new wife? That was not fair, and I hoped the judge saw this.

They finally called us in. I pushed all of my hair inside of my hijab, so the judge, whose job is to judge, would not judge me on my appearance. My mother and I sat on the right side of the court, and my father sat on the left. We were all facing the judge and one other man who would take notes as we all talked, and occasionally handed some documents to the judge. The room was lit from the large windows facing the major street, but it did not help the stagnated air filling the room. Client after client had come to this very room, shout their disappointments, and talk about their dead dreams. This room was filled with negativity and hatred. Every tissue in my body could feel it.

They read the purpose of our suit; it was to get monthly child support from my father for me. The judge asked my father how much he makes, and he had brought his lowest paycheck to show that he has no money to support us. I just wanted to ask the judge; how can he have two wives and not enough money to support them both? Is not that against the Islamic law? But I was not in the fairest court in the world; I was in front of a man who probably had multiple wives himself, most likely had no education, followed his daily mood more than the actual laws, and was definitely appointed by a revolutionary supporter.

My mother showed documents to the judge to prove that my father was lying about his monthly income, that he had a second wife, and that it had been a couple of years since he had paid a penny for child support. The judged looked the documents over and ruled 30,000 Toman per month as child support for me. To put that in perspective, that was equivalent to $27 per month, at the time. With that much money I was not able to do much. I might have been able to rent couple of movies and buy some chips and dips to go with it. I was shocked. I knew my father had more money because after my father had cheated, my mother had found out how much money he really made. He was making much more than he was bringing home for almost thirty years, his entire career. Every time he went on a work trip, he would receive a bonus, which we did not know about until after he moved out. He never brought that money home.

I asked the judge, "How is that amount fair?" He said, "Young girl, do not be rude. Be thankful."

I asked, "Would your daughter be thankful with 30,000 Toman a month? Would that buy her clothes? A school uniform?"

He was shocked that I spoke up and replied, "You do not have to buy anything expensive." I was furious and was shocked by how unfair this judge was. My heart was racing, and all the blood had rushed to my face. My hands were shaking and were so cold that I could not even feel my fingertips. Did he have no understanding of the life expenses of a teenager? Was he not a domestic judge? Did he not judge people's income and life expenses on a daily basis? I said, "Where do they sell cheap clothes that would cost 30,000 Toman? Tell me so I can buy them, too."

My mother stopped me from getting into a verbal fight with the judge. What I had said was insulting and sarcastic. I did not want my father's money, I wanted justice. That rusted court room and rotten judge was enough for me to learn that there is no justice in this country, especially not for women and more specifically, not for women who spoke up. No one helped us take our right after my father had left us. All the judges were male and ruled in my father's favor in almost every court and there was nothing we could do to teach him a lesson to hold him accountable for his awful and destructive actions.

I was so emotional that I burst into tears at the court. I hated myself for the fact that I was weak and had cried in front of men in charge of the court, and in front of my father who had no regard or empathy for my tears. Later in life I learned how to hold my tears back and not cry in front of my enemies. That day I cried, not because there was not enough money, but because of the unfairness that other women and I had to endure in that closed-minded country that I had to call home. I was born in an unfair land, where men were right regardless of their actions, and the newly made-up constitution by the government was never followed.

My mother did not say much on the way back home. She asked if I wanted her to buy me something to eat and I told her that I did not need anything, and that I just wanted to go home. She knew I was embarrassed because I had cried, and that felt like I had let her down. She did not make me go to any courts after that event and we never collected any child support or alimony from my father. She soon realized that this was all too emotional for a young teenage girl.

My mother had a lawyer to help her with the divorce proceedings. She had hired Ava's son-in-law, who was married to the oldest daughter from Ali's second wife. What a small world! Ava's entire family was on our side, and if Ali had the slightest inclination to take my father's side, the women in his family would stare him down. Ali was just disappointed that my father did not learn from his own mistakes and had to experience the mess by himself. My brothers were in shock at first, but then they started fighting against my father. They were looking at it from a man's standpoint, and they would treat him as a man who had listened to his lust when he decided to marry the other woman.

In the beginning, my father would occasionally come to the house, fight, and leave for weeks. My father would say that he wanted to come back, but my mother had ruined his reputation by telling everyone. I thought that he had burnt all his bridges with us and that was more important than his reputation among the family and friends. He did not want to divorce his second wife, but he still wanted to come back to us. He would tell my mom, "She has nothing against you. She is older than you, and she is not even pretty. Let her be."

When my mother saw the second wife for the first time, she realized that my father had married a much less attractive woman whose left eye was bigger than the right one. The second wife was a retired teacher who was supposedly never married and therefore she had no children. There were rumors that my father had a son with her who was ten years old, but that was never proven.

I would hear all of my parents' conversations through the shared bedroom wall whenever my father would return. Some nights my father would tell my mom that he missed her, and that he wanted to come back, but that was followed by a loud fight and he would soon storm out. She would tell people that my father had told her that he could not divorce his second wife because he felt badly for her, and that she was alone in this world. How that was an excuse to tear apart a family of six, I will never know!

During one of the fights that we had with my father, my brother asked him to leave the house indefinitely. I stepped in front of the front door and told my father that he had to go over my dead body to leave. He picked up my bicycle that was by the front door, threw it into the middle of the living room, and said, "I will go over your dead body if I have to, but I will leave." That was a turning point for me, I knew that he was gone; he was emotionally and mentally gone.

My father stopped coming over after a while, and we continued to receive pitying looks and hugs from family members and close friends. My mother would sit on one side of the living room, and our guests would sit on the other side and ask my mom about my dad and what she wished to do next. They would ask how she found out, what she thought actually happened, or how long it had been going on. I had no power to stop them from asking her. It was rude to tell the guests to mind their own business. These questions were new to each guest but old for my mother, and giving the same repetitive answers bothered my mom as if she were picking at a newly healed wound. I would just observe her go through a range of emotions on a daily basis; I can only imagine how she felt.

There was gossip in our house twenty-four hours per day, seven days per week. Most of the people hated my father for what he had done to my mother, and to all of us. I could not believe after all the things that she had done for my father, giving up practicing her religion and staying behind in Iran when her siblings left as religious refugees, that he would cheat on her and leave her for another woman. What could he possibly want that my mother did not have? She gave him the best and the most important things loyalty, honesty, and attentiveness.

One day when my mother was at the court, completing some divorce papers, the clerk told my mother that he just saw another woman filing for divorce from the same man. She begged the clerk to tell her what the other woman looked like. The clerk felt bad for my mom and told her what the other woman, the second wife, looked like and what hijab she was wearing, and my mother managed to find her in the crowded court building. My mother confronted her, and the second wife told my mom that she had not known that my father was a married man, and that she wanted to divorce him now.

How was that even possible? At the time it was very unlikely for a man in Iran, in his fifties to be unmarried and childless. She knew my father's family; her mother was a good friend of my grandmother for years and that is how they had met. Even after she found out about my mother and that there were children involved, she still did not file for divorce until a couple of years later, and when she finally did, she did not follow through. The few encounters that my mother had with the second wife were always brief and sad, and my mother would end up feeling bad for the other woman. We soon realized that the other woman had to live with my father now, and he was her punishment for tearing apart a family of six.

My mother, my brothers, and I did not have any communications about our new situation after my father left. We all just avoided discussing it with one another. I do not think it was wise to avoid one another and to seek support from outside, but we did not know better.

My mother would go to court almost every day of the week. She would sue my father for different reasons, and she was trying to get a divorce, but my father would not divorce either wife. I believe he enjoyed the drama and torture that he was causing. Maybe this was his retirement game. My mother had to prove to the court that he had lied to the government and had gotten a second, illegal birth certificate in order to marry the second wife. Thanks to me, she had his original birth certificate to prove that he had cheated the system. But the judges were all men. They did not care about my mother's pain, and they would rule in my father's favor most of the time and that would force my mother to go to more court hearings.

The government had recently announced that everyone needed to get a government issued identification card, with a specific identification number. In order for us children to get the government-issued identification card, we had to provide them with our parents' birth certificates. Our names were on both parents' birth certificates, as in Iran the birth certificates hold details of one's spouse and children, and that is how we would prove who our father or mother is. The tricky part was that my mother had to make sure she had applied for the new identification cards before my father applied for his, so she could use the original birth certificate that had our names as his children, or we would have been considered illegitimate. My mother was a strong woman who had lost her sword and now she was fighting with her nails. It did not look good on her at times, she seemed desperate, but maybe I would have done the same. At least she had a plan and was on top of her game, trying to protect her children's rights and future in a country that had no regard for women nor for religious minorities.

I did not feel too bad about my father being gone forever. I just felt bad that my mother would not have any support from now on, even though he was not an involved dad when he was around. I had my own little world, reading Shel Silverstein's poetry, writing love novels, and listening to Western music, trying to mimic their accents and dance moves. Even though my older brothers moved back, soon after my father left, to support the house, most of the time they were gone to their friends' homes to stay away from the drama. My oldest brother was in his twenties and felt responsible for taking care of what was left of the family, and I think that was unfair to him.

I was in disbelief that a man would just turn his back toward his wife of twenty-some years, and on his four children. I could see that my mother and brothers were all hurt. I knew that because they were older, they were supposed to be stronger, but they were more damaged than I was. We all dealt with the pain in our own way. I am not sure why they were hurt by the void created after my father left us; we did not even want him in the house anyway. It was always better when he was gone on his work trips, as we all were able to express ourselves freely, dance, sing, create, and invite friends over. When he would come back home from his trips, there was a strange silence in the house, as if a black cloud were over the household. We had to hold our breath and hide in our own corners. With the knowledge that I have now, I wish we had all attended regular family therapy sessions to express our feelings and maybe work through the hard times, but back then any type of therapy meant one was clinically insane and, therefore, it was frowned upon.

Now that he was permanently gone, we would not see my father for months at a time. Even though he was living less than thirty minutes away from us, at his second wife's house, he would never come to check on us. We had no way to get a hold of him because he did not have a cell phone and he would always say that he was at his mother's house, yet every time we would call his mother's house, she would say that he was not there, or that he just went to the local supermarket to buy something. Everyone was in denial.

My grandmother was very bad at covering up for him, and while she hated to lie for her son, she did it anyway. There was no caller ID yet, but after a few minutes of us calling my grandmother's home phone, he would always call back and say, in an angry tone, "What do you want from me?" We had nothing to say to him, and most of the times it was my mother who had instructed me to call and see whether or not he was at my grandmother's house so she could either serve him with court papers or just torture him by having us call him and check on him. He never called for birthdays or New Years. He did not know what our daily routines were or if we had enough to eat, or enough to buy school supplies. He just left and shut down his brain and father instincts.

After a while I told my mom that I was ready to go and see what Baháʼís have to say. I wanted to see the difference between the Baháʼí Faith and Islam. I felt the need to rely on something strong that made sense for the day and age we were living in. Whenever my mom would talk about the Baháʼí Faith, when she prayed or read the sacred Writings, she had more inner peace and seemed more calm and encouraged.

She contacted some of the Baháʼís we were acquainted with in our neighborhood. There was a Baháʼí woman who was married to a man from Afghanistan, and her husband was usually away for work. They had some Baháʼí gatherings and activities at their house, and we started to attend. Soon we realized there were so many Baháʼís in our neighborhood, but we had not known because they were not supposed to make that information public.

The fascinating part was that I met some of my own classmates who were Baháʼí, but I had not known it before because Baháʼís were not allowed to volunteer such information at school. At the time, if Baháʼís were asked about their religion, they had to tell the truth, but if they were not asked, the wise thing was to not bring it up. Baháʼís were in a lot of danger, and it was not safe to go around teaching the Faith or voluntarily telling everyone that they were Baháʼí.

Baháʼís were labeled as unclean and untouchable by Muslims, and there were many rumors about this new Faith. My mom and I spent time with the Bahá'í community and started to attend their gatherings, without my father's knowledge. All of the gatherings were hosted by the Bahá'ís, in their homes, in a quiet and secretive manner that would not get the Muslim neighbors' or the government's attention. There were no Bahá'í centers where we could go to attend gatherings since the government had demolished them all after the revolution. The Bahá'í community had asked my mother if my father knew of my participation in the gatherings. She answered that he had left the house and was not aware of us attending the gatherings.

The Bahá'í community was concerned about my father finding out the fact that I have been attending the gatherings since I was under eighteen years of age, and technically needed my father's permission to attend the Bahá'í gatherings. My father had threatened my mom and me that if he found out that I participated in any Bahá'í activities, he would give the location of the gatherings and of the neighborhood Bahá'ís to the government agents so that they would arrest the Bahá'ís in our community. That did not stop us from attending the gatherings, but it sure scared us as a community. My mother and I had to be more discreet and not draw any attention to ourselves, especially my father's attention.

While attending Bahá'í gatherings, I realized how boys and girls are comfortable with each other, and how they maintain a healthy relationship, which was nothing like in the Muslim community that discouraged any relationship between men and women. That was refreshing. I enjoyed being friends with the opposite sex, and it felt as if there were something missing in our social lives since boys and girls were forbidden to interact with one another by the government and highly discouraged to do so by the society.

In the meantime, since my mother had sued my father for alimony and child support and gained access to my father's paystubs, she found out that my father made way more money than he had claimed for years.

My mother was furious to see that my father had denied funds for my brother's university education, due to his low income. She had to sell her wedding band and some Persian rugs to pay for it, when in fact he had enough income to support the university costs. She had to be frugal with everything throughout their marriage because she thought my father was making much less than what he was actually making.

Even though my mom was not the guilty party in this new situation, she was under a lot of pressure and ashamed of her husband's actions. She was ashamed of walking on the street in the neighborhood or shopping at the local stores, since all the vendors knew my father and had been friends with our family for years. The whole neighborhood knew that my father had left, and they would stare at her as if she was responsible for it. As a woman in Iran, she was not in an appropriate situation.

Later in life, my mother told me that some neighborhood men had offered her temporary marriage.[38] Those were hard days for all of us. I did not like the way people judged my mother or our family's situation. Living in our neighborhood was getting harder every day. It was true that things had changed, and they would change more in the upcoming years, but I wanted to act like nothing had happened, and I did not want to leave my comfort zone.

My brothers were old enough to be married, but instead my father had gotten married for the second time. That had ruined our reputation and made it hard for us kids to get married in the future. My brothers and I did not even want to talk about the betrayal or its effect on us. Sometimes we joked about the hard and unfortunate situation caused by our father's desires and stubbornness, but we did not want to have a serious conversation about what it meant to not have our father in our lives anymore.

---

38 An Islamic practice that unites men and woman as husband and wife for a limited, pre-determined, duration. This duration could be for hours, days, weeks, months or years.

My hurt and distressed mother had to ride the bus or the city metro to the court almost every weekday, wear the full dark hijab, and try to get the judge's attention and hopefully some sort of justice. The judges, instead of justice, would offer her other things as soon as they would find out she was left alone by her husband and was most likely vulnerable. She had to be both a woman and a man in the house and in public. She had to defend her right more than anyone else in the court because in addition to being a woman she was also a religious minority. My father had documented to the court that she was a religious minority and that he had remarried because she was not Muslim, that she did not count as a wife since she never converted to Islam upon their marriage. Even the Muslim judges did not think his claims were valid because he knew she was not Muslim when they married twenty some years ago, before the revolution.

She had to go from one office to another to get a single legal paper signed. Due to her religion, the court would not treat her as a normal citizen of Iran; they would treat her like a foreigner who had no rights in this country, and they would purposefully delay her court dates and more. My father would not show up to my mother's court appearances. He would not give the right mailing address to the court, and he would not sign papers from the court or respond to the mails, just to delay the divorce. This way my mother would go back and forth to the court but get no results, no alimony, no child support, and not even her divorce. In the meantime, my brothers and I were left alone at home, unattended, and there was no emotional support structure for us. We just witnessed my mom fall apart, and get older, both internally and externally.

HOLY BROTHERS
AND SISTERS

Between 2003 and 2005, many mini revolutions took place in Iran. I remember people would go out to the streets to protest against the regime, the economic crisis, the lack of freedom, and the constant oppression. Sometimes the Iranian TV channels streaming from America would host anti-regime and pro-Shah activists, and they would dictate a specific time and date and encourage people living in Iran to go out to the streets and take charge of the country, as if it were that easy. It was overwhelming and stressful to leave the house knowing you could be arrested, killed, or worse, tortured by the supreme leader's guards. Parents would not allow their children to go out to the streets because they did not want their children to get arrested and disappear. The worst was that after people got arrested, families would not know their loved ones' whereabouts for weeks; meanwhile the government would be torturing and executing the arrested youth with no consequences nor court appearances.

I had curious, energetic young brothers who would want to get involved in the activities, but I was not allowed to leave the house since I was still very young. As a matter of fact, I was not interested in the pro-Shah activists on TV. I was more interested in listening to the Persian Music Channel (PMC) or watching American movies instead of getting pulled into politics. Young people would talk in public chatrooms on the internet about going out and changing the regime. It was common knowledge that the government agents were probably prowling the chatrooms and would know where and when the next protest was going to take place.

My mom had seen the 1979 revolution. She knew what this regime was capable of, and she forbade us from joining any protests, but my brothers would not listen. One of the days when people had gone out to the streets to protest against the regime, my youngest brother had left the house without our knowledge. He had taken his fancy new Nokia cell phone to take pictures of the protesters. To photograph the protests was an unforgivable crime by the regime. It was one thing to participate in a protest, but it was another thing entirely to actually document and take pictures of it. Iran did not and still does not want the rest of the world to know that so many people went and still go out to the streets to protest against the regime. The regime wants to keep everything under wraps and to suppress all the protesters. My brother did not follow the advised hair and dress style in Iran. He grew his hair long, wore foreign brand shirts that were too tight, and wore the baggy pants that were in style in the 2000s in Western countries. The Islamic Republic of Iran considered anything that was Western to be evil and, therefore, suppressed it.

The day my brother went missing, my mom and I tried calling him several times after he left the house, but he never responded. We were extremely worried and did not know where to begin our search for him. I do not remember how long it was before we got contacted by the police, but I think it was sometime between twenty-four and forty-eight hours from the time he had left the house. We were expecting the worst. I remember we had all gathered in my mom's bedroom and were sitting on the floor surrounding the red home phone with its curly black wire.

My youngest brother had changed a lot after my father left the house. He would play loud music in the house, sometimes in the middle of the day. He did not pay a lot of attention to us or to family plans and events. Most of the time he was in his bedroom, either playing video games, participating in group chats, or working on his inventions. He had his own life schedule, he dropped out of high school, and his friends would come over any time of the day or night to hang out with him. His eating and sleeping schedules were reversed. He was technically on United States time, and we were all concerned about his health.

Finally we received a call, It was a warning that he should never participate in protests or there would be harsher consequences, and my brother was given permission to leave the police station and come back home. When he came home, he said that they had him arrested almost as soon as he joined the others in the protest, as he was taking pictures. He said they kept him and the others in a dark room, in a remote location, for hours before they questioned them one at a time. His hands had been tied behind his back, and they did not give him or the others any food or drinks. After hours spent in the dark, they brought them out, one by one, and questioned them. He just told them that he had nothing to do with protesting against the regime, and when they searched his pockets and found his phone, they found no pictures on his phone. If there had been pictures on his phone, he would have been in serious trouble. He told us that while he was in the dark room, he reached for the phone in his back pocket and knowing what buttons to push, he accessed the picture gallery and deleted all the pictures he had taken that day. God knows how many teenagers were held against their will and without their families' knowledge, and how many of them were actually let go after these protests.

It was a horrible situation in Iran. There was no freedom, and every move was monitored by a very small percentage of people who were following the regime blindly. They had started a Guidance Patrol, basically the Moral Police. It was constructed by the government, but they portrayed themselves as a non-government organization, and they mostly registered volunteer people who would patrol the town for sinners. Members of this Guidance Patrol would wear full Islamic clothing and would patrol the streets, cinemas, parks, and coffee shops, looking for boys and girls hanging out, holding hands, or God forbid, wearing clothing, makeup, or hair styles that were un-acceptable to the Islamic Republic of Iran. We would be stopped and questioned at any time or place, just for incorporating colors in our clothing or for using Western style behaviors in public.

Female members of this Guidance Patrol program would wear the full black hijab from head to toe, and nothing but their nose was visible. These women would not wax their facial hair and would look scary and unpleasant. They were mean and would give a hard time to who was not married and had waxed their facial hair or were not dressed in a way that the Guidance Patrol deemed to be even slightly immodest or Western looking.

Male members of the Guidance Patrol would wear buttoned-up, mostly dark-colored shirts with ugly baggy khaki pants and closed-toe formal shoes. These men would close the buttons of their shirts all the way up to their chin, would not shave any facial hair, and would wear the traditional Islamic cologne made from essence of rose flower or other herbs, as if they had bought it from the organic section of the Whole Foods store. These men would always wear their hair to one side, and would play with a prayer bead in their hands as they looked for sinners in the neighborhoods.

The Guidance Patrol would address everyone on the street as sister, brother, holy sister, or holy brother. In return we would address them as Holy Sh…t when we would come across one. They would drive a decent sized van, and sometimes, they would park the van on one street, close to a school, a cool coffee shop, or other public place that young people would go to hang out, such as a mall, movie theater, or a park, and they were out to get everyone who did not meet their extreme Islamic standards. As soon as one had to cross paths with the Guidance Patrol team, makeup was wiped off, hair was shoved into the head scarf, and sleeves would roll down. If one was with a boyfriend or girlfriend, they would separate, change their paths immediately, and pretend they did not know one another. One would deny all relationships with the opposite sex and would do exactly as the members of the Guidance Patrol would ask in order to avoid arrest.

It would have been the end of one's freedom and reputation if one would have gotten arrested, for whatever reason, by the Guidance Patrol and taken to the police station. The police would call the person's parents and ask them to come to the police station with some kind of proof of identification. The parents would be told the manipulated version of what the circumstances under which one was upon arrested. They arrested many young married couples and would hold them in jail until their parents showed up with the marriage certificate, and only then the couple would be let go. That is why, starting in the 1980s, most young married couples would carry their birth certificates, which included marriage information, with them at all times as a proof of their marriage, in order to avoid getting arrested, being humiliated in public, or even spending the night in jail. In some cases, unmarried couples captured on the street were forced to get married at the police station against their will and in absolute humiliation.

I had the pleasure of interacting with the Guidance Patrol several times. Once when I was in high school, while walking with my mother in Tehran from my uncle's house to the main street to catch the bus to go home, I was stopped by a Guidance Patrol member. He was a young man standing on the side of the street, staring me down from a distance. He was a volunteer, working for the Guidance Patrol, barely capable of growing a beard, and was dressed in a white, ironed, buttoned-up shirt with Khaki pants and a baton in his hand. As we were getting closer to approach him, my mom asked me to adjust my pants' hem, which were folded up to display my young, white ankles. I told her, "What is he going to do if I do not? Kill me? I'll gladly die for my freedom." I was young, and with the mini revolutions happening here and there, I thought I had to do my part by disobeying their hijab enforcement. My mom shook her head in a disappointed way as we approached the young man. She knew I had the revolutionary spirit, and that sooner or later I would get into some kind of trouble.

In those days the style for women who wanted to push some boundaries was to fold up their pants' hem to show some ankles. We would even bejewel our ankles by wearing an ankle bracelet. Of course, the young Guidance Patrol man stopped me, saying, "Sister, unfold your pants to cover your ankles."

I stopped walking, stared at him for a few short seconds to display my disappointment, and I pushed out my chest, then with reluctance bent over and unfolded my pants to cover my ankles. I looked up and said, "There! Does this make you happy now? Did this solve any major problem in this society?"

He said, "No, but thank you. You can go now." I walked away with my mom, filled with hate and revenge.

Not too far from him, I stopped on the side of the street and folded my pants up to showcase my sinful ankles and, more importantly, protest for my freedom of expression.

The government would stop the youth on the street to monitor our personal relationships. If boys were walking on the street in a group, they would not attract any attention, but if a group of girls were walking together or boys and girls were even walking in close proximity, as determined by the Islamic Republic, they were questioned. If they tried to stand up for themselves they were arrested, and often beaten up on the street. Some families would force their young girls to get married as soon as they graduated from high school so the neighborhood and the family would not gossip, or so their daughter would be protected from the Guidance Police. Men definitely had more freedom than women, and it felt unfair, but there were times when men would get arrested even for having long or Western-styled hair and the police would shave their head, set their hair on fire, and humiliate them in public or at the police station. Those were scary times to be in love with the opposite sex or try to modernize the society by pushing the boundaries on the hijab.

GENETICALLY
TRANSFERRED OPINION

Even though I was attending a girls-only high school, we were not allowed to take off our head scarfs inside of the classrooms or in the yard, which was surrounded by hundred-feet-tall walls and other adjacent buildings. We would get in trouble if we removed any facial hair or dyed our hair. If our nails were long or had any type of nail polish, we were in trouble. If we would wear anything other than the uniform supplied by the school, we would get in trouble. If we would walk into the classroom after the teachers had already entered, or if we ran in the schoolyard or hallway, we would get in trouble.

We were not allowed to take cell phones, CDs, or makeup to school; only school supplies were permitted. No calculators were allowed in school, or ever used during exams. In short, there was nothing modern or non-Islamic that was allowed in school, but that was how we grew up. We were okay with it at the time because we did not know freedom could be defined differently. We did not understand unfairness, and we were sheltered from Western ideas and fed anti-West potions in schools and through the media, by courtesy of the new regime.

School was a place to be tortured and punished for being a human, a woman, an Iranian, or for having feelings and opinions. We were forced to be Muslim and supporters of the regime's ideology. During the thirteen years of schooling in Iran, I only met one Christian classmate. She was allowed to skip the Quran course and hang out in the hallway, but that was because both of her parents were born and raised as Christians. I never met a Jew, a Zoroastrian, a Buddhist, or a Hindu. I am sure they existed, but they never advertised their religion.

In high school, we were not forced to pray in the prayer room as often as we used to in elementary and middle school, but we were often asked to attend mourning events and lectures in the prayer room. I had learned my lesson to keep a low profile in school when it came to religion and prayers. I did not want to get expelled from high school, but I wanted to tell everyone that religion is a choice and not a genetically transferred opinion. I wanted to tell everyone that I knew of a different religion, and what they taught us in school about the Bahá'í Faith was not true, but even though I should have kept a low profile, I had a lot of energy and wanted to find ways to express myself.

Our public high school had a horrible reputation, and most students attending this high school did not have decent grades, behaviors, or futures. The school did not charge much as an annual fee, and we all knew that we would not get hired by NASA[39] after we graduated from this high school, but it was in our neighborhood and it would allow us all to stay together and make memories. We would be able to love and laugh and grow up together. It was an amazing experience, and I would not want to exchange it for a better education at a different school.

I grew my hair long in high school and would braid it into cornrows, and my schoolmates began to call me "Dony Fashion." Even though I would wear the boring uniform provided by the high school, which was ugly and intentionally made of a less desirable brown color fabric, I would wear it in a fun way. I would roll my sleeves up or wear my head scarf in a way that would not be ordinary and repetitive. I wanted to stand out, and I

---

39 National Aeronautics and Space Administration, U.S.A.

had to get creative with what I was forced to wear. My schoolmates would always follow my style; they believed that I would always bring the new fashion and trends to school.

My schoolmates would mimic me when I cut my bangs short, rolled my uniform sleeves up in a creative way, or dyed my hair with a temporary hair dye. It was Paris fashion week almost every month in our public high school, somewhere in the middle of crowded, suppressed Tehran, and I was the fashion designer, in my own way I created fashions within the limitations we had, for my own clientele with the courage to push boundaries.

The public high school fashion catwalk would start the moment we were finished for the day and would exit the school, walking home surrounded by teenaged, hungry, hormonal boys, who waited by the school door, taking mental pictures of our young body curves and fashionable hairstyles that were barely visible from underneath the mandatory school hijab. The prettiest girl was often followed by a group of boys, as they commented on her courage to display her Western style or beauty. Sometimes boys smuggled their phone numbers written on a small piece of paper torn from a notebook page, to schoolgirls in the hopes of getting a phone call.

The school principal would often stand by the school entrance/exit gate and monitor our uniforms or faces to ensure we were not disobeying the Islamic and school rules, showing more hair than we should, or God forbid wearing any makeup. But we always found a way to push boundaries despite their efforts to control our every move.

High school was fun for me. I loved going to high school and being away from home. I used to listen to Linkin Park's full *Meteora* album, which was about thirty-seven minutes long, every day before I went to school. I did not know a lot of English, but I knew enough to mumble the words. The fact that I listened to the latest Western music set me apart and automatically portrayed me as the coolest kid in school.

On the last day of the school week, Thursdays, we would take longer to go home. We would check out the young boys starving for our attention and laugh at their cheesy comments. They would get in trouble if school staff would find out about them hanging out by our school gate. Young boys and girls only had a minute or less to make an impression on one another and some of those "street" friendships lasted years and even ended in marriage.

WEAK

My father had already moved out of our house during my high school years. In the second year of high school, my mother was still extremely angry with my father and was constantly plotting revenge. She had nothing to use against my father other than us children, his paystubs, and his pension. My older brothers would not go out of their way to cause difficulty for my father; therefore, my mom had no one but me to use against him. A few days before the second year of high school started, my mother told me to go to my grandmother's house and stay there until the first day of school, when my father would have to take me all the way from the southern part of Tehran to the middle, and this daily exercise would supposedly teach him a lesson.

That Fall, my mother dropped me off at my grandmother's house. I took my newly bought schoolbooks, uniform, and some clothes with me. My grandmother was surprised to see me, as she let me into her house. My father was not there at the time, as he was at his second wife's house and my grandmother had to call and ask him to come to her house.

I immediately felt alone, left behind, used, grossed out, and sick to my stomach for being there, away from my mother, and stuck in what appeared to be a bad situation. I had some friends in that neighborhood and knew that I could hang out with them if I felt lonely. My father came to my grandmother's house later that day, and he immediately began to fight with me. I did not get a warm welcome or a "Hey, it's good to see you after months of abandoning you." He yelled at me, asked what I was doing there, and was mad at his mother for letting me in. They were speaking Azeri, and I could not understand a word. I did not feel bad for my grandmother at the time, because she was helping him live a lie. Frankly, she was probably scared of him and that is why she would lie to us that my father had always stayed over at her house.

I did not enjoy staying at my grandmother's house, without internet, computer, my close friends, satellite TV, and all of my toys, or the little freedom I had. My father slept at my grandmother's house that night, pretended that this is where he has always been.

The next day, he gave me some money to buy school supplies from a nearby bazaar. Of course, the money was not much; he just wanted to silence my needs. I did not feel loved or welcomed during the time that I spent at my grandmother's house. I felt like I was putting on a brave show as I internally shattered.

I told my father if he did not want me there, he could very well take me to his new house. He denied that he had a different house and said that his mother's house was where he had always been. I am not sure why he would deny the second wife and second house! What was he accomplishing by lying? Trying to make my mother look like a liar? Why would she make up such a lie? What was more hurtful throughout those years was the fact that he never admitted to having a second wife or that he was sorry for tearing the family apart. He continued to accuse my mother of lying to us about him having the second wife and claimed that he was living at my grandmother's house the entire time. That lie was insulting.

The first day of my second year of high school arrived. As one entered the second year of high school, there were three options to choose from based on one's grades from the first year: Math and Physics, Biology and Chemistry, or Literature and Arabic. I was not interested in any of these, but I was forced by family to choose Math and Physics as my major in high school. I was terrible in Math, but I loved Physics and Astronomy. On the other hand, I loved writing and wanted to become a writer, but I did not want to take years of Arabic.

The first day of school, first day of fall, September 23, coincided with my mother's birthday. My father dropped me off at school and went to work. I was happy to see my old friends and talk about the events that happened during the three months of summer. Tera attended a different school for the last two years of high school, therefore the only friend who knew my problems was not there to hold my hands.

Around 12:30 pm or 12:40 pm, when school was over for the day, I went through the yard to leave the school and ran into my mother waiting for me underneath a shaded area by the snack bar. I was not expecting her there and asked what she was doing. She hugged me hard and said that my brothers had celebrated her birthday at the house the evening before, and she had brought me some left-over birthday cake. I told her I did not want any cake and I just wanted this situation to be over so I could go back home. She did not want me to give up that easily, and as she forced some birthday cake in my mouth, she advised me to be brave, strong, and to have some patience. As I chewed on the delicious birthday cake, a mix of the famous Persian banana and walnut hit my taste buds, and I felt betrayed that they had had a birthday party without me. I had to be brave, strong, and independent, so I told her that my current living situation was not hard at all and I could continue longer.

I held myself together, held my head up, and suppressed my tears and my many complaints about the situation. I know my mother was waiting for me to show some weakness so she could tell me I could go back home; I could see it in her body language and the tone of her voice. I told her that I would not let her down and would stay there until my father was tired of me being there, got frustrated, and caved into my mother's demands. She asked if my father had been coming to my grandmother's house after work. I told her that he was. Even though he did not have a lot of clothes in my grandmother's house, he still claimed that he lived there.

I told my mom that my father was probably waiting outside of the school gate and I should go before he got suspicious. She stayed behind in the schoolyard, as I left to meet my father outside. I found my father outside of the school gate, among other parents, waiting for me to come out. He looked upset and disappointed, and took me back to his mother's house. My existence was inconvenient for him, and it seemed like it was the first time that he had an actual responsibility and had to take care of another being.

He knew that my mother had talked to me. He had seen her around the school. He said some nasty things about my mother on the way back to his mother's house and made me feel like I was a burden. He said that he had to leave work in the middle of the day to pick me up, and that this could not go on for long since he had to work all day. I told him that I was going to live with him and grandma, and I was not planning on going back to my mother's house again. He did not make me feel safe or wanted, and he made that obvious, maybe too obvious. He just wanted to be free and did not show much interest in me or my feelings.

My father had set some serious and strict rules in my grandmother's house and forbade me from seeing my friends or doing anything else other than house chores and schoolwork. He was trying to take all my freedom away from me, so I would get tired and give up this challenge. He made sure to tell me that my school schedule was inconvenient for his job as long as I stayed there, I told him that his second marriage was inconvenient for everyone, but he continued to deny his second marriage and called my mother a liar.

For the first week of school, I did not learn much and I did not know what to study. All I wanted was to go back home to my own bed and be in charge of my own life. I just wanted to go back to my mom, but I did not want to seem like a loser and give up on this mission, which was actually her mission. I wanted to make my mother proud, and just as I had said when I was a little girl as I pretended to wash the silverware standing on the stool by the sink, I wanted to ruin his life, and his new wife's life.

During that same week I found out that my last maternal cousin was leaving Iran to become a religious refugee in Turkey. I was devastated when I found out that during her last days, she was coming to Tehran to stay at our house and I was not there to say goodbye to her. I had always been there for the family members who were leaving the country, and I wanted to see her for the last time. I knew that we would never leave Iran and I would probably never see her again.

Just a week after I had gone to my grandmother's house, I felt so sad and lonely that I asked my father to take me to say goodbye to my cousin. It was a Thursday; I had survived around ten days of emotional torture by my father, and he had not given up. By the time we got to my mother's apartment, everyone was saying goodbyes to my cousin downstairs, on the side of Sattar Khan Street. She was on her way to the train station that evening to go to Turkey. I got out of my father's old, light blue, Paykan car and rushed to hug my cousin one last time. She was already crying as she said goodbye to my mother, who had played the mother role for her for years, and I broke into tears.

I cried in my last maternal cousin's arms for a few minutes, confused as why I was crying. Was it her leaving us or me living with my father that caused my tears? She was leaving for the same reason that others had left. She left to be able to study, progress, and have a better future instead of staying in Iran and marrying a Muslim man who was going to keep her away from practicing her religion. God only knew when the next time would be that I would get to see her again. She got into the taxi and left for the train station. We were standing on the sidewalk of Sattar Khan Street, making small talk. My father was standing at a distance. As I cried hard, I told my mother that I did not want to live at my grandmother's house anymore.

I confessed to her that I was weak and was ashamed of being weak. I did not really want to live with my father anymore. He had hurt me enough by telling me how much of a burden I had been and how inconvenient his life had become since I was dropped off at his mother's house. He never celebrated or acknowledged that I was closer to him now that I was staying at his mother's house. He did not take an interest in my future or my development and constantly reminded me that I was not going to be happy living with him and grandma.

My mother said that she does not want to hurt my feelings by getting back at my father. She knew that I was weak, and I hated that now it was proven to her. As a child, when I told him that I would sabotage his second marriage if he ever cheated on my mother, I did not know that it could ever be real, and now that it was, I was scared and very weak. My father was relieved when he heard me say I wanted to go back to mom's house and immediately packed my belongings and delivered them to my mother's apartment.

After moving back to my mother's house, I was both happy and disappointed. I was disappointed in my courage; I knew that my father was back at his second wife's house and that it broke my mother's heart. I wanted to be close to my mother, to my school, and to my friends. I was only a teenager. I wanted to be able to attend the youth Bahá'í gatherings, watch satellite TV, and listen to the Linkin Park album every morning before going to school. I was weak.

DRUMMER

After months of trying to take revenge on my father, my mother ended up in the hospital because her high blood pressure had caused her eye to go temporarily blind. She was weak, depressed, and defeated by the male-favored social and legal laws and by my father's betrayal. I was attending school and was not able to get to the hospital on my own, but we visited my mother during her stay at the hospital and even smuggled some pizza to her room to cheer her up.

For the second year of high school, Tera was attending a private high school, which had high fees, but great teachers, and it would help her get ready for the university entrance test. We did not have the chance to hang out at school, or on the walk to and from school anymore; therefore, we had to find some other time to catch up on life events. We talked on the phone a lot more than before and met up at their new house on the weekends or sometimes weekdays after school. In the meantime, I was not doing so well at school. I would get decent grades in Physics or English but not in Math or Arabic. I was not there to learn; I was there to hang out with my friends and stay away from the depressing house in which I was forced to live in. My mother even hired my Math teacher to give me some extra attention, but I was not improving, perhaps maybe because Math reminded me of my father.

I obeyed almost all of the high school's strict rules, except one. I played drums for my friends to dance around the class when we were on break. After trying to learn to play Santoor for a couple of years, I became interested in Tombak, the Persian drum. I used the school benches and table in the class to play drum-like noise for my friends to dance and sometimes I even used the classroom's door.

When I told my mother I was interested in learning Tombak, she bought one for me without hesitation. Tombak by itself was not an expensive instrument, but my mother hired a young man to come to our house and teach me how to play the drum. He only came a few times, taught me the notes, and after that I could play the Tombak with or without notes. Soon I began to take my Tombak to school, which was highly illegal. Our floor principal knew about it and would allow me to bring it to school and play uplifting music for my schoolmates during recess. She wanted us to have some fun at school. She was an open-minded woman who thought there should be more freedom at school, and she was not as strict as the other school staff.

Every recess, we would sing, clap, and dance in the classroom. This was a way to let out the anger, frustration, and oppressed energy of youth. We would dance for a few minutes or sometimes only at recess, and some classmates would keep lookout for the school staff and would inform us if they saw someone coming. Even though our hands would hurt from clapping hard or playing drums using the classroom doors and tables, we looked forward to those moments at school because there was no other time to have fun.

During the recess, we were naughty. Our hijabs would fall off of our heads, and we would not adjust them. Sometimes we would take them off and let our wild hair loose. All we wanted to do was to dance, sing, express ourselves, and let off some steam, but all these acts were forbidden in Islam, in Iran's society after the revolution, and at school, especially if you were a woman, a drummer.

I even played my Tombak in collaboration with another friend who played the Santoor at a high school event honoring the birthday of Imam Ali. I wonder what they would think, or if they would even let me play Tombak for this event if they knew my mother was a Bahá'í.

ONLINE REVOLUTIONARY LEADER

My mother was still working on her divorce paperwork. My father had made it very hard for her to get a divorce. Legally he had to agree to divorce her, and there was nothing she could do to bypass that law. I was left alone in the house most of the time, and there was only one space where I could be myself, talk about the changes that society needed, and get my generation to listen to me and initiate change. I was not political and did not want to start a political revolution. I just wanted change and freedom for our society and for my generation, and I needed others' support.

Thanks to dial-up internet, I would enter the public chatrooms and start conversations about freedom and how it could be achieved. That's where I met Kooshan and Sam, two young boys who showed interest in me and my ideas and we became close friends.

Aside from the social justice conversations, I needed a listener about my family situation and the boys found me fascinating. I was very smooth in chatting online and could easily make the young boys fall for me and give me attention, which I lacked at home. We were not allowed to meet up, but we could talk online or on the phone. Again, relationships with the opposite sex were frowned upon in the society and I was in no situation to meet up with strangers I met online. I was fifteen or sixteen years old when I started talking to boys online or on the phone, and at first I was scared of being caught by my family members, which could result in losing internet or phone privileges followed by a strict stay at home rule.

With no caller ID, I could freely call people without risking the exposure of my home phone number. I would talk to Tera and my cousin, Assal, about the boys I had meet online and the subjects we had talked about. We were not allowed to meet in person and walk together on the street, but we figured out a way around it. I had told Sam where I went to high school, and he told me what he would wear on a specific day, waiting for me outside of the school gate. We were able to see one another by just passing each other and getting a few seconds of a look. There were no cellphones, and no social media to see what people looked like. We were at the mercy of those few seconds, passing by one another and memorizing how each other looked.

I had a secret; a very small home phone that kept by my bed and used to make phone calls after everyone was asleep in the house. I just had to make sure I spoke in low tones and did not draw attention to myself. They did not want us to talk to the opposite sex, but we would find a way to talk, to meet, and to fall in love. Even though the government and society forbade us from doing it.

Our parents did not want us to make a mistake. I understand that they wanted the best for us by keeping us away from the opposite sex. My mother always told me that a girl's reputation is like a white cotton cloth and once it is stained, it can never be restored into its original condition. I learned that from her and kept it in my heart. I tried to honor her trust and refrained from risky behavior, especially in our neighborhood.

In Iran my generation would meet each other on the street and exchange phone numbers. It was either after school or at the shopping mall. The way it worked was that girls walked in groups in public but never engaged in a conversation with the boys, and the boys would find a way to give their phone numbers to the girls.

Sometimes a boy would make a comment to a girl as they passed by one another, and if the girl was interested, she would make eye contact, or answer his comment, unless she was shy. The body language was clear. If she wanted him to give her his phone number, she would make eye contact and slow down so he could catch up and give her the small piece of paper with his phone number on it.

My brothers were actively watching my moves to see if I had any relationships with the opposite sex. Sometimes I would tell my mom that I was going out to the shopping center with my friends, and I would get followed by my brothers. I think they were hypocrites because they would give their phone number to the girls they met, just like the boys who were interested in me and wanted to give me their number, but they did not like it when that trick was played on their own sister.

Even if my brothers were not watching or following me secretly, their friends, indeed the entire neighborhood, would watch me. I had to make sure I erased all my tracks, so my family did not find out about me talking to the opposite sex. The other girls and I would cover for one another and make sure we did not get caught dating boys because our parents would talk to each other about our dating activities. If one of us would get caught talking to a boy, we would all be punished.

It was harder in Tera's house. Her father was very strict, and because he was self-employed, he would often come home in the middle of the day, to everyone's surprise. The government was already keeping us boys and girls away from each other by building gender-segregated schools, and by having the secret police surveil the parks and streets to catch us even looking at the opposite sex.

The universities did not have gender-segregated classrooms, but men and women had to sit separately from each other and most of the times the men sat at the front and the women sat at the back of the class. This way the men were not able to easily look at the women or get distracted by them.

Universities had onsite hijab and behavior committees, moral police, who would give warnings to women and men who did not follow the proper Islamic clothing guidelines, or who engaged in conversations with the opposite sex or, God forbid, had a relationship.

Even if opposite sex students were seen studying a subject with each other, they were reported to the principal's office and were given a warning. If they did not take the warnings seriously, they would be expelled, and banned from education for life. Most of the universities were run by trusted revolutionary followers and they would set the rules, completely made up. Most students who fell in love with a fellow classmate were not able to reach out, talk, and get to know one another, and if they did, they were risking their education and reputation.

Living in such a closed-minded and fearful society, I am not sure how we avoided criticism. If a group of girls would go to the mall to walk, to shop or just to get ice cream, they would be considered loose girls and people would not have any respect for them. A girl who laughed out loud on the street was not considered a decent girl, not a girl that a decent boy would want to marry down the road.

I was still not allowed to go to my friends' houses, unless I was escorted there and back. It was not that my family was strict, it was the entire society, and my family was doing what they had to do to protect me and my reputation. I guess that is why they controlled and monitored my phone conversations and escorted me everywhere. At least in the Bahá'í gatherings boys and girls were free to converse without getting questioned, but in the Islamic world and gatherings, conversing with the opposite sex was a sin, was frowned upon and forbidden. Even cousins could not speak confortably to each other if they were opposite genders.

FAMILY REUNION

At the time I attended high school, it was three years long. I was still in the second or third year of high school when I finally had the "pleasure" of meeting my father's new wife for the first time. That day, my mother and I had gone to my grandmother's house to eavesdrop on my father. My mother knew that my father's sister had come to Tehran to visit, and despite the fact that my father's siblings had said they did not approve of his new wife, my mother was sure that the new wife was at my grandmother's house visiting my aunt.

My mother and I surprised the family with our presence. I knocked at my grandmother's door, and when they asked who it was, I confidently announced that it was me. My mother was hiding in the alley. The plan was that I would go in, and then if my father's second wife was there, I would open the door for my mother so she could come in and call the police on my father. My father had continued to lie to the court and to the family about the existence of his new wife and was accusing my mother of being delusional.

There was a long pause before my father opened the door. He was in his pajamas; they were not expecting anyone. Once he opened the door, he calmly invited me in, and I entered the front yard. I was young and wanted to find a reason to hurt my father because he had hurt my mother and my siblings. He had to pay for his mistakes, and I wanted to help my mother get her rights. I went inside. I saw my grandmother by the outdoor kitchen door and soon my aunt walked out of the house and entered the yard to greet me. I said hi to them and kissed them both, but I was not there to see them. This was not a family reunion. I was on a mission to find the woman who ruined our lives.

I looked around the yard and noticed that they had lowered the curtains in the guest room. My dad invited me to go inside and rest, and maybe have some tea. I went inside, but not with the intention of resting. I was there to start a revolution, and there was no time to waste. As I entered the small living room that was one of the two rooms that shaped my grandmother's house, I saw a woman standing by the back wall, directly facing me. I paused by the door and stared at her. She was short, wearing a long dark skirt and a colorful hijab over her head. She was fixing her hijab as I continued to stare her down. In a very low tone she said, "Hi." I did not make a move and just stood by the entrance door to the living room and stared at her some more, not saying a word. She was the woman that ruined our lives. I had finally met her.

My aunt walked in the living room, passing me by, and said, "Come in, dear. Why do not you sit down!" as if nothing had happened and there was nothing abnormal. I knew it was her. I had never seen her face before that day. My mother had told me that she was at least five years older than my father, unattractive, and overweight and one of her eyes was physically larger than the other one.

The woman was looking down, staring with shame at the flowers of my grandmother's old, handmade, and thinned out Persian rug. I was not going to join them in the living room. I did not want to give the pleasure and satisfaction of my presence, which would mean my approval of this disgusting choice. The Persian rug had witnessed us growing up in this house, playing on the tiny flowers as my father and mother accompanied us together, not with the second wife. If the rug could leave the house, it would have already done so, ashamed of the situations it had to witness.

I went back to the yard, asked my dad, in a high-tone voice, "Who is this woman? Is she your second wife? The woman who ruined our lives?" He did not expect this reaction. He had always viewed me as a weak little girl. He stood in the yard and did not say anything.

I walked towards the yard door and opened the door, called my mother in, and in a loud tone I said, "Come in, mom. Dad's second wife is here too." By the time my father realized what the plan was, my mother was already in the yard, yelling at my father and the fight had started. The other woman was scared, and I think she was hiding in the corner of the living room, trying to stay out of sight. Since my grandmother's house consisted of only two rooms, one living room and one bedroom, there was no place for her to hide, and no emergency exit door through which she could escape. She was stuck in the house. My father went towards my grandmother's living room, and through the open windows, he grabbed the home phone to call the police. I took the phone from him and told him that he needed to face his worst nightmare and he could not escape it.

I told him to man up and acknowledge the two wives he has. The other woman started to cry, and my father acted as if he wanted to protect her against us. My aunt was shocked, and all I could say to her and to my grandmother was that I could not believe that they had accepted his mistake and were backing him up on this unjust act.

There was a lot of yelling and screaming; by the time the police arrived I was on the roof. I did not know how I got there. I did not know what was going on. All I knew was that I was on the roof and everyone was worried that I might jump down, killing myself, which would just have made life easier for my father. I was not suicidal; I was emotionally hurt and that had led me to make a scene. The police were there to control the situation, but they could not do anything to resolve or undo the mess my father had created. If the court and the judge could not determine that my father was a fraud, what could the local police department do?

They asked my mother, my father, and I to go to the police station, but did not make his new wife join us. I kept asking the police to understand that we were not the ones who needed to go to the police department, and it was the second wife who needed to go and explain why she ruined our lives and married my father using the fake birth certificate. The police were not listening to me; they did not care what came out of my mouth. I was a teenaged girl, and they had no regard for women or children. They just wanted to take my mother and me away, so that the neighbors would not find out what my father had done, they were trying to save a fellow Muslim men's reputation. I was hungry for justice for women, but I soon learned that was a dream that that was never going to come true.

At the local police station, we had to wait in the yard for a while. My father was smoking cigarettes and was yelling and cursing at us from across the yard. I had to explain all that had happened to the local chief of police, but all he saw was an outraged teenager yelling, accusing her father and demanding justice. He did not listen to a word I said. My mother explained to him that my father had lied to the government to get a fake birth certificate to marry another woman, had left his four children, and was not paying a penny in child support or alimony.

My father's counterargument was that we had interrupted his afternoon with his family by yelling in the yard and had ruined his mother's reputation in the neighborhood where everyone knew them as the family of a martyr. It seemed like the chief of police was on my father's side. After all, they were both men and had to back one another up in rough situations such as this. My father was born and raised in the same neighborhood and the chief of police was not going to listen to me, who was from the upper side of Tehran. A few times my father even mentioned that he was the brother of a martyr, and he would try to prove that he should be considered in the right, and that my mother, a religious minority, was wrong and had no rights.

It was close to sundown when my father's brother showed up. He talked to the police chief, and then he came and stood in front of my mother and me, sitting down under a tall green tree, which was obviously tired of all the things it had to witness in that yard on a daily basis. My uncle stood in front of us, tall and riotous, and said, "What is wrong with you two?"

I did not even let my mother catch her breath to respond. I jumped up with an answer and said, "What is wrong with us? We want what is our right. Your brother takes his second wife to your mother's house, and then your sister is also there as a support. He has not paid a penny to help us and support us over the years, and he refuses to divorce my mother."

My uncle said, "Then you have to go to my mother's house to take your right? My sister had to go to the Emergency Room because of the stress."

I said, "Well, I hope she has learned that supporting her brother's mistakes costs her as well."

My uncle said, "Well, brothers and sisters support one another, and if I ever learn that you have done something like this again, I will send you some place where no one can find you." I knew he was capable of doing such things. He worked for the court system himself, and he was deep in the Islamic Republic's system at the time. He could probably get rid of me in no time. A few minutes later, after my uncle was done talking, on other words, "telling the chief what to do," they took signatures from my father, mother, and me, and told us to follow up using the court system. Then they let us go.

They advised my mother and me against disturbing my grand-mother's house again. I was hesitant to sign. I said to the police chief, "My father does not even come to visit us. He is either at his new wife's house or here at my grandmother's house. Are you telling me I cannot come here and see him anymore?"

The chief said, "You can see your father, but do not start a fight again."

I took a long look at my father. He did not care to see me. He wanted all of us gone so he could be with his mistake in peace. He did not seem to miss his children or feel guilty for ruining our lives.

He had sunk so deeply into his mistake that he would never apologize for it, or try to rebuild his relationship with his children. It did not seem like he had any fatherly feelings towards us. My mother and I left the police station that day disappointed in the Islamic system and in our gender. It was past sunset and it took us a while to get home. My mother was upset. The police chief had dismissed her complaints and told her to follow up with the court instead of giving her a police report proving that he has a second wife. The police chief and my uncle both knew that the Islamic Republic's laws are in men's favor and my mother would never get what she was asking for, her right.

My mother witnessed how angry I was that day. It was proven to me that the Islamic Republic of Iran did not care about women nor their rights. Women were never going to be treated as equal to men in Iran. I wanted to know what my uncles, who supported my father's decision, would do if the same thing had happened to their precious daughters. Sometimes I wished that very situation upon the people who supported my father and who took his side or visited his second home. My father's family did not protest his actions. If they had, maybe my father would have left the other woman and apologized for his actions.

That night, my mother was sad, not because she did not get what she wanted, but because this event had shown me how unfair life was for women in this country. She had the fear of losing her children when we were younger and that was why she had not left my father, but now she had to raise us all by herself with no financial help. That night, on the way home, my mother asked me what kind of food or dessert I wanted. She wanted me to have a little treat to forget about the pain. I did not want anything. I did not want my cheating father, or his fake family, or money I just wanted a long hug from my mom.

A few years had passed by since my father had cheated, and due to him not helping us financially, my mother was forced to rent out our apartment and move us to a smaller and cheaper apartment. We were still in the same neighborhood, so I did not have to change my high school, but I definitely lived farther from my friends and had to walk a much longer distance to get to school every morning.

One time my mother allowed my father to come back to the new apartment for the Persian New Year to see if he could stay long term. I am not sure what they had talked about or what the deal between them was. I believe that my father was negotiating terms with my mother and wanted to prove to her that he loved her and did not want to divorce her. After the New Year, on the first day of Nowruz, my father wanted to go to visit his mother. As always, none of my brothers agreed to go with him. They all said that they had something to do, and of course I was the only girl and the baby, so I had no choice. Other people had already decided for me that I would go to my grandmother's house.

I did not want to go there because my grandmother had lied for my father and she had not disowned him or kicked him out of her house for his obnoxious actions. Later I found out she did not have a choice either just like I did not. They forced me to sit in the car and go along for the visit. In the middle of the ride to my grandmother's house, as I sat behind my mother, on the passenger's side in the car, the conversation was steering towards my father lying. I added a comment about the fact that he had cheated, and now he was back, and that I did not like that very much.

He could not believe that now, his youngest child and only daughter, was pointing fingers at him and speaking out against his harmful decisions. As he was driving on the freeway, he turned around and slapped me across the face so hard that my tears fell one after the other from physical pain. My ear was ringing, and the print of his palm and five fingers were hacked on my face. My mother reached with her right arm, between the seat and the window to calm me down, and I pushed her arm away. He was the one who had made a mistake, and he thought that he could just fool my mother and come back to this life without apologizing to anyone else? I did not even think he had apologized to my mother. He owed us all a big apology, and even if he gave one, I would still ask him to beat it.

As my face was hot and burning, I kept telling myself, "I will never forgive him." He had just come to ruin another New Year. He could not just walk back into this life and regain his father status, for which he never really worked hard anyway.

I decided that I would be strong, I would not cry, I would learn from this and grow up. Pain brought tears to my eyes, but my pride swallowed them back down. I grew up more with that slap. I discovered who I wanted to become, and it was not a moaning, weak woman like his second wife; I would be a fighter, a strong and determined woman. I did not want to become a woman who needed a man to take care of her; I was going to become a woman who take care of herself and her family. My father only lasted a week back at our house, and then he left my mother and us again, this time for good.

THE REAL BLACK HOLE

I do not have a vivid memory of my high school graduation day. Graduating from high school was not a major milestone in our lives. Virtually everyone graduated high school, and no one dropped out or failed unless they were extremely poor or unintelligent. There were no parties or gifts, just exchanging phone numbers and saying "goodbye for now" to high school friends. The majority of my friends were eager to study for the university entrance test, which left a sour taste in my mouth because I knew that I would not be accepted into any university because of my religion. Technically I had not yet become a Bahá'í because I was waiting until my eighteenth birthday to officially declare my belief, but by the time I would be applying for universities, I would check the religion box as "Other – Bahá'í" on the application, and therefore would receive a rejection.

We had recently moved to a new apartment and neighborhood, which gave me the feeling of a fresh start. I shared a room with my mother while the two brothers who lived at home, each had their own bedroom. I still was not eating much and mostly watched satellite TV. Sometimes I rode my bicycle in the neighborhood, which I would have done more often if not for the fear of being arrested for a violation of the Islamic Republic's rules that "women should not be riding bicycles in public". Apparently, a woman riding a bicycle aroused man, which made it illegal.

I did not have a plan for my future. I wrote poetry and stories, watched American and Indian movies, and barely contributed to household chores.

I did not consider finding a job or learning something new, since job applications would also ask for religion. I was interested in taking some courses, but my family could not afford it and I did not want to put my mother through the pain of borrowing money for my pleasure.

I attended Bahá'í gatherings in people's homes and engaged in discussions about our futures as religious minorities in Iran. There was an underground university, the Bahá'í Institute of Higher Education (BIHE), where Bahá'ís could attend to earn a bachelor's degree, but only a few degrees were offered at that time and I was not interested in any of the offered majors. Plus, at that time many students and professors were arrested and jailed simply because of their association with BIHE. I did not want to risk my arrest and unknown imprisonment terms with no hope of a fair trial. Also, most people that graduated from BIHE were not able to find jobs with their degrees since having a higher education did not affect their choice of religion and the government did not accept their education as a legitimate degree because BIHE was not associated with the Iranian Government.

Several weeks after I graduated high school, my mother and I ran into Tera and her mother while out in the neighborhood. Tera said she was taking courses at a very well-known institution that would prepare her for the university entrance exam and improve her chances of being accepted. She encouraged me to do the same, and I told her I would look into it. When Tera walked away, my mother told me she could not afford to send me to that institution.

The summer that I graduated from high school, the United Nations (UN) had informed the Iranian Government that they were not allowed to discriminate against Bahá'ís by preventing them from taking the national college entrance exam or applying to universities. The UN told them they needed to guarantee the same civil rights to Bahá'ís as the rest of the citizens of Iran.

In response, the Iranian Government announced that Baháʼís have always been allowed to take the national college entrance test or to attend universities and that nothing has or will in the future prevent them from doing so. As a result of this statement, many Baháʼís began to study for the university entrance exam that year. I knew some Baháʼís who were over fifty years old and were still studying for the entrance exam. The whole community was enthused. I was very excited about the possibility of going to university and keeping my religion. I did not want to sit home until some Muslim boy wanted to marry me so he could then forbid me from practicing my religion, as my father had done. I did not want to repeat my mother's history.

The university entrance exam was proctored once per year for five hours and covered all of the material studied during our twelve years of primary education. It was nerve-wracking because of its importance in determining our immediate future. Everyone who passed the university entrance exam could select a major based on their test score. The higher the test score was, the better the majors one could pursue, such as medicine or engineering, and one could pursue them at better public universities. Students who did not pass were forced to wait until the following year to retake the test. Every year there were, and still are, many young men and women who commit suicide because they did not pass the entrance exam, causing them to lose hope in their future.

Even though my mother had told me, after running into Tera, that we could not afford for me to attend the expensive exam preparatory institution to get ready for the entrance test, she borrowed the money needed and registered me at that institution. She did not want me to lose my opportunity of entering the university and getting a quality education, she always came through. At that point there really was no alternative to borrowing the money, aside from not attending the program. I certainly was not going to ask my father for money. He had never paid any child support for any of his children for years, so there really was no point in asking him for anything now.

I was back in the same class with Tera. We traveled back and forth together to the institution every day, and I loved spending time with her. She was a good influence since she was smart and determined to do well on the test. I did not really learn much in high school, and within one year I needed to learn everything that I had missed, plus additional material that would also be covered on the test. Tera was academically ahead of me because she attended a private high school the last two years, majoring in Math and Physics, and had studied hard in preparation for the college entrance exam. While attending high school I did not have much motivation to prepare myself for the college entrance exam because I did not realistically believe that the government would acknowledge Bahá'ís as normal citizens with rights and allow us to enter university.

Tera and I attended several classes per day at the institute, arriving in the morning and leaving in the evening. Various subjects were reviewed, and we had to learn new material as well as take tests in short periods of time to sharpen our test-taking skills. We spent six days per week at the institution, it was hard work. On the weekends, we met at Tera's house to study or take tests and check our results. Sample test books were expensive, so I would either borrow them from classmates or ask my mom to buy them for me so I could practice my test-taking skills. The books were expensive but we would manage to find a used version from the previous year to save money. This whole college entrance exam seemed like a big scam to make money off of desperate youth.

During the year I was preparing for the test, I was introduced to a young man named Amin. His older brother was dating a close friend of mine at the time. I was not interested in dating him when we first met, but I began to like him over time. I first met his brother, who was dating my friend, and thought he was a decent fit for her. When I was asked out on a double date, I hesitated for a moment, but went anyway.

When teenagers born in the 1980s planned to go on dates, they had to make sure it was in a different neighborhood, and they had to walk with fear in the quiet alleys of Tehran with their date. People on the street would look at us with shame if we ever walked with the opposite sex in public. We would be considered disobedient, wild girls with loose morals. All we wanted to do was to experience love, find a partner, and possibly plan a future. How else could we learn who would be compatible and well suited for us?

It was risky to hang out at coffee shops because the guidance police would raid those places and arrest the youth. Every one of my friends had to hide their relationship from their parents. Some girls were forced into arranged marriages immediately after high school, before they had a chance to develop a voice and use it to ask for some type of freedom. They were essentially exiled from one prison to the next. Most girls were happy to get married and move on; they could live in their own place and enjoy the freedom to have tea parties with other married women or spend time with their husbands.

I did not want to be sold like sheep in an arranged marriage, nor did I want that for my friends, therefore I covered for them in front of their families if they went on dates. Tera did not have much experience in dating either, and her father controlled her life more than my three older brothers did mine, which is saying a lot. I was not dating anyone at the time, and I needed to focus on my courses. I felt I could not let my family down since my mother was spending borrowed money on me by paying tuition and purchasing books.

The day I went on the double date with Amin and his brother was a hot summer day, and our young, hijab-covered bodies were cooking. It was so sunny that our exposed hands and toes would tan in no time. We met at a coffee shop in Tehran, a few neighborhoods away from our new apartment. My friend and I did not want to risk being recognized and eventually reported to our families that we were found with strange men. We told our parents that we were going out shopping at a mall. My friend picked me up from my apartment, and we went on the double date. I was considered the fashionable and cool friend in my group of close friends and they had always consulted me about their boyfriends. They often asked to go on double dates or join them when they were with their boyfriends in order to observe and give feedback.

My long hair was corn-braided and was exposed from beneath my short headscarf, which was against the Islamic public laws, and was widely considered a Westernized look. I was bold, and fearless, and wanted to stand out in public. I usually did. I was wearing a modern, short, hijab that was covering most of my upper body, well above my knees. My brand-new fashionable, white, leather sandals exposed both my ankles and the summery color of my newly polished toenails.

My friend's boyfriend showed up with Amin, a young and handsome man. We met outside of the mall, and they followed us to the coffee shop we had picked out, on the top floor of the mall. Amin had long, dark, thick hair, tied at the back of his head in a low ponytail. He had dark skin and thick, dark eyebrows. He was not much taller than me and had a skinny body. He was well-dressed, and it was obvious that he had spent a good amount of time preparing his physical appearance for our double date. He seemed funny and outgoing but a little reserved.

We had fun conversations and ordered a simple cold beverage, which we finished very quickly since it was such a hot day. We were usually in a rush to get in and out during a date, fearing that the Guidance Police would show up, arrest us, and call our parents. It was nice to spend time together in the calm, uncrowded coffee shop on the fifth floor of the mall, enjoying each other's company. I was facing the large windows and soaking up the bright rays of light, sweating underneath my hijab.

We could not stay for long. We had to go back home so our parents would not get suspicious. We did not have cell phones at the time, or we would have received calls from our parents every fifteen minutes, questioning our whereabouts. The two brothers offered to give us a ride home, and we accepted. I had made it clear that I was not interested in Amin, a man with long hair, and said I did not want to date anyone at that time since I needed to focus on my studies. While at the coffee shop, Amin was staring at me the entire time, and even commented that I resembled Shakira, the famous singer. I did not share his opinion, but maybe my long-braided hair and curvy hips reminded him of Shakira.

The next day, my friend called me multiple times and insisted that I call Amin. I told her that I did not know him well enough and was not interested in dating anyone, and especially not a man with long hair. Men with long hair were flashy and drew more attention to themselves than others, and I would not have wanted to walk around the city with him, which would have increased the risk of us getting arrested. Plus, my family would never take seriously a man with long hair, if we were to decide we wanted a future together. He had spent years growing out his hair and did not want to cut it unless I was interested in dating him. He sent me a message through his brother and my friend that if I agreed to go on one date, he would cut his hair.

I agreed to the date; he had dared me, and no one had done that before. The date was set to be a walk home from the institution. I was not allowed to spend time with boys, so this would have to do. He brought me flowers on the first date and joked that he had considered bringing me a cactus instead, to go with my unyielding and strong personality. It was a short walk. We talked about our interests, and soon we had to say good-bye since I was approaching home. He did not have my phone number, but I told him that I would call him when I could. I found him funny and wanted to tell my mom that I had met a boy who made me laugh, but even four years later, she was still busy with court appearances. I was not bold enough to tell her I was dating a man.

I had been asking my mother for a cell phone for a while. She would not buy one for me because it was expensive and unnecessary, she did not even have a cell phone herself. After seeing how upset I was, and knowing that even Tera had one, she surprised me with a sim card one day when she picked me up from the institute. My first cell phone was an old Nokia 3310, as basic as it gets. It was able to make calls and send text messages, nothing else.

Amin cut his hair before showing up for our second date, and again brought me flowers that I could not even take home. It would have been difficult to explain the source of the flowers because I was not supposed to have a boyfriend. He was a musician who played drums with a band every once in a while, at weddings and other events, and they made a decent amount of money. He was only a couple of years older than me and was not enrolled in any universities. He still lived at his mother's house, as most children did until they got married.

As Amin and I went on more dates, and talked on the phone in secret, I spent less time studying and more time daydreaming about a future with him. His father was much older than my parents and had two wives and children from each marriage. His father owned a grocery store and lived with his first wife, not Amin's mother, on the same street as his store. I encouraged Amin to study for the university entrance exam as well, but he said he had already been accepted to study psychology at a university in a different province. He did not want to attend the university because he wanted to be near me and either get a job or start his own business with the help of his father.

Amin's half-siblings were older and married with children. He and all of his siblings had healthy relationships despite having different mothers who were still married to their father. Amin's mother was the second wife, who rarely got a visit from her husband. Amin and his siblings lived with her in a two-story house.

They were all Muslim, and his mother even wore the black, long chador, similar to a cloak. Amin was not a religious person and did not really practice Islam, similar to people my age. Most Muslim-born youth completed the symbolic rituals but did not emotionally participate; we were only going through the motions because of the government's rigid encouragement. Those of my generation would go on the street for the month of Muharram[40], dressed in black, wearing subtle, matte makeup, but our purpose was to check out the opposite sex. Many youths met this way.

Around that same time I declared as a Bahá'í. I had just turned eighteen and was legally allowed to decide my own religion. I enjoyed hanging out, praying and meditating with my Bahá'í friends. I had a fire inside of me and was high on the joy of becoming a Bahá'í. I would pray by myself and wanted to memorize prayers and read the writings with other youth in the community. My mother and I would host devotionals at our house but feared my father's interruption. He was aware of the dates we had gatherings and would threaten to leak our event's locations and times to the secret police.

I told Amin that I had become a Bahá'í and even gave him some books so he could familiarize himself with my Faith. I did not expect him to become a Bahá'í, I just wanted him to know what it was, and hopefully he would be okay with me practicing my religion, unlike my father. The last thing I wanted was to end up marrying a Muslim man who would prevent me from practicing my religion. He found the Bahá'í Faith interesting and

---

40 The first month of the Islamic calendar, it is typically considered very sacred

read the books I provided to him. I do not think my mother would have liked me making the same mistake that she did.

He declared his love for me less than a month after we started dating and wanted to come and propose to my family. I knew that our relationship was moving too fast and did not want to rush into anything, but in our society, with the laws and rules preventing us from getting to know each other, dating someone for a long time in secret was not possible. The government, society, and Islam would not allow two people to date or get to know one another unless they were legally or religiously married.

We were young, and our families were not going to allow us to get married before we had some type of higher education and financial stability. Worst of all, he was stubborn and would not listen to my plans for our future, but would not come up with his own plans. At his age, he had two choices: attend the university, or serve in the military. At that point, I was not even sure if the government would allow me to study at the university, but I was trying my hardest to study and score high enough to get accepted. I wanted him to do the same so he could enable himself to get a job and become more independent.

Amin and I would spend time with one another, often after I left the institution for the day, daydreaming about our future, until my family members became suspicious. My mother was not supportive of me having a boyfriend at the time, mostly because she was concerned that my brothers would become over-protective and try to forbid me from ever leaving the house again.

My father would probably have liked the idea of me marrying a Muslim, and I am sure he would have advised my future husband to prevent me from attending any Bahá'í gatherings. Almost every day after the institute, I would meet up with Amin on the way home. Sometimes we had lunch together in between my classes. He was becoming a safe place for me; he filled the void of a male figure in my life.

He knew all about my family, that my father left the house, and that my mother was trying her hardest to make ends meet. He listened to my problems and became the support I needed at the time. I was tired of being monitored by my brothers and having to lie, even at eighteen years old, to see my boyfriend.

At this point I had my own cell phone and did not have to wait until everyone left the house to call my boyfriend. Usually teenagers in love do not realize that their intentions are made obvious by their behavior, and my brothers had become suspicious and constantly asked my mother who I was texting, or why I was often on the phone behind a closed door. She would come and ask me the same question, and I would always make up some story and then lay low for a while.

My oldest brother was becoming worried and would ask me or my mother questions about my behavior, or about where I was going every day. He became very suspicious and asked my mother to show him my cell phone records. For some reason my mother obliged and requested the records, which showed page after page of phone calls and texts to one phone number, Amin's. This created a big elephant in the room, which meant I had to try to get home on time or cut down on the number of text messages I sent. My family began to limit my movements, but I would still manage to see Amin, to work on a plan to make our families see eye to eye.

About six or seven months into our dating and I was already on house arrest; my brothers were very harsh on me. They monitored and inquired about my every move, especially phone calls, and even tried to interfere with my visits to Tera's house. They interrogated me incessantly, and even questioned my friends, which caused my relationship with Tera to end. Her father became suspicious and would not even let her leave the house. We were both on house arrest, but I felt betrayed when I learned that Tera had told my family some of my deepest secrets. I had lost my best friend and was not able to even meet or talk to Amin anymore.

Soon after that, we received a phone call from my maternal grandmother, saying that there was a potential buyer interested in buying my grandfather's car shop property. My mother told her not to sell. During the following weekend, my grandmother was talked into selling the property, and signed the paperwork without my mother's knowledge. She had the power of attorney from all of her kids except from my mother and from her youngest son. When my grandmother realized that she had been fooled into selling her property for one tenth of its actual price, she had a stroke.

My mother left Tehran to go to her hometown to take care of my grandmother, who was in the hospital at the time. She also wanted to see if she could sue the buyer who tricked my grandmother and get the property back. Since my mother had not signed any documents, they still needed her signature as one of the owners, so she thought there was a possibility that she could reverse the sale. I had to stay back and was left alone with my brothers, against their wishes, because I had a lot of material to study for the entrance test which was coming up that spring.

There was so much pressure on me: I had to study as hard as I could, had recently lost my best friend, I had to cook for my brothers, and I was not able to communicate with Amin. When my mother returned home to check on us, she saw that I was under a lot of pressure, so she helped me pack my books and took me back with her to her hometown. All of my mother's siblings living outside of Iran traveled back to visit my grandmother since she was in a horrible physical and emotional condition. I was the only grandchild in her house at that time and was able to spend time with all of my aunts and uncles. I took a lot of pictures of my aunts and uncles with my grandmother and did not study as hard as I should have.

Amin was obsessed with me. He could not be separated from me, and it was very distracting to think about his well-being as well as my family's trust, respect, and reputation. On many occasions I told him that it was best for both of us to end the relationship, but every time, he would respond by attempting to take his own life. I was torn because I wanted my wishes to be respected by my family, but Amin was acting like a child, upset that we were apart, while my family was acting like a team of investigators.

I came back to Tehran with my mother when it was time for me to take my college entrance exam. I studied hard until the last day, hoping the government would keep their promise and let Bahá'ís get access to higher education. My mother arranged for a taxi to pick me up early in the morning on the day of the test. The five-hour test began early in the morning, and there were no breaks. No one was allowed to bring anything to the test besides a birth certificate for identification purposes. Everyone had to show up to the test wearing the full hijab, and all were searched before the test to ensure no one was cheating. The entrance test was gender segregated, which lowered the types of distractions.

The test covered all subjects taught in high school, including Math, Science, English, Arabic, and Islamic studies. Because we could only take this test once per year, I had to make sure I passed it the first time. If someone did not pass the entrance exam, they could be considered unintelligent.

One of the many new majors added to the list of the possible degrees offered by the universities that year was Physics Engineering, and I knew that most students would list this as their first choice. This would leave the old common, plain Physics major wide open for me. I would have to study physics as a bachelor's degree in order to study astronomy in graduate school. I had high hopes and wanted to be the first Iranian woman to go to space or to discover a new planet or star. I would often read magazines and newspapers on the latest astronomy discoveries and wished that one day I could work for NASA. Because we had to declare our desired degree program before the test began, I selected Physics as my first choice, with some others as a back-up plan.

The nerve-wracking day had finally begun. I was not able to sleep at all the previous night, thinking about the test. I am sure half of the country was awake that night, those who would be taking the exam, as well as their relatives, who would be praying. I woke up at five in the morning and waited for the scheduled taxi to pick me up. For some reason I have always been on my own during major events in my life, and the college entrance day was one of them. There were hundreds of girls waiting by the gate, along with some parents who had accompanied them as support. They all seemed exhausted and hopeless.

Tera was not taking her test at the same test center as I was. I felt alone and alienated because I did not know anyone there. I had nagging doubts about whether or not I had studied enough, and I was not hopeful that the government would allow me to take the test or attend a university. I was imagining the worst-case scenario in which I was either forbidden from taking the test or rejected after I had taken the five-hour exam for which I had studied for during the past year, due to my religion.

I remembered that months before, when completing the test application, I had penciled in my religion as Bahá'í, under the "Other" option in the registration form; the other choices were Muslim, Christian, and Jewish. Bahá'ís were advised to write their religion on the form and not misrepresent themselves to gain entrance into the universities or the job market. In hindsight, I am sure that the Islamic Republic of Iran was able to get a good count on the number of Bahá'ís living in Iran by allowing them to take the test.

We waited for nearly two hours before being called to go sit in our designated seats. I was shivering with fear and just wanted it all to be over. I just wanted to take the test and go home to sleep; I was exhausted after one year of non-stop studying and uncertainty.

The test was hard, though I had seen these types of questions before. I second-guessed myself many times but tried to finish the test and then go back to answer the questions that I had left blank. I only had an average of one minute for each question. I did not use the restroom for the entire duration of the test, was not allowed to eat anything, and did not leave my desk to take a break. I am not sure if I would even have been allowed to do so. I finished the test before the five-hour time limit. I turned in my scantron paper, walked outside of the building and into the green yard behind the testing center, and immediately felt relieved, as if a heavy weight had been lifted from my shoulders. The yard was full of blossoms and young leaves as it was still spring. There were others that finished early and were walking around in the backyard of the testing center. I took some time to sit down and unwind from all the stress and hardship I had gone through in the past year. I was not allowed to have my cellphone on me during the test so I called my family using a payphone outside of the testing center and asked them to pick me up.

I sat on the sidewalk curb for forty-five minutes, contemplating on my future, as I watched other students come outside of the testing center, received by their parents. All I wanted was to be united with Amin and tell him about the test and how stressed I had been lately.

Unfortunately, I was on house arrest and was not able to see him. My family was against the relationship, and I see now why they were keeping me from him. At the time it was hard to understand, and the more they restricted me, the more I wanted to escape and be with him. He was just not right for me and I could not see it then, but I see it now.

I waited for weeks to get my score. On the big day when they were available, I went to the designated government office with one of my Muslim friends to pick up my score. I will never forget that day. I was shaking and overwhelmed with mixed emotions of anxiety and relief as I received the envelope containing my score. I quickly peeled back the flap and frantically scanned the results.

First, I made sure the results had my accurate name and information printed, before my eyes darted to the score. Then I saw it. My eyes were looking for the score that I needed to get into the physics program at the university, but there was something wrong. There was a bright red, foreign looking stamp intentionally placed in the middle of the page. I clumsily read the words aloud, I had been rejected on the basis of my status as a religious minority and was banned from studying at any university in Iran.

An existential emptiness tore through the pit of my stomach. I became weak and speechless. All of my facial muscles frowned, and I became so heartbroken. My friend approached me and reached for my test results. She stared at the page, and as she uttered the words, she huffed and puffed in confusion. She told me to ask the testing committee for reconsideration. The government-run admissions office was not a safe place to talk about religious subjects, so I took her hand and led her outside.

As we headed for home, I told her that she was Muslim and was not aware of the treatment of Baháʼís in Iran. I told her to keep quiet and not to mention the day's events to anyone. I walked home, broken-hearted and disappointed in my country's decision. I shared the news with my family and Amin at the first opportunity. I was sad. My mother had spent so much money for me to take the test for no reason.

I did not plan on taking the test again. Most people who failed would take a month off and start all over in preparation for next year's national test. I had run out of patience and courage; the glass was no longer half-full. I had to think outside of the box. My dream of becoming an astrophysicist had died due to my choice of religion.

I pulled myself together after a few weeks of mourning. I knew that I was not the only one who had been denied a university education due to religion. My name was Donya, after all, and I wanted to honor my name and to demonstrate that there was a better future for me. I was a new person, a new girl who had an even greater thirst for knowledge and courage to learn.

I gathered some of the local Bahá'ís who were in the same situation as me, and organized several teams, each with its own research topic, and we started studying independently. I had more energy and determination than before and was eager to share my findings with others. I partnered up with a young boy who was also interested in physics and astronomy. I became a member at a public library and borrowed thick physics books to study and learn theories and formulas. During my studies, I realized that the books were published over fifty years earlier and I wondered if there were new articles I could access. There was no way to find articles online, especially in Iran.

We prepared summaries of our studies for our own Bahá'í community on the research topics we had chosen and presented them to the rest of the group. My research topic was on black holes, which was my new obsession in astronomy.

Since our old apartment had been rented to an English language institution, I signed up for English classes to keep busy. I also signed up for driving classes to get my driver's license. I had to busy myself with classes and chores or I would go insane being alone at home all the time. I tried to see Amin but was not allowed to contact him, so our phone conversations were all in secret.

I had lost hope in life. I told Amin that he had to complete his two years of mandatory army duty because he was not attending the university. I was very disappointed in him for giving up on attending the university just because he did not want to be apart from me. I told him that either way we must be apart for a while. It was very important for our prospective future that he do one or the other.

He registered for the two-year service in the military and was lucky to get assigned to a location near Tehran. He called me nearly every day for the first two weeks he was there. He hated being apart from me, but I told him that it did not matter because no matter where he was, stationed at the military or sitting at his mother's home, we could not see each other anyway. He was obsessed, and it did not even last a full month before he left the army to visit his family, and did not return to the service. He was considered a deserter according to Iran's policy, and was responsible for two days of service for each day that he was missing.

He was stubborn, he did not want to be away serving in the army, and he was not listening to me. I told him that I did not want to continue the relationship because he was not sticking to the plan, but then he would take a bunch of pills and attempt suicide. One time his mother told me to let him die because she did not want to call the ambulance anymore.

I finally convinced my mother to meet with Amin's sisters and mother in a park, there was too much pressure on me and deep down I wanted his family to receive the rejection from my family. This way they would convince their son that this was not the right match for either one of us. After meeting with them, my mother walked away disappointed in my choice. She pointed out that they were a very religious family, and his mother was wearing a full chador. She did not want a future for me in which I was denied my personal right to practice my religion.

One day, I had a total meltdown and broke everything in my bedroom. My mother calmly sat in front of me on the floor while I was at the edge of my white, twin bed. She said it was normal to have boyfriends at my age, but that I did not need to feel forced to marry him just because we were together, and he was insisting on the union. She told me a story about a friend of hers who was with a man once, and she thought she had to marry him. Her friend had four kids from that marriage, before he left her, but she was never happy. That story sounded like my mother's life, but to this date I have not had the guts to ask her if she was telling me about herself.

On the other hand we were barely surviving the current situation, due to lack of proper income and the fact that none of us as religious minorities had a decent future. My family decided that it was best for my youngest brother to leave the country and seek refuge in Turkey. He left soon thereafter, and I moved into his bedroom and finally, for the first time, had a room to myself. I inherited his old computer, and I would type my short stories on that computer or use it to do research about astronomy online.

Some of the Bahá'í youth were going through some Bahá'í books called the Ruhi Institute, and I was excited to meditate with my fellow Bahá'í friends since I was not attending any more classes. We went through three out of seven of the Ruhi books and were so happy to meet at each other's homes and discuss spiritual topics such as human virtues and the importance of truthfulness. One day we were instructed to stop the Ruhi book gatherings because the government of Iran had found out about them, and had warned the Bahá'ís to stop meeting in private.

The winter after I was rejected from university, my mother and I went to visit my brother in Turkey. He had been living there by himself for months and missed the family. We spent almost three days on the train to get to Kayseri, a small city in Turkey. At the border of Iran and Turkey, we had to show our passports, then get on a small ship to cross the Van Lake. After our passports were stamped, I noticed two young foreigners traveling with us. They looked European and were speaking English to one another. I told my mom that I wished I could speak to them in English, and my mother encouraged me to approach the foreigners and talk to them. As she stood back to watch me, I approached the two young men. I had to be careful. I was still near the border of Iran and Turkey, and I did not want to be flagged for inappropriate behavior and arrested by the Iranian police.

As I approached them, I said, "Hi, my name is Donya." They immediately welcomed me with a smile and started talking in English. They both had nicknames, Ziggy, who was from Holland, and Roy, from Ireland. This was as close as I had ever been to the Western world, and it was exciting to communicate with people from across the world. For a moment, I forgot my problems and concentrated on trying to speak English.

My mother soon joined us and mostly smiled as she watched me speak broken English with the tourists that we had met. I tried to translate our conversations in Farsi so she could be included, but I am sure I was not doing a great job. The two young men had been visiting Iran and were on their way to visit Turkey. Roy said he had been to Shiraz, Isfahan, Yazd, and Tehran and he loved the Iranian food, nature, and people. He mentioned that he had been to Afghanistan and many countries in Europe over the past couple of months and he would love to go back to Iran very soon. We all shared some of the food that my mother had packed from Tehran and sat in the small train rooms. I tried to tell them about Iran, and about the Bahá'í Faith as much as I could. We all became very close in just twenty-four hours, took many pictures, and exchanged email addresses.

In the middle of the night, sometime around one in the morning, we arrived in Kayseri and were welcomed by my brother and his friends. We went back to his small room, which was in a store a few steps lower than the street. It was extremely cold and dark inside the store. It had a small kitchen that could not be used for much and a very small bathroom combined with a shower.

Winters in Turkey are much colder than those in Tehran. After a heavy snow, a thick smog would blanket and darken the sky because coal was burned as the primary source of heating throughout the city. The smog could fill your lungs and make breathing difficult. The coal was called komur, and it was burned indoors in a metal stove- like fireplace, which was usually located at the center of each house. The burnt coal would heat up the house almost immediately, but after it was extinguished, the stove would need to be re-supplied or the house would quickly lose the heat due to poor insulation. This was definitely not the most economic or best engineering solution to dealing with the cold weather, but people who lived in Kayseri were generally from the lower middle class and could not afford a better energy system to deal with the brutal winters. Even though it was very unhealthy to walk around the city filled with smog, I enjoyed the very small amount of freedom, and I finally felt free to express myself.

My mother and I did not have to wear hijabs in Kayseri, so we did not. We took off our head scarves as soon as we arrived in Turkey, although we still wore our hats because it was very cold. Most Turkish people are Sunni Muslim, but the country does not have the mandatory hijab policy like Iran does. People were free to choose for themselves if they wanted to wear a hijab. I did not know much about Turkish people, their culture, or their rituals, but I was fascinated by their way of life when I went to visit my brother.

My brother had found many Iranian and Turkish friends since he had moved to Kayseri and almost all of the Iranians living there were refugees, either religious, social, or political. One of his Turkish neighbors became very close to him and had even taught him to speak Turkish. They invited us to their house for tea and cookies and included us at their small parties. It was true that we did not know their language, but my mother and I managed to communicate with them.

The cold and smoggy weather was hard on my mother, and she got sick after only a few days of staying in Kayseri. My brother's lodging was too cold and humid for her, and when the Turkish neighbors noticed she was ill, they offered us their home and their extra bed. My mother, brother, and I stayed at their house for the next few weeks, and we made sure to help them purchase groceries, cook food, and complete chores.

We learned how to make Turkish baklava and other dishes as we helped them in the house. I remember that before I went to Turkey, I did not know what to think of their people. It was mostly because my father and my grandmother used Azeri language as their secret language and Azeri resembled Turkish. When I went to Turkey, I fell in love with their hospitality and kindness. Turks were just like us Iranians, and we were embraced as family. I learned to speak some Turkish and even to crochet. It was a memorable trip, and I felt wiser upon my return to Iran.

Taking showers in the Turkish family's small and unequipped apartment was a long process. There was no running shower or tub. We had to use burning coal to heat the water vessel, wait for the water to get hot, and then dilute the hot water with the cold water from the faucet in a different bucket. Once the water temperature was decent, we had to use a small bowl to pour the water on our body, lather up our bodies and shampoo our hair, then rinse. Since the entire water vessel was heated, we all had to wash briskly so there would be enough hot water for everyone to shower one after the other. Otherwise, the water vessel would cool down, and the hot water in the heater would get cold. I still remember how painful it was to rub my goosebumps covered skin with the soapy loofah.

I spoke to Amin only once during the one month that I was in Turkey visiting my brother. He thought my mother was taking me to Turkey to leave me there and he would never be able to see me again. My brother asked me to stay with him in Turkey, but I refused and told him that I was not interested in leaving my home country. I could not bear the thought of living without my mother. I was used to my friends and Tehran and I loved my friends, so I could not imagine a life outside of Iran. It was my comfort zone and my very own black hole.

GREEN TOP WITH
WHITE POLKA DOTS

Before we left for Turkey, Amin's mother contacted my mother to see if we would allow them to come to our house for a formal proposal. Amin had left the military service and was eager to marry me before returning to complete his two remaining years of mandatory service. My mother consulted with my brothers, and they were not interested in having Amin's family over. When we came back from Turkey, Amin's mother called to inquire again.

My mother was not pleased with his family the first time she met them. They were wearing long hijabs and did not fit our modern family profile at all. Being Bahá'í, we would dress modestly but would never cover our entire body with the black chador. I knew they did not fit, but I wanted to be with him because he expressed such deep love for me. It felt wonderful to know someone wanted to give me a brighter future in the country that was hopeless for the youth. Love is blind. The truth has a different meaning when one desires to be with another.

Finally my brothers allowed Amin's family to come and propose. We cleaned the house and prepared bowls of fruits and pastry. My mother made tea, and we waited. They were supposed to be there before 9:00 pm. My mother, my two oldest brothers, and my sister-in-law joined us for this event. Nobody had informed my father because this was a charade to just silence me; this was not a serious proposal in their minds.

I was so anxious and shy in front of my brothers that I did not come out of my bedroom almost all day. For the proposal, I wore a sleeveless green top with white polka dots and tight white pants that would expose my ankles. My hair hung straight along my face; I had cut it short, just below my ears, a few months before, out of frustration and anger. None of the women in my family were covering their hair which was normal for us, but most likely not normal for Amin's family. I wanted them to see who we were, and how we behaved in family settings.

It was 9:30 in the evening, and they still had not shown up. My mother urged me to call Amin and find out their whereabouts. I called him on his cell phone, and he said they were on their way and would be at our place shortly. They did not show up until 10:00 in the evening. I was embarrassed in front of my family, but at the time I just felt like I had to marry him since I had come so far. Everyone knew about us, and I thought he really loved me. My mom told me many times that it was okay if I wanted to change my mind and refuse to marry him, but I knew he would make a big deal out of it and ruin my reputation. He was obsessed with this relationship and would not let it go. More importantly I did not have a clear understanding of what love truly was. I am not sure I do even now.

I do not remember much about the proposal ceremony. I was very stressed out and sweaty. I tried to smile throughout the night and glimpse at Amin when my brothers were not watching me. I had not seen him in months and had not talked to him for a long time. He had his sisters call my house a few times, pretending to be my friends, so he could send messages to me, but that was about it.

He had come to the proposal ceremony with his mother, father, older stepsister, and her husband. During the ceremony they talked about every possible subject except the marriage between Amin and me. His family did not bring up the marriage, which was an insult to my family and probably the worst-case scenario at a proposal ceremony. My family did not bring up the subject either because traditionally they were supposed to be receiving the proposal. My mother brought the tea instead of asking me to bring it. This also meant that my family did not take this proposal seriously.

They left after 11:00 in the evening, and I was extremely embarrassed in front of my family. I wanted the earth to open its mouth and swallow me whole. Amin acted shocked that nobody from his side brought up our union. When they left, my oldest brother said, "Well, that was awkward. They did not mention anything about you two getting married!" He was right, but it was not what I wanted to hear at the time.

During the proposal ceremony I felt like sheep. Even though I thought I had chosen my future husband, I was still far from being in control of my own destiny. Marriage in Iran was a transaction, it was not about love. I could not make any decisions for myself. I was not allowed to marry Amin, and he would not agree to let me go. Even though my family was considered, open-minded and forward-thinking, they were making all of the decisions for me and I had no say. I was starting to sound like my mother: she had always said that she saw how much my father wanted her and she married him to feel wanted and loved forever.

That same spring, the presidential election had taken place and many people were saying that the new president, Mahmoud Ahmadinejad[41], would be ordering all women to wear a national uniform. The standard uniform would only be available in black, dark brown, and navy blue. They said that he was going to create new hijab laws, new restrictions for religious minorities, and to order the secret police patrols to enact harsher punishments for the public. He wanted to empower the under-privileged religious communities to push out the rich and open-minded.

---

41 Sixth president of the Islamic Republic of Iran

It sounded like a horrible idea to have Ahmadinejad as a president immediately after Mohammad Khatami[42], the first open-minded president, at least in appearance, after the revolution. Khatami served for eight years and tried to give some basic freedom to the youth of the country. He was pro-youth and even allowed students to clap after his speeches at universities. At the time clapping was considered to be "haram," forbidden, by Islam and by God, as prescribed by Islamic laws after the revolution. No one was allowed to clap in public at any event for any reason, which sounds insane and it sure was.

Ahmadinejad was a surprise to everyone, and I'm not even sure how he was elected. His political followers would call him Doctor Ahmadinejad as if he were a brain surgeon. No one took his candidacy seriously, and many joked about him running for office, but this turned into a cautionary tale about how things could get very serious and very out of control quickly. From day one of his presidency, he made absurd statements about other countries, which constantly received international news coverage. I am sure similar situations have been experienced around the world, even in the modern-day United States.

It was a bad time to be a minority in Iran. It was a bad time to be a woman. It was a bad time to be in love. It was a bad time to be an Iranian living anywhere else in the world. It was a bad time to be an Iranian even in Iran. To be a woman, Baháʼí, young, and in love, was considered a crime all by itself.

---

42 Fifth president of the Islamic Republic of Iran

THURSDAY TRAINS

After we returned from visiting my brother in Turkey, my small family and some paternal cousins traveled to northern Iran for Nowruz to celebrate and to visit my father's oldest half-sister. I was able to relax and forget about the embarrassing proposal and the fact that I had no plan for my future.

Over the course of the previous several months, my family had lost a significant amount of money. Nearly the entire family savings had been lent to a trusted businessman who went bankrupt and lost all of his money. My mother was the first of several lenders to find out and she filed a complaint against him, though nothing ever came of that. As a result, we lost the small stream of money that was paid monthly as interest by the now bankrupted businessman. Now, our only income was from our old apartment, which was rented to the English teaching company and that was not enough for our family.

The days that my mother was not running around the civil court to get her divorce from my father, she was running around in a different courthouse to recover some of her lost money. That was her life savings, and we were running very low on cash. I knew it and would try my best to not ask for any money even though I still had the same old hijabs and I had not bought new clothes in a very long time. I was also aware of the hardship that my brother in Kayseri was facing and knew that my mother had to send him money as well.

In Iran, if one declared bankruptcy, the government would seize all of one's assets and distribute them among the people to whom money was owed. The businessman was running from the police and had signed over all of his assets to his mother so no one could claim his assets. We were able to recover less than one sixth of the money he had taken from my family, but not more.

There was talk at our house about moving out of Iran. I was never involved in decision-making, but I would listen hard from my corner of the house. Being a religious minority had made it very difficult for all of us to work, study, or even survive one day to the next. The fact that one of my brothers was already living in Turkey and on his way to the United States was another motivation for us to leave to keep the remaining members of the family together. Soon after the New Year, my family decided to move to Turkey and apply for refugee status.

I was shocked and shaken by the news. They decided we were moving out of the country and no one consulted me for my opinion. I was not in charge of my own future. They just informed me that in two weeks we would be leaving. I had two weeks to say goodbye to my close friends and I was not able to share where I was going or why because if the word would get out, we could have been flagged and stopped at the border, and our passports would have been taken from us. We also had very little time to sell or donate our things, since we were forced to pack very light for Turkey.

My mother asked the owner of the English company renting our old apartment to vacate so she could sell it. She would have liked to have kept the house that she spent so much time and effort on, but my father had threatened to take it from her. He wanted the house, and in return he would finally sign the divorce papers. He had even brought up the fact that my mother stole the house from him in one of their court appearances, and mentioned that my mother was a Bahá'í, so it was within legal rights to take her house without permission since she had no citizenship rights.

We all knew this was just what he did for attention; he would never sign the divorce papers, even if my mother gave him the house. If any money needed exchanging between my mother and father, it was the money that my father owed my mother for years of alimony and child support as well as the money he had promised her upon marriage as a marriage tradition. All my mother wanted was the signed divorce papers and her freedom after five years of going back and forth to the court.

It was on a Thursday afternoon that I was informed we would be moving in two weeks. The train tickets were purchased later that day. As hard as it was, I packed my personal belongings and then left some items with my mom. She also promised to keep my Physics and Math books so she could send them to me if I needed them. I was only able to take some of my clothes, my childhood pictures, my favorite poetry books from Shel Silverstein, my own writings, and a Farsi to Turkish dictionary.

The plan was for my oldest brother and me to leave first, with my mother joining us after she sold the apartment and the rest of the furniture. Our landlord had asked us to empty the rented apartment around that time anyway because their son and German daughter-in-law were coming to live in Iran and would take the upstairs apartment where we lived.

It was unimaginably hard to let go of my hometown, I was leaving behind my friends and the only place I had known for a new country where the people, the language, and the future were all unknown. Iran was my home, even though they did not accept us Bahá'ís as citizens. I was born and raised in Iran. I knew the people and the culture, and had many memories here, both pleasant and unpleasant.

I was sure my youngest brother was excited and could not wait for us to join him in Turkey. He was experiencing a hard time, being all on his own in Kayseri. I was allowed to invite some of my close friends to the house one week before my trip so I could say goodbye to them. I reached out to some of my high school friends and told them I would be leaving the country and would like to see them one last time. I asked them not to share this information with anyone because I would be in danger if this information were leaked. I was not even able to say goodbye to my father's family members because if they would say anything to my father or others, they could have stopped our journey.

A week before our departure date, some of my high school classmates gathered in my small bedroom and we all took pictures to capture the night's essence. We talked about the high school days and about future plans. I told them that when I reached the United States, I hoped to study Astronomy after all and maybe even work for NASA. I took many mental pictures of my friends, held them in my arms, and joked around. I did not know the next time I would be able to be in their presence again.

My mother had to go to court to fight for clearance to exit the country since she was still married. Any man in Iran can legally stop his wife from exiting the country with or without a valid reason. I was over eighteen years old and unmarried; therefore, my father could not legally stop me from leaving the country, but he sure could cause chaos.

My mother suggested that I call my father and let him know that I would be leaving the country. She did not want me to leave without saying goodbye to him. I wanted to see him one last time just to have closure. I had not seen him in months, and he would never reach out to see how I was doing. That day I sat on the precious, colorful Persian rug in my bedroom, and faced the red home phone with the curly black wire. I had sat down on that rug so many times, but this time the floor and the rug felt harder, more rigid, and very uncomfortable. I never knew which number to call to reach my father. He was not at my grandmother's house, and I did not want to call his second wife's house to validate his betrayal.

I called around and finally got a hold of him, and I told him that we had decided to leave the country and join my brother in Turkey. I told him that this could be the last chance that we would be able to see each other. He was calm and paused for a few seconds, which felt like an eternity, before giving me a response. He said that he disowned me. He said that I was not his well-behaved Muslim daughter and that he wanted to have nothing to do with me. He quickly followed by refusing to see me and hung up the phone. I was still holding the phone to my ear, traumatized. Warm blood rushed through my veins and up my face. Suddenly rivers of tears flooded my eyes, and I burst into tears. I was still holding the phone to my ear, just a flat tone on other side.

My mother, who was just outside of the bedroom eavesdropping on my phone conversation with my father, rushed into the bedroom and held me tight. She put the phone back down and ran her fingers through my hair. I blamed her for it and told her that she had forced me to call him, but I knew deep down that I wanted to call him so he could prove to me one last time that he was cold-hearted.

I attempted to say goodbye to Tera. I tried reaching her home phone, but she was not there. I had just acquired my driver's license and was running an errand a week before leaving the country. I decided to run by her house and say goodbye. It was mid-day, and Tehran was hot. Again I was sweating under the hijab that I had to adjust every five minutes while I was driving. I rang the bell, and her mom opened the door, and I told her that I was leaving the country and wanted to say goodbye. She said that Tera was asleep at that moment, and that she would tell her to come and see me. I told her not to worry and there was no need for Tera to contact me. I was angry because I knew that they were trying to keep us separate. I got in the car, reversed, and immediately hit an electric pole in their alley and damaged the trunk of the car. My brother was not happy that he had to spend his last days in Iran fixing the car.

Later that day I received a call from Tera, and she said she wanted to see me one last time. I told her I had come by to see her because I was in the neighborhood, but it was not necessary for her to come by, we could just say goodbye over the phone. I was still mad at her because she was not there for me when I needed her the most. Even though I was angry, I still wanted her to know that I cared enough to say goodbye, but I did not need to see her anymore. I still felt betrayed by her. I had kept all of her secrets, but she had not kept mine. I expected her to have my back after twelve years of friendship, but I soon learned to lower my expectations.

When I told Amin that we were leaving the country, he asked if I could take him with me. I told him that if he had finished his military service, he could come with me as my fiancé or husband, but since he still had to serve his mandatory military time, he was not able to legally obtain a passport and leave the country. He was hopeful that we could maintain a long-distance relationship for a while and maybe reunite in the future. He said he wanted to see me before I left the country and asked what I would like as a parting gift.

My family was afraid that Amin would do something stupid such as kidnap me before our departure date. I talked to Amin on the phone and told him that if he wanted to say goodbye face to face, he needed to get my oldest brother's permission. Then I handed the phone to my brother and walked to my bedroom, so he could talk to Amin alone. I tried to hide my shadow while I listened from my bedroom. After a minute, my brother called my name and handed me the phone. Amin said that he had my brother's permission to visit with me one more time before I left.

A few days before we were to leave the country, my maternal uncle and grandmother came to visit us and say goodbye. My uncle was my mother's only sibling left in Iran, and he had no plans of leaving. My brother and I reminded him that his daughter had left, and now that we were leaving, he would be alone with my grandmother. We said he should consider coming to Turkey with us. He had his passport with him and decided to join us. He bought a ticket for the same scheduled train, and my grandmother went back to her hometown to sell his store and pack.

It was Thursday, the last day in Iran. I had mixed emotions. I felt like I was seasick and lost in a tornado. Amin and I had decided to meet that morning for the last time. I was supposed to meet him somewhere on the street, close to our rented apartment. I had walked out of the house and into the alley when my mother opened the kitchen window, which opened into the alley, and asked where I was going. I told her I was going to meet Amin for the last time, and I had my brother's permission. She asked me to take a cell phone so they would be able to reach me and that she was not informed that I had permission to see Amin. I took a cell phone and started to walk as fast as I could to where Amin and I were supposed to meet.

My legs were hurting from walking so fast, and I was overwhelmed with emotions and fear. I was dying to see Amin and ask him if he actually had my brother's permission to visit me one last time. I saw Amin from a distance, standing at the end of the alley. He had some wrapped gifts with him. He noticed me from the distance and started to walk toward me to meet me halfway. He was dressed and groomed nicely and smiled as he approached me.

We had not seen one another for months, since the proposal gathering which had gone south. When he opened his mouth to say hello, I immediately cut him off and demanded to know if he had lied to me. I did not believe that he had ever asked for my brother's permission to allow us to see each other one last time. He stopped smiling and assured me he had. I told him that neither my mother nor my brother knew we were meeting up today. He paused for a second, and we stared at each other. My phone rang, and it was a call from home. I knew I was in deep trouble. I answered it immediately and walked a few steps away from Amin. Sure enough, it was my brother, worried, screaming, and demanding to know where I was. I knew he was worried about me getting kidnapped or running away from home.

I told my brother that after Amin and he had talked, Amin had said that I had permission to say goodbye in person. My brother said Amin had never asked him to meet with me and that he was lying. I was stuck between Amin and my brother. I had no idea who was lying, but one of them was. I stared at Amin as I held the phone to my ear and listened to my brother's demand to return home immediately. I told my brother that I would be home soon. I hung up and told Amin that I could not believe he had lied to me.

I walked away from Amin as he yelled my name and asked me to come back and accept his gifts. I looked back and saw him throw the gifts on the ground and they slid under a parked car. I walked away as fast as I could. My bony legs were hurting by the time I got home. My face was red and wet with tears. My heart was pounding hard. I was mad at Amin and at my brother, who was waiting for me in the living room and yelled at me as I walked into my now empty bedroom, crying.

It was just a few hours before we would be leaving the country, and I had not even said goodbye to the people I cared about because it was dangerous. My mother tried to calm me down but was not successful. I was very hurt and confused as to who was lying to me.

Our shower was right next to my bedroom, and my brother was using it prior to our trip. He called my name from the shower, so I cracked the door open and asked him what he needed. He shut off the water and stuck his head out of the corner of the shower curtain and said he would take me to the coffee shop nearby to say goodbye to Amin. I knew that he felt guilty and wanted to make it up to me. I stared at him for a few seconds and told him that the right time had come and gone. He asked again, and I assured him that I was ready to move on. I did not want to see Amin anymore. He had lied to me so many times, and I was numb to the kind of love he had for me.

CANNED BEANS AND TUNA

At the train station time was passing quickly. I made my mother promise she would join us as soon as possible. I was so scared to be on my own for the very first time in my life. I was only nineteen years old. Our dear family friends, Ava and Ali and their family, came to say goodbye. We boarded the train, and as we rode to Turkey, I said goodbye to my country town by town, little by little, as the train passed through mountains and valleys, through the heart of Iran. The mountains did not know why we were leaving, and I bet that they would not understand anyways. They would not understand discrimination or prejudice. They would not believe that humans could treat one another differently based on beliefs, color of skin, or gender. These mountains and valleys had seen many wars, untold bloodshed, and ancient humans either traveling through or settling nearby for a season. They did not know I was not coming back, but I had a feeling that it would be the last time we would see this beautiful country.

I wished I were a mountain, so I would never have to leave. I wanted to be a glowing star in the desert and stare at my hometown forever. It was such an emotional experience to leave my country town by town, as if it were a slow, painful death. I wished we had taken the plane instead, that way I would not have to see the beautiful countryside with it's wonderful people before leaving for good. I had no idea what the future held for me on the other side of the mountains, and that was a scary feeling.

We each had a couple of pieces of luggage, and in one I had stuffed my pillow and blanket. I had had that blanket for years and was not ready to let go of it. It felt like I was trying so hard to hold on to a part of my past and my childhood. I did not want to grow up or let go of my home, but if I would sniff my blanket and pillow, I could be instantly taken back there.

My oldest brother, my uncle, and I were on the train for two days. I remembered meeting Ziggy and Roy as I had my passport checked the last time I crossed the border into Turkey. This was the first time I was going to be completely alone with my brothers, without my mom. I knew my youngest brother would be waiting for us at the train station in Kayseri. I was attached to my mom, and I needed her to be there for me and to tell me there would be a better future waiting for us. I needed her so I could have someone to talk to.

I began forgetting about Amin as I was on the train moving toward my unknown future. It was so clear that he was not the one for me, and that I should not waste more time with him. Maybe I was tired of being questioned by my brothers, and I wanted their friendship and approval more than a stranger's love. Amin had lied to me too many times, and I have always been sensitive about liars. My father was a liar, and I did not want to be married to one.

It was cold outside and had recently snowed in some of the towns through which we passed. The sun's reflection off the snow made it hard to look outside as the train passed by. The Iranian train had a better bathroom and sleeping quarters than the Turkish train. The Turkish train employees were disrespectful and greedy, they even charged us for hot water, which we needed to make tea. Some of the other Iranian passengers mastered the art of making hot water in their sleeping quarters and would provide hot water to the other Iranians, free of charge.

When the train stopped in the city of Van it was snowing. We found a young Bahá'í man and delivered a bag of food that his mother had given us to deliver to him. Most of the young boys were living in Van because they had escaped from Iran without a passports and crossed to the Turkish border to seek refuge in Van. The Iranian government does not issue passports to anyone who has not finished his military service, therefore they had to pay a smuggler to accompany them across the border to Van, a city located on the Iran Turkey border. Van had a United Nations office where refugees could declare refugee status.

When we arrived in Kayseri the weather was very cold. We were not as prepared as we would have liked. My younger brother was very happy to see his family after months of living alone. He was also surprised by my uncle's decision to join us. We all made our way to the same cold, humid little store where he had been living for the last nine months.

I slept on a very small love seat the first few nights, on which I could not even straighten my legs. I felt like I was a shrimp on that love seat. Every morning my body would ache from sleeping on the uneven and short love seat. I could not stretch my legs or arms throughout the night and even if I would have, they would be sticking out into the frigid air. I clasped my hands together all night and buried them between my legs while hiding my nose and ears under the blanket to prevent losing body heat. I would try not to move too much, so I would not let the cold air in under the blanket. This weather felt much colder that Tehran's winters, especially in an uncomfortable store a few steps below the street level. In Iran my mother had always ensured we had the proper insulation and a good heating system, but this was not even close.

My brother had tried so hard to accommodate us, but the store's tiny shower was not working properly. The shower was combined with the bathroom in a small room in the corner of the store, as if it had once been a coat closet. The Middle Eastern toilets are nearly flush with the floor, requiring one to squat over them. His shower was right next to the toilet, and just big enough for a person to stand in. If I dropped the soap, it most likely would have been swallowed by the toilet before I could get to it.

The thin stream of water coming from the faucet was too cold for me to wash my bony body. The water pressure was so low that it would take a long time to wet my body, and then, to not waste too much hot water, I would turn it off to lather my body and shampoo my hair. The cold air would find its way inside of the shower through the uneven metal door, and I would have to stop soaping my body because the goosebumps hurt my skin. I was lucky if the water was still warm when I was ready to rinse.

After the shower, I did not want to leave the small, semi-warm, steamy bathroom because it was much colder in the store. There were no other rooms where I could go to put on my dry clothes or to change my clothes at any given time. There was just one large room that I was sharing with three adult men. I had to change in the small shower and do it carefully in order to avoid dipping my dry clothes in the leftover water on the bathroom floor. I would try to blow dry my hair as soon as I was out of the shower to not catch a cold. I used the blow dryer to blow the hot air under my shirt, trying to warm up my skeletal body. None of us wanted to end up in the doctor's office, or to spend all of our savings on doctors or medication. Our living conditions were very poor, and we definitely needed to get out of the store and into a more proper house with bedrooms and a functional kitchen.

A couple of days after our arrival in Kayseri, we all went to the UN office in Ankara to declare our refugee status. It was a five-hour ride on the bus from Kayseri to Ankara. As we stood in line outside of the UN office, we noticed other Iranians who were also waiting to declare their refugee status and stay in Turkey. We had to show our passports and announce that we wanted to become religious refugees. Since my brother was already living in Kayseri, we requested to remain in the city of Kayseri so the family could stay united. The UN accepted our refugee status and sent us to Kayseri, where we waited for our first interview.

It was fun being in a country that did not require women to wear a hijab nor men to wear long-sleeved shirts and pants. Ankara seemed like a developed and open-minded city. It felt like I was still at home, in Tehran, but I did not have to cover myself or hide my beauty from men. We had lunch on a busy street in Ankara and took some pictures to capture the moment. Then we went back to Kayseri.

The next day we reported to the police station in Kayseri, produced our refugee paperwork, and received refugee residency cards, which allowed us to stay in Kayseri until we were given a refugee visa to go to a different country, or our refugee application was rejected, in which case we would have been deported to Iran. We were not allowed to have a legal job in Turkey, or travel outside of Kayseri unless we were asked to do so by the UN, at which time we had to let the police station know and get permission to leave the city.

Three times per week, we had to go down to the police station and sign our names in a giant notebook proving that we had not left the city. Since my oldest brother and I arrived in Kayseri at the same time both our pictures were stapled to the top of the same page in the giant refugee notebook, so only one of us had to go to the police station and sign in on both people's behalf.

Shortly after we came back from Ankara, my oldest brother decided to look for an apartment. The cold and cramped space in that store was unbearable, and we had decided on an apartment that would accommodate the entire family. We did not know the language, but I asked the Turkish friends that I knew from my last visit to Turkey, and they recommended a real estate agency close by.

We found an apartment available, move-in ready for the next day, but still had to spend the cold night somewhere. A couple of young Bahá'í boys who had been accepted as refugees in America, offered to give us one of the bedrooms in their apartment for the night. My oldest brother and I accepted their offer and went over to their apartment, sat in their warm living area, heated by the Komur, and chatted for a while. My brother and I were sure that we would finally get a good night sleep in their warm apartment that night. When it was time for bed, they pointed us to one of their own bedrooms.

My brother and I walked to the bedroom and thanked them for their generosity as they closed the door behind us. For a moment we were quiet and studied the room. There was only one bed, and we had to share. We changed into our pajamas and approached the bed in silence. The mattress was pushed up against the wall under a windowsill, adjacent to the street below.

I slept against the cold wall. We did not mind that our bodies were touching as we shared a blanket. The bedroom was freezing cold as the heat from the Komur had dissipated in the living room before reaching the bedrooms. I did not make a comment about the room temperature at first, but we both knew it was extremely cold. I was just happy that I did not have to bend my knees and neck all night to fit on a love seat at my youngest brother's store.

The cold was becoming unbearable again. I looked at my brother, and his eyes immediately acknowledged that it was cold but did not say much. I turned my frosty face toward the wall and noticed a little yellow plastic container by the windowsill. Out of curiosity I reached for it, even though I knew moving my limbs would most likely let the heat escape from under the blanket. When I picked it up my brother's silence encouraged me to peek in the container. He was curious to know what it could have been that was left by the cold windowsill. There was butter in the yellow container.

Butter! They used the room as a refrigerator to store their butter. We were both shocked, looked at one another, and said "Butter?!! They keep their butter here?" My brother laughed uncontrollably and let out all the heat from under the blanket. We both pointed to our nose to inform the other to be quiet. I put the butter back on the windowsill and went back under the blanket. It was definitely a turning point for both of us. We knew that we were on our own and had to face the cold weather, and the language barrier, for God only knew how long.

The next day my oldest brother and I moved our things into the new apartment. It had two bedrooms, a kitchen, and a bathroom which was separate from the shower. The shower was large, and the shower head kept a consistent water pressure. It had a living room with large windows facing a small alley, and a glass door that led to a small balcony.

My brother called my name and asked me to hurry and check out the shower head after we moved in. He knew I would appreciate it since I had longer hair and had a bad experience at the last place we were staying. I still needed to take quick showers because there was a limit to the hot water but at least I did not have to worry about a toilet right next to me, or dipping my dry clothes in the leftover shower water. However, the shower floor did not slope towards the drain, and after each use it had to be mopped in order to direct the water towards the drain and to avoid standing water stagnation in the shower. I was happy about a bedroom with a door as I could finally change in a bedroom instead of a bathroom or a living area where I had no privacy. The apartment was located on the second floor of a four-story building, and like other rented apartments in that area, it was owned by a Turkish family who lived in Germany. The apartment floor was concrete and had no carpet, so we had to find our own floor insulators.

The first day that we moved into the apartment, it was just my oldest brother and I, and we purchased an electric stove and a used pan to warm up the canned beans and tuna that we brought from Iran. We bought a big loaf of Turkish bread, Ekmek, and ate the whole thing with the beans and tuna mix. Ekmek was a delicious, fluffy, French-looking bread that we could not get enough of, and we ate it almost three times per day. I have tried mixing beans and canned tuna many times since then, and it has never tasted as delicious as it did that day.

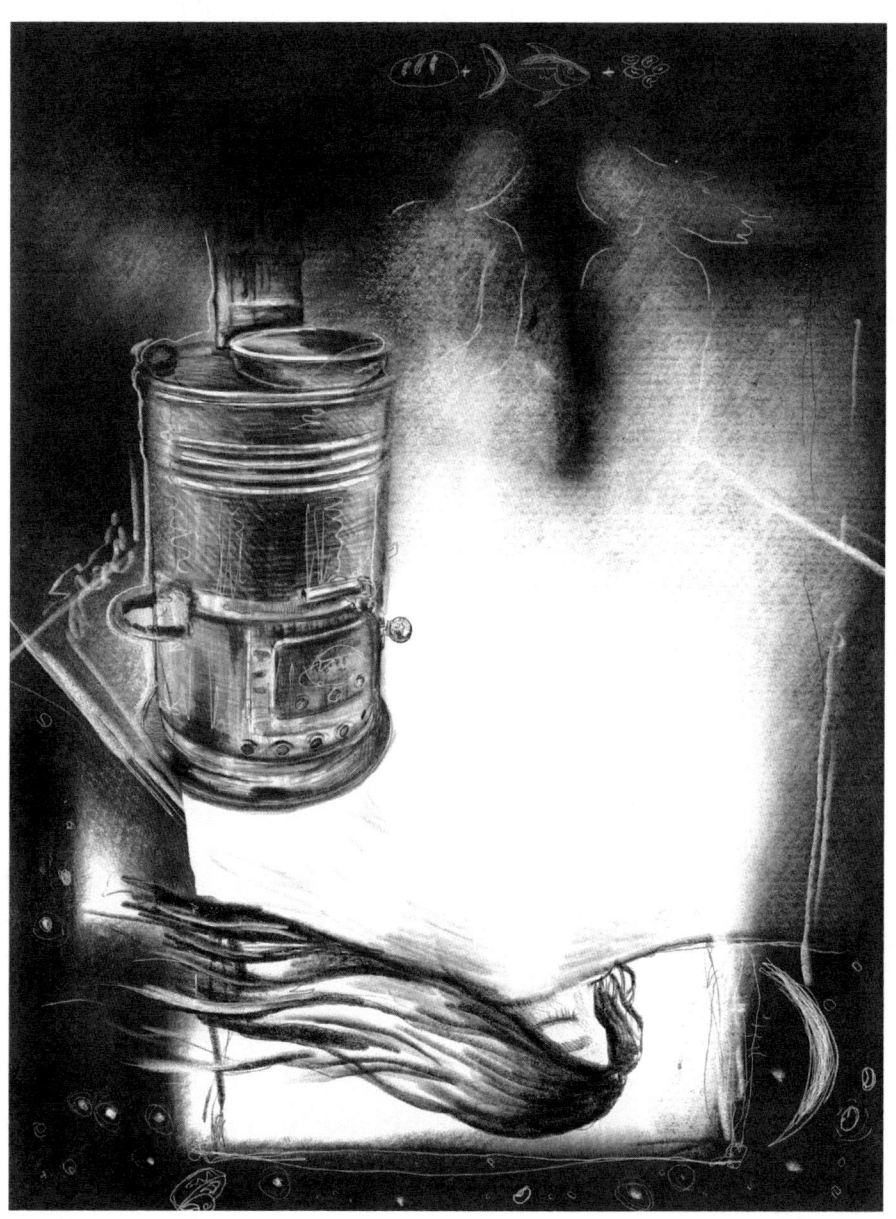

We were cold and had no blanket or carpet to sleep on. We put some rags on top of each other and slept under the only blanket we had, the one that I had brought with me from Iran. We did not move much all night so our bodies would not touch the cold and naked concrete floor. We joked about our pitiful situation all night and laughed hard. We hoped our situation would get better as we would buy more furniture and settle in, but at least I was much closer to my oldest brother than I had ever been.

We soon acquired some furniture and carpets from other Iranian refugees who were selling their belongings as they were moving onto their final destinations as determined by the UN. Most of the couches that we considered could be converted to beds and we could kill two birds with one stone. Even Turkish people used the convertible couches in their homes in case they had guests from out of town who needed to spend the night. The couch I used as a bed for the first six months was light green and had a little storage compartment underneath. I had to lift the couch's cushion up, and it would lock itself in position and I would be able to access my clothes. There were no closets in the bedrooms.

I was more focused on learning Turkish, and on how to survive on a daily basis. I learned how to pay the bills and rent, and to shop at the local farmers markets to save money. We attended some free concerts by famous Turkish musicians during a three-day annual festival, and for the first time, I danced outside of our home without fear of getting arrested. I was free to remove my hijab although Kayseri was a religious city so I would dress very modestly to ensure that I respected their culture and rituals. It was nice knowing that I was not going to be stopped on the street and questioned about my clothing.

My oldest brother shared the room with me, and his bed had a headboard against the wall, on which he placed some of his books and documents, and a coin jar. Whoever woke up first in the mornings had to take one Turkish lira out of the jar and go buy Ekmek, bread for breakfast.

Shortly after we rented the apartment, my younger brother left the store that he was living in and moved into the other bedroom of our apartment. My uncle rented his own apartment not too far from us since my grandmother was going to join him in a few months. Like most other refugees, we either walked or rode our bicycles, regardless of the weather. I would ride the bicycle to the farmers market every Thursday and hang the plastic shopping bags on the handles while riding back to the apartment. I had to cross the railroad tracks each time on my way to and from the market, which required me to get off the bicycle and push it across the tracks.

I was learning to cook, clean, and prepare food for my brothers, and to make sure the refrigerator was always full. I had to think hard to remember my mother's recipes, or at least to guess, since I was not very experienced in cooking. My mother often left me notes in the kitchen when I was a young teenager, giving me step-by-step instructions as to how the food had to be prepared. After burning many chopped onions, I remembered that my mom always said that sautéing onions to perfection needed continuous stirring with patience. Turning the stove on high would not cook the onions faster, it would just burn them. This always sounded more like a life lesson than a cooking lesson.

I enjoyed cooking in that little kitchen overlooking the street. I had decided to grow up, fast. My priorities were no longer about doing my nails or watching TV. Now they were about keeping the house clean and hitting all the weekly markets to shop for fresh, cheap produce.

My brothers were picky eaters and liked variety in meals, and I would often ask our Turkish friends for tips on cooking instead of my mother. She would get emotional if I asked her for cooking tips, thinking the worst that her children were helplessly starving to death without her in a foreign country. I also learned to cook Turkish dishes by helping our Turkish friends in the kitchen.

Some nights we joined our Turkish friends. After helping them cook or do house chores such as washing the carpet, planting vegetables and herbs, or painting the walls, and we would stay over for dinner and socialized with them until late in the evening. I had started eating every meal, unlike when I was in Iran. Sometimes I would eat at home, then go over to my Turkish friend's house and eat there as well. For the first time in my life, I was hungry for food, maybe because there was no one to feed me or beg me to eat.

This was the first time in my life that I had taken on real responsibilities. I even washed everyone's laundry, either by hand or by using a very basic washing machine, which was practically just a vertical vessel with an opening at the top. It had to be manually filled with water using a hose. All it would do was rotate the clothes that were dumped inside of it. I was careful not to electrocute myself while using the open vessel as it spilled soapy water around the shower floor. I still had to take the spun clothes out of the vessel, rinse them with running water from the shower head, squeeze them as hard as I could to get the water out, and then hang them on a thin string out on the balcony to dry under the sun.

I learned enough Turkish from our friends that I could communicate with them and even translate for the Kayseri police station whenever I was there for my mandatory refugee sign-in three times per week. Just a few months after moving to Kayseri I learned that I had a talent for languages, and I enjoyed the ability to communicate with all people.

My mother did not call as often as I would have liked, and when she did, she hardly talked to me. On a weekly basis, she and my oldest brother exchanged updates and talked about future plans on the phone. A few times she sent us canned food and cash through other Bahá'ís traveling to Kayseri. Every time she sent a package, she left a note addressed to me on a small piece of paper, most likely found at the last minute at the bottom of her busy purse, repurposed for her message. She would write that she missed me, and was dealing with a lot, and would soon join us.

In one of her care packages, she sent me a small plastic container containing a black stone ring given to her by Tera. Tera had run into my mother and told her that she missed my friendship. I had not called Tera after I left Iran because I was still angry with her for betraying my trust.

I was under a lot of stress, which caused me to lose some of my eyebrows and break out with pimples. I was also stress eating and had gained some weight. We watched the currency exchange rates on a daily basis and traded our US dollars for Turkish lira when the rate was favorable. On one memorable day in particular there was a two to one ratio, much higher than normal, so we exchanged a bunch of dollars. Because of the constant fear of running out of money, we had to be extremely careful with our limited supply of it. We would only buy what we needed and would try to reuse items as much as possible. Most of the time we would buy used items from other refugees who were leaving Turkey for their final destination.

THURSDAY CALLS

My oldest brother and I attended and hosted many Bahá'í gatherings at our small and humble apartment in Kayseri. Since many of our friends in Kayseri were refugees, just like us, and were living on limited budgets, refreshments served at gatherings were simple, mostly biscuits and Persian black tea. To this day, tea and biscuits have never tasted the same. Only when you are a refugee living on a limited budget, you do truly enjoy the plain, black tea with Turkish chocolate-flavored biscuits.

Many Bahá'ís lived in the same neighborhood as we did, and we would often get together for birthdays, dinner parties, and backgammon, which was usually pretty competitive. My younger brother would rent the local disco room and play Persian music for the Iranians to dance. As refugees we did not have much to do. We were just waiting for the UN to give us news about our cases.

The waiting was not the worst part of our lives as refugees. The worst part was having to call the UN office in Ankara or Istanbul every Thursday afternoon, provide our case number, and hope that it was our turn for an interview. We had a strategy where all three of us, my brothers and I, would call simultaneously until one of us got past the wall of busy signals. Whoever was able to get through to a representative would ask for the status on each of our cases. We would inform them beforehand that we were three siblings, and would provide them with each of our refugee case numbers. Sometimes we would get the busy tone for forty-five minutes before getting through, and after they had looked up our cases, they would say "No, call back next week," and would abruptly hang up. They did not wait for us to ask for more information about the cases' progress because they were busy answering other calls.

My grandmother moved to Turkey three months after I left Iran, and she moved in with my uncle. I was excited that she was with us in Kayseri, especially because she was such a great cook. Now that she was with us, I could request homemade Persian food from her or at least get recipes to make myself. It was nice to have my grandmother close and listen to her talk about my grandfather in such a loving way. She always had stories to tell about the old days, and I was interested to listen to her stories now that we were in the same town. I had not gotten the chance to spend a lot of time with her throughout my life since she lived in Rafsanjan and I lived in Tehran. She smelled like my mother, and I would hug her and smell her every time I missed my mom.

My grandmother would often tell us that her late husband had asked her three things before he passed away. The first was to not get remarried after he died. The second was not to ever dye her hair. The third was not to never move away from their house in Rafsanjan. Now that she had moved to Kayseri, away from her house, she felt guilty because she had not fulfilled all of my grandfather's wishes. I reassured her that my grandfather would have forgiven her for leaving because it was better than being separated from all of their children and living alone in Iran. I often helped her shop for fresh produce at the Thursday bazaar, and carried her groceries to her apartment. She lived in an apartment that was a level lower than the street and was always humid and dark, causing her to have joint pains, but she refused to move to a different apartment.

My oldest brother was in charge of the limited amount of money we had brought to Kayseri with us and would give me an allowance to buy groceries. If there were good sales on clothing, we would buy clothes that we needed, but if there were no sales, we would wait. Most days we all wore nearly the same clothing to save money. I was not ashamed, especially because I had become accustomed to wearing the same daily uniform growing up in Iran and knew that this was a very minimal sacrifice for a possible better future.

Most of the refugees in Kayseri were in the same situation as we were, if not worse. At least we had my mother sending us money every once in a while, which was virtually her life's savings. Some people had no one to send them money and had to work for cash. Most of the refugees who had come from Tehran had found jobs in Kayseri. There was a young girl around my age who was working at the local bread bakery and would get paid cash. I am sure she got free Ekmek as well.

There was a constant fear of being rejected by the International Catholic Migration Commission, ICMC, the organization working alongside the UN to help us relocate to America. There was also a fear of being accepted and leaving this place that we were learning to like. We would have to move again, this time to America, somewhere I had never been, and I was not sure I would to be welcomed. It was a whole different continent, halfway across the world, and I had only seen it through the small magic box, television.

What was awaiting us in America? What would I have to do? What did it look like? Did it smell the same when it rained? Of course, like everyone else who has never been to America, we all thought we were moving to a paradise where jobs were unrestricted, and we would make unlimited amounts of wealth and have the life that Hollywood superstars displayed in American films. I watched many American movies while growing up in Iran and while living in Kayseri, and to me the whole country looked like New York and Los Angeles, with tall buildings and comfortable homes. It was a place where teenagers were spoiled and threw parties at their parents' mansions and danced all night.

I knew that once I had migrated to America, I would not be able to go back to Iran anymore and I would not see my friends and family who were still in Iran. We were planning on going to New Mexico to join my aunts, uncle, and cousins, but I did not know whether or not that would make me happy. I even had yet to meet some of the cousins we would be joining because they either left the country before I was born, or they themselves were born outside of Iran.

I was still in touch with Roy from Ireland, the tourist I had met on the train traveling from Iran to Turkey several months before. He was happy when he learned I had moved to Turkey and was waiting to migrate to America. He even sent me some traditional Irish music that I would listen to on the old CD player that I had brought from Iran. He sent me some postcards showing a bit of Ireland's natural beauty. He had even gone back to Iran after I had declared my refugee status and had taken back some special Iranian cupcakes for his father. I knew that with an American passport I would be able to go and visit almost anywhere, but it would be risky to go back to my home country.

I did not know much English and often referred to the dictionary as I was writing emails to Roy. The English courses in Iran were not as helpful when it came to communication. Some Bahá'ís had started English classes in their homes and would help us learn useful phrases. I had a dedicated notebook for all of the new English words I learned, and would review them almost daily to memorize them. I was fascinated with the English language, such words as "accept," "expect," and "except" or "hair" and "her"; words that sounded similar but had different meaning. In Kayseri we had a satellite dish, and I was able to watch some English-speaking movies with Arabic subtitles, which did not help me learn much English but kept me entertained.

I did not contact Amin after I moved to Turkey. I guess I was done with those types of troubles. There were many young Bahá'í men in our refugee community, and some were interested in me. With little in the way of daily responsibilities, many refugees fell in love during their time in Kayseri. We had neither jobs nor big plans, and we were full of hormones.

For the first time I existed outside of Iran's cage and I knew that I was free from the nightmares of Amin. I was wounded from that breakup but was happy that I did not have to take sides anymore. I no longer had to give advice to an immature boyfriend who wanted to disagree with everyone; a child who could not protect or control himself.

I would visit with the many Iranians who lived in Kayseri on a daily basis. Some were homosexual and had left Iran to freely express their sexuality, some, Like my youngest brother, were born into Muslim families only to later convert to Christianity and have their lives threatened, and others were political refugees who had spent time in prison or had their lives threatened by the government. I became very close to a girl who had moved to Kayseri as a political refugee with her mother and younger brother. Her father's family had served the Mujahedin-e khalq, and the government had targeted her family. That was the very first time I ever met someone who had a connection with Mujahedin-e khalq.

A few months after we settled in Kayseri, on one of those stressful Thursdays, the UN granted us our first interview. Both my brothers and I had our own case numbers. I was over eighteen years old and had to defend my own case since I had no parents with me. It was not too hard to justify my refugee status as I simply told them that I had been rejected from the university because of my religion. The stress and tension before the interview sapped a lot of energy. We took the night bus to Istanbul and arrived in the morning. We took the city bus to the famous Taksim Square and walked to the UN agency as we ate a small breakfast. We checked in with the reception and waited in the lobby while they met with each case in the scheduled order.

When it was my turn to go in, I held a piece of paper in my hand on which I had written down my thoughts.

The interviewers were English speakers from the United States, and the translator was from Turkey and spoke Farsi, Turkish, and English. The interview panel asked about my family and how I had become a Bahá'í. They even asked why I had not lied about my religion on my university application in order to get in. I told them it was against my religion to lie or pretend that I was Muslim when I was not. During the UN's first interview I was exhausted by emotions and fear; it were as if I was on trial in front of the judge.

The UN representatives knew about the condition of Bahá'ís in Iran, but I still wrote my statement in Farsi prior to the interview to prepare. My brothers and I all stated that we wanted to move to America because we had close family members living in New Mexico, and we were able to prove that they were expecting us and would sponsor us. My oldest brother and I celebrated the end of our stressful day by eating at a restaurant in Istanbul, and we got on the next bus back to Kayseri the same night. This way we did not have to pay for a hotel.

After a twelve-hour bus ride, we arrived at the outskirts of Kayseri early in the morning as the sun was coming up. As the bus was taking us through the small city of Kayseri, I said to my brother, "Nowhere is like your own home," a thing Persians often say as they enter their own home or hometown after a long day or vacation spent away. I watched the sun rise over this magical city through the small window of the bus. My brother smiled and said, "You just referred to Kayseri as your home, so do you finally feel like this is your home?" Suddenly I realized, this small new city had become my home. My second home after Tehran. I was happy to be home; I was happy to be back in Kayseri.

Six months had passed from the day we had moved to Kayseri. There was no news on my case. There was a strange silence throughout the night every Wednesday, as we were all awake knowing that the other refugees were also restless, hoping for any news when we would all call the UN office the next day. We were all anxious about the possibility of being rejected or not getting a second interview. We were worried about getting stuck in Turkey and running out of our limited money.

On some Thursdays as we were calling the UN office to get news on our cases, one of our refugee friends would send us a message that they had gotten a first or second interview. We would be happy for them, but we would get more nervous for ourselves.

I busied myself with painting classes offered by a young Bahá'í from Shiraz. He was a truly talented and patient artist. I took my painting lessons seriously and started a three-month pencil project, which upon completion I sent to my father, attempting to forgive him in my heart. Painting supplies were very expensive in Turkey, so I asked my mother to send me my colored pencils from Iran. She asked another Bahá'í woman who was coming to Kayseri to visit her son to deliver them to me. The Bahá'í youth also offered Math classes, and I signed up to refresh my mind in case I would be accepted to go to America, where I hoped to attend the university.

I kept myself busy most days. I wanted to learn how to make cakes and borrowed an electric oven from our Turkish friends, and with the recipe that my mother gave me, I baked a cake almost every week. The cake would be gone almost as soon as it was brought out of the oven, and it reminded us of the days when my mother baked homemade cakes and we fought over the batter.

SMALL BAG AND FLIP-FLOPS

Sometimes my oldest brother would ask me to give him my hairbrush so he could brush my hair. It was extremely calming, and I really enjoyed it, as this kind gesture made me feel precious. I was beginning to form a healthy bond with my brothers, and I was excited about it. Winter was close, and my mother still had not yet joined us in Turkey. We often joked about the cold weather, and I told my older brother that he could leave me in the cold to die and save himself if we ever got caught in a winter storm, since we walked almost everywhere.

My mother had decided to sell the house and move to Kayseri, afraid that my father would take over the property after she left. Even if my father would not have claimed it, the government could have easily taken her property since she was a Bahá'í and had left the country. Many times since the 1979 revolution the properties of Bahá'ís were seized by the Islamic Republic of Iran without any notice or valid legal reason.

My mother and my second brother had said their goodbyes to friends and family and were finally ready to join us in Kayseri. She had talked to a judge who gave her a one-time chance to leave the country even though she was still married to my father, who had the legal ability to prevent her from exiting the country. Based on an Islamic law, in Iran and after the revolution, a husband could legally and officially deny his wife the right to study, to work, to travel internationally, or even to socialize.

There were butterflies in my stomach; I missed my mom so much and she was finally going to join us in Turkey. In the past six months I had only read a few small letters and only heard her voice a few times during very short conversations, which were not private because my brothers were always standing around waiting for the phone to be passed back to them.

My mother sold our apartment. It broke my heart, and it felt like this was too real. There was nothing waiting for us in Iran anymore. My mother and second brother had packed their belongings and were waiting for the following Thursday to catch the train and come to Kayseri. They chose train travel over flying because the train would allow them to bring more luggage and was a cheaper form of transportation.

My oldest brother and I cleaned the apartment in preparation for their arrival. That Thursday, the day of their departure, when my mother and brother arrived at the train station along with some family and friends, my father showed up with a police officer to arrest my mother for illegally leaving the country without her husband's permission.

My mother had prepared herself with the judge's letter that granted her permission to leave the country without my father's approval. My father embarrassed my mother in front of her friends, some of his own family members, and complete strangers at the train station as he made a scene. He accused their mutual friends and family of taking the wrong side and providing shelter to a woman who was leaving her husband and removing his children from their home country. In the heat of the moment, my mother was not able to find the copy of the judge's order.

She was forced to go to jail that day, and since my father was acting very disrespectfully, he was also taken to jail. Once there, my mother requested that the police let her go home, but they denied her request. She handed over her identification document and passport and told the guard, "I am going to leave these documents here and you know there is no way I can leave the country without them. Let me go home to find the judge's letter." The police officer believed my mom and allowed her to go home for the night.

My brother, along with all of his and my mother's belongings, had gone to Assal's parents' house. Since my mother was arrested, he did not continue the journey to Kayseri without her. My mother took a taxi to my uncle's house and surprised everyone. After calming down, she attempted to find the letter and she soon realized that the letter had been in her purse all along. Later that evening, she called us in Kayseri to give us the bad news, and then she discussed a new plan with my older brother. I was devastated and wanted to go back to Iran and give up my refugee status when I found out that she was arrested, and that my father was preventing her from reuniting with us.

I hated my father for torturing us for this long. He had cheated on my mom and was currently holding her hostage. I was terrified; what if she could never leave the country to join us? Should I continue my journey to America with my two brothers, or should I go back to Iran to stay with my mother? I could not leave her behind in Iran, a slave to my father's demeaning and childish behavior. In Iran, she had no family, no children, and no law to protect her against my father's actions. He knew that separating her from her children would not only hurt her, but also us and yet he did it.

The next morning, she went back to the jail house, presented the judge's order to the guard and police officers, and was able to claim back her passport and other identification documents. After my mother moved to Turkey, she told me that she had been approached by my father a few months prior to leaving and that he had asked her to stay and live with him in his newly built house just outside of Tehran. He had promised to divorce his second wife. My mother did not accept his offer because she did not think he would ever change and she did not trust him anymore. She believed he was saying the things she wanted to hear to manipulate her to stay because he knew she was the best thing that had ever happened to him.

That Friday, my mother reassured us that she was safe and actively looking for a way to exit the country. She had to attend the mandatory follow-up court appearance because of my father's initial accusations, even though she had already shown proof of her right to leave the country to the jail house. The next day, Saturday morning, she went to court and was arrested again because of my father's accusations against her. Later that day, she bailed herself out for the second time and explained to the judge that she had been issued permission to leave the country at any time, but that it had been specified as a single exit. She would not be allowed to re-enter the country and leave again at a later date.

The new judge recognized her situation and empathized with her. After my father heard that the new judge honored the initial judge's order and gave permission to my mother to leave the country, he began to yell at the judge, "But she is a Bahá'í!"

The judge very calmly replied, "So what? Did you not know she was a Bahá'í when you married her?"

My father acknowledged that he did, and the judge replied, "Then go away and do not waste any more of my valuable time."

For the first time, my mom witnessed my father lose his power, as a lion losing his teeth and claws. She told us later that as they exited the courthouse, he began crying and begging her to stay. After they argued on the street, she returned to my uncle's house for the remainder of the day.

The next morning, Sunday, she woke up early, before anyone else was awake and rushed to the airport. She suspected that my father would assume she would be traveling by the weekly train to Istanbul due to her having too much luggage so he would have time until the next Thursday to stir up trouble again. He would not suspect that she would fly to Turkey, the more expensive and less traditional way of traveling for refugees. The female employee working at the ticket kiosk at the airport informed my mother that there were only two tickets left for that day's flight to Istanbul. My mother reached into her purse and immediately realized that she forgot to bring my brother and her own passports to purchase the tickets.

She became extremely anxious and pulled out a stack of cash, asking the woman at the kiosk to reserve the tickets so she could go back to my uncle's house and retrieve the passports. The woman at the kiosk agreed to hold the tickets for only one hour and took the cash. My mother rushed back to the house, woke my brother up, got the passports, and asked him to pack a small bag of necessary items to fly to Istanbul. She then rushed back to the airport on time to get the tickets. She packed herself a small bag, said goodbyes to my uncle's wife and Assal, but told no one else of her plan. They took a taxi to the airport, this time with two small bags of clothing and no luggage.

That Sunday I was so depressed, constantly thinking about my father trying to keep my mother away from us. To lighten the mood, my older brother and I went to our Turkish friend's house to hang out, watch some soccer on TV, and to keep our minds off of the current distressing situation. After a while, witnessing my sadness and lack of interest in the soccer match, my oldest brother told me that we needed to go home and clean up, but from his tone I knew he was hiding something. On the way back to our apartment, he made me promise not to speak a word to anyone, then told me that my mom and second brother were arriving in Kayseri that same night. My mother had called him that afternoon and had informed him that she was planning to fly to Turkey instead of waiting for the Thursday trains. She was not sure if she would be able to leave the country by air, and did not want us to get our hopes up, and so she had only told my oldest brother. My older brother did not even want my younger brother, grandmother, or uncle to find out that she was coming to Kayseri by air, scared that one of them would accidentally spoil my mother's plans to my father.

Later that night my oldest brother went to Kayseri's small airport to receive my mother and second brother. I was extremely excited and relieved to see my mother after six months. I was waiting for them at the apartment, watching through the kitchen window, waiting for their arrival. I had cooked some food in case they were hungry. The moment finally came. My mother arrived by taxi. She got out of the car, and I ran towards the front door and rushed down the stairs to receive her. She was relieved to finally join us, but was heartbroken by the way my father had treated her in Iran. I looked her up and down. She had lost weight and was wearing flip flops and holding a small bag of clothing. She had run away from my father and had not even packed herself decent shoes. It was cold outside; winter had arrived, and all she had on was a thin layer of hijab and flip flops. I squeezed her in my arms and reassured her how much I missed her, and the first thing she told me was that I had finally gained some weight.

The next day, before she was reunited with my grandmother and uncle, my mother and second brother went to Ankara to declare refugee status. The UN combined her case with mine since I was under twenty-one years of age and now had a parent present. This meant that she would have to assume the responsibility of defending my case for the second interview and could skip her own first one, though I was still required to be present during the second interview. Since we already lived in Kayseri, my mother and brother also requested the same city to keep us all in the same location while our cases were processed. My mom's and my brother's belongings were sent by train later that week.

My uncle, who had moved to Turkey with us six months earlier, was not aware of my mother's desperate flight and arrival in Turkey. He went back to Iran a day after my mother got back from Ankara because he thought that she was not able to come to Kayseri and he also missed his life in Iran. My mother was devastated and speechless that her brother had gone back. She blamed us and my father for this unfortunate event. Maybe if she had gotten to Kayseri by train or had told my uncle and grandmother that she had finally made it to Turkey, he would not have gone back. But then again, we do not know the consequences of our actions or decisions until after those decisions are made and some time has passed.

The first time my mom and I went to Istanbul for her interview at the UN, we tried to find the house of our Prophet, Baha'u'llah, who had lived in Istanbul in the 1800s under house arrest. It was hard to find that house. It was in the Fatih Mahal neighborhood, a very religious neighborhood that was located on a hill in Istanbul. After hours of walking around, we found the house, but it was past the visitors' hours and no one was there to let us in, therefore we just sat by the house and said our prayers.

NOWRUZ

Spring cleaning, or "khaneh tekani" in Persian, literally translates to "shaking the house." This was always a big deal to my mother since the living room windows in our fourth-floor apartment in Tehran faced the major Sattar Khan Street. A lot of pollution residuals found their way into the house through those large windows. My mom would prepare a cleaning solution and spray every window in the house while we wiped them clean using old newspaper. We had a lot of furniture and had to meticulously clean all of it, like detailing a car, as a part of spring cleaning.

We removed the curtains and separated all of the small hooks so she could wash the fabric. After the curtains were cleaned and dried, we would repeat the process in reverse and hung the curtains, making sure that the hooks were evenly spaced and that, overall, the curtains looked tidy and clean. We had big, shiny chandeliers that gathered dust through-out the year, slowly losing their shine as debris formed a thin layer on the surface.

Because I was the shortest in the family, someone else would bring down the chandeliers so we could disassemble the crystals and wash them with soap and water. Each crystal was delicate and had to be gently washed, one after the other. We would then rinse, dry, and re-attach the crystals in the same arrangement. I can assure you that every year I would forget a few extra crystals that needed to be re-assembled, and we would save them in a bowl, kept at the bottom of the china cabinet. We also changed out the light bulbs if they were missing or broken.

We had to hand wash our delicate handmade Persian rugs every year, all of which were of high quality. We carried the rugs up to the roof of our apartment building to wash and dry them under the weak, late winter sun. The rugs had witnessed a full year of happiness, sadness, and history take place, and now it was time to get their souls cleansed before the new year arrived.

The larger rugs were very heavy, so my father or brothers took those to the roof, and I would carry the small ones that were placed in the kitchen or used as a welcome mat. All the rugs were a part of a matching set. My mother had made sure that our furniture and rugs matched throughout the house. I would wash the smaller rugs all by myself and would help my family wash the larger ones. Our neighbors also brought their rugs up to the roof, sometimes on the same day as we did, and we all washed them side by side.

Spring cleaning was fun unless we were experiencing a colder than normal winter. Not everyone in our household would participate in the spring cleaning since it was not desirable to complete chores for weeks before spring. During the spring cleaning, everyone donated old clothes or other items to the needy. This ritual was supposed to cleanse our hearts, and help us make peace with everyone around us.

The first day of spring is the celebration of the New Year, known as Nowruz in Iran and many other countries in that region. In Iran, Nowruz, which literally means "new day," is a thirteen-day holiday where schools, government agencies, and most businesses remain closed. Families and friends get together for a celebration of the very moment that the earth enters the spring cycle, the moment that the sun crosses the equator, whether it is sometime during the day or the night.

Every Nowruz we would get new outfits, picked out by my mother, and we wore the same outfit for every house visit we attended throughout the thirteen days. Families congratulate one another and give each other hugs and kisses at the predetermined time of Earth entering the spring cycle. Most of the time, if it is not in the middle of the night, people call the elderly and wish them Happy Nowruz.

Prior to the New Year celebration, the last Tuesday night of the year, which is called "Chaharshanbe Suri," meaning festive Wednesday. It is celebrated by jumping over fire and participating in an activity similar to trick-or-treating. People gather outside in the open and jump over the fire as they sing, "Let your ruddiness be mine and my paleness yours." They offer one another "ashe reshte," a traditional legume and rice noodle soup, and "ajile moshkelgosha," which is mixed nuts with roasted chickpeas and raisins, as well as pastry and tea.

A night before Nowruz, the immediate family members gathers for a special dinner of "sabzi polo ba mahi," which literally means herbed rice with fish. Each Iranian province prepares this dish a bit differently than the others, but they all use the same name. This is the one night that almost every Iranian is eating the same dinner, if they can all afford the fish.

People mostly exchange monetary gifts unlike in the West where gifts are purchased and wrapped for Christmas. Most of the time adults only give money to children and do so by handing them money that has been buried in the Quran's pages, meaning the money is blessed. If we keep it in our wallets, it will bring us abundance.

Days before Nowruz, the family sets up the "haft sin," an arrangement of several items on the table in the family room of the house. Haft sin means seven S's, and the table includes at least seven items that starts with "s" in Persian, such as wheat sprouts, apple, garlic, sumac, vinegar,

Persian olives, coins, and more. Over the years people have added other items to this arrangement such as candle holders, mirrors, goldfish in a bowl, flowers, pastry, mixed nuts, or a poetry book by Hafiz, and some people even add the Quran, which is not a part of the Persian culture but represents an individual's religion. We were advised to refrain from touching or eating any of the sweets or nuts that were set on the haft sin table, as they were only for guests and they had to last all thirteen days of Nowruz and feed all the guests that came over for home visits.

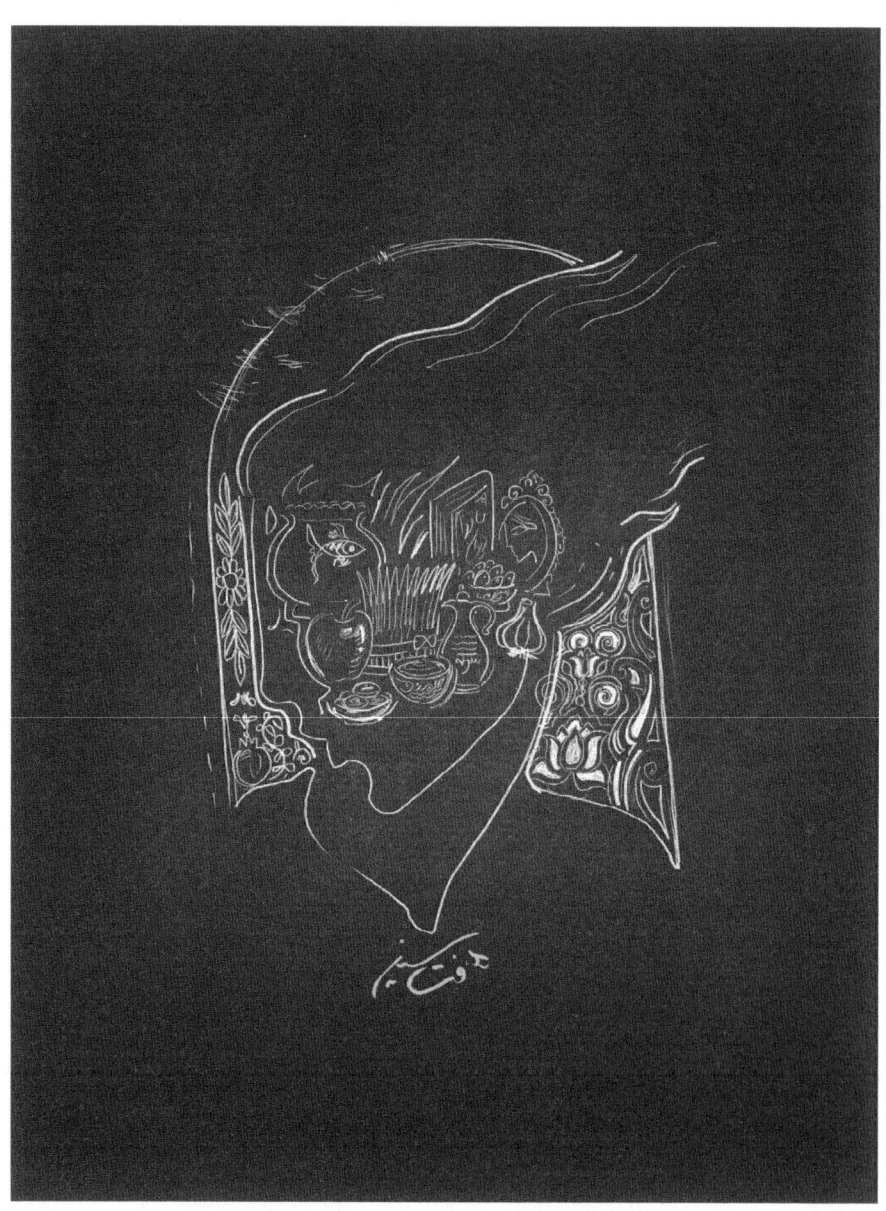

On the first day of the New Year we would go to my paternal grand-mother's house to visit. It is tradition to start the thirteen days of Nowruz by sequentially visiting relatives, from oldest to youngest. The second day everyone would go visit my oldest uncle, and the third day everyone would come to our house because my father was the second oldest son in the family. After Assal's father passed away, we changed the order and moved our home visit to the fourth day of Nowruz and visited Assal's house on the third day, in memory of, and out of respect for her father.

As we grew up the order kept on changing; some families began traveling for vacation out of state instead of visiting each other in Tehran, and the rest of the family had loose home visit schedules. It was not the same happy, warm Nowruz with the same spice and excitement anymore. I do not have a lot of memories of my father coming to my mother's hometown with us for Nowruz, but there were some years that we traveled to Shiraz or Rafsanjan for the Nowruz celebration.

The thirteenth day of Nowruz, recognized by the national govermnet, is Nature's Day when every family carries goldfish and wheat sprouts outside, into nature, for a picnic. The goldfish are set free in a river or a pond and the wheat sprouts are set outside among the newly grown grass. Everyone makes either ashe reshte or barbecue. People often meet new friends during the picnic, and play backgammon, bridge, or badminton, or participate in another sort of social entertainment.

School would give us a lot of extra homework before the holidays. It was sardonically called the "happiness message"; but it caused more anxiety than happiness. We always left our homework for the last day of Nowruz, the day before school was to resume. This extra-large package of homework was filled with Math, English, Farsi, Sociology, Geography, Religion, and other subjects.

I wished we knew the answers, or were at least familiar with the questions, or could find the answers somewhere hidden in our books. The questions handed out were always the hardest material, and no one could find the answers in our books. It was like we were trying to troubleshoot NASA's latest and most sophisticated project in thirteen days. "Tehran, we have a problem." For the first couple of years of elementary school my mom would remind me every day of the Nowruz vacation that I needed to complete the package, but I always left it for the last day. I would then experience this terrifying feeling of panic and would rush over to Tera's house, to copy her answers as we got closer to the thirteenth day of Nowruz. I think failing to manage my time in completing the homework package taught me to become more organized and self-disciplined later in my life.

At the end of the Nowruz holidays, I would always turn over the money I had collected from my house visits to my mother so she could use it, but she always bought me a small piece of gold jewelry and saved it for me to use when I was grown.

In high school I was a pretty well-organized revolutionary leader. When I was in tenth grade, one day I asked the entire class to stop showing up a week before the New Year. This way we would get an extra week of Nowruz vacation. At recess I had given a speech to my classmates and assured them that if we all do not show up at once they could not expel all of us, but if even one of us showed up, they would deduct points from the behavior scores of the ones who did not show up to school. All students had a behavior score which was assessed throughout the year based on the number of missed school days missed, overall behavior in class or during recess, and it would have an effect on the Grade Point Average (GPA) at the end of the year. It held the same weight as Math or English.

That year, during the last week of the Persian year, no one from my class showed up to school, not even one person. They all listened to me and trusted that my strategy would work. One of the other classes had heard of our plan and had tried the same approach, but a few of the classmates had showed up to school and betrayed the rest. Our floor principal took a few points off the behavior scores of the ones who showed up. She told them that they were not united, and that they had betrayed their fellow classmates.

By deducting points from their behavior scores, she had made the point that they were naughty by not listening to their leader, and breaking trust and causing disunity. She later told both of our classes that if there is one thing they should learn, it is to be a team player and be united. Our floor principal did not deduct any points from my class's behavior scores, instead she used us as a positive example. She later told us that she admired our unity, and if we had learned anything from high school, it would be the fact that with unity more can be achieved. I believe she was training us for the future.

Our floor principal trusted me with important tasks. She would even put me in charge when she would take her young son to the hospital for dialyses. I was always fighting bullies in school, listening to students' problems, and trying to improve the quality of our high school experience. Our floor principal had a magnifier in her office, and she was instructed to go to each class, unannounced, once or twice per year, to examine our facial hair. If we had plucked any hair from our face, meaning eyebrows, mustache, or any other part of the face, regardless of how ugly it was, or if we had dyed our hair, she would note it and take points off of our final behavior scores. It seemed like it should have belonged to the *Black Mirror* series.

Our floor principal would not look at my face for very long, or even at all. She knew I had not touched any of my facial hair. I did not have a lot of eyebrows to pluck, and I did not care enough to pluck anything off of my face. She just trusted me, and I had gained her respect. She knew I had far more important things to accomplish in school than pursue beauty fads. I would use my hair style, folded uniform sleeves, or bulky shoes to express myself. My behavior score was always perfect. I needed school as a platform to build my confidence as a future leader. I was going to make a change. I still do not know what that "change" will be, but it is coming.

STOMACHACHE

I had been looking for a job in Kayseri for a while. I wanted one that would at least cover my weekly phone bill. Everyone knew I was good at manicures and pedicures as I had done many people's nails before. Nine months after I had moved to Kayseri, one of our Turkish friends took me to a hair and nail salon to introduce me to the owner. The salon did not have anyone for nail art, and, even though I did not have a license, they tested me out on one of their regular customers who would come in every week to get her hair done, and she liked my work.

They asked me to start that same week. I would work every day for twelve hours starting at seven thirty in the morning. I either walked the ten miles to and from the salon, or rode my bicycle to the salon, and the winter snow made the commute challenging. I was making less than twenty dollars per week, but I continued working there because I was learning some basic haircuts, as well as the Turkish language.

I started working at the salon three weeks before the Iranian New Year, and I was not home most of the time. I would wake up at six in the morning and leave quietly so no one else would wake up. When I came home from the salon after working twelve hours, I was so tired that I would barely check emails or talk to my family, and would instead go straight to bed. I would carry my breakfast and lunch because with less than twenty dollars per week, I could either afford to pay for my weekly phone bill or to pay for two meals per day. I would have loved to eat Turkish food but just could not afford it. Once my mother cooked some Persian food for my coworkers, and I took it to work and shared with them at lunch. They had never tried Persian food before, and once they tried it, they loved it.

My duties at work were cleaning the hairbrushes and sweeping the floor every morning and after each haircut, assisting other hair stylists who were giving haircuts, blow drying, hair dying, giving manicures and pedicures, and plucking eyebrows as needed. Most of the youth working there were cosmetic students and needed the hours to complete their studies and earn their license. They were used to standing around the salon and did not sit down very much, but my legs were killing me all day from standing for hours and then walking or riding my bicycle to and from the salon.

Some of the male students who worked at the salon asked me to cut their hair when there were no customers at the salon, and the female students asked me to pluck their eyebrows. Most customers asked me to pluck their eyebrows in a way that theirs would resemble my own eyebrows, but that request sounded insane when the customer had thinner eyebrows to begin with.

One day, an older American woman came to the salon for a haircut. She did not speak any Turkish and was trying to communicate with our best hairstylist on what type of haircut she needed. I was the only one who knew some English; therefore, I was called over to translate. I successfully translated her needs from English to Turkish and when she asked where I was from, I told her that I was from Iran. She was impressed by my translation.

As the American customer left, I thanked her for coming in and said goodbye in English. One of the Turkish girls who had seniority in the salon approached me with a big smile and handed me a five-lira bill, saying it was a tip from the American lady for my translation. I was amazed: my knowledge of another language had finally been of use. I cherished that money; it was the best money I had ever made. I loved working there and felt like

I was getting ready for a better future, training myself to work long hours and to take orders from people. I was learning self-discipline.

Three weeks into working at the salon, on the first day of the Persian New Year, I barely said Happy Nowruz to my family. The moment the earth entered the spring cycle was in the middle of the night. I was passed out after my long shift at the salon, but my mother woke me up at the time of Nowruz and videotaped me as she said Happy New Year to me. I said Happy Nowruz to the camera and fell back asleep.

My mom had signed up for a jewelry-making class weeks before. The art classes were located in a school close to the police station, and some of our friends had also signed up. My mom was invested in the class. She enjoyed arts and crafts, and it was much better than being bored at home or watching TV all day. By coincidence, the last day of the art class was on Nowruz, and they celebrated the last day with a potluck luncheon. Everyone had brought a traditional dish from their country of origin to share with the class, so my mother prepared a certain Persian dish and took it along with her for her class potluck.

On the first day of Nowruz, I went to work and did not stay home to celebrate the New Year with my family. I was dedicated, and enjoyed having a schedule. Even though it was tough, I enjoyed it and was very committed to the salon team. Later that night, tired as always, I went straight to bed, and did not even eat dinner. The brutal commute in the winter was taking a toll on me. It was tiring to walk or ride my bicycle in the snow, and my body took a long time to thaw out after arriving at home.

The next morning, I woke up early and went to work. As I was walking to my job, one of our friends called to ask how my mom was doing. That was an odd question at seven in the morning! I told him I was going to work, but that we were all doing well. He then specifically asked how my mother was doing since last night's incident. I said we were fine but followed up by asking him what was wrong with my mother. I stopped on the side of the street, looking toward the house, breathing out hot air, which instantly turned to steam in that cold winter weather. My friend informed me that my mother had gone to the emergency room the night before due to a severe stomachache, but she was okay now.

I started to walk toward the house, but my friend told me that it was unnecessary to do so since she was okay and possibly resting now. I had slept through my mother's trip to the emergency room and return. I thought to myself that she must have overeaten at her art class and she just needed to rest.

I went to work and forgot to call my mom all day. My mother was a superhero, and I never felt that she needed someone to check on her. She was always worried about us, making sure we had everything we needed. I never thought I had to worry about her health or her needs.

That day, I worked another twelve-hour shift, then walked home, did not eat dinner or talk to anyone, and passed out on my older brother's bed. I had always considered myself a heavy sleeper, but that night, I woke up to the sound of my mother's screams. She was yelling, "God, take this pain away!"

I was halfway between waking and sleeping, and was shocked; it was like a dream or a movie. I could barely open my eyes. From my brother's bed, through the hall, I could see the living room. From the corner of my half-open eyes, I saw my mother on her knees, moving her upper body up and down as if she was bowing, yelling, "God, please take this pain, take my life, I am ready to come to you, God!"

I felt the adrenaline rushing through my veins, as if my body was hastily re-starting itself. I jumped up like a rabbit and ran to the living room. I was fully alert, sat in front of her, and asked what was going on. "Are you okay, mom? What happened?" I did not know she was in physical pain. I thought maybe she had a fight with one of my brothers or someone had died in the family and she was mourning.

At that very moment, I did not even remember that she had gone to the emergency room the night before. I was no longer sleepy, but some parts of my brain were still shut down and were slowly waking up to the ongoing situation. I kept asking about the pain as I sat in front of her, but she looked through me as if I was a ghost and did not reply to my questions nor acknowledge my existence.

As my brain was warming up, from where I was sitting, I looked around and saw no one in the house. Her tears were falling down her young face, and I did not know if they were due to physical pain or mourning. This all happened so fast, probably less than one or two minutes, but it felt much longer. When she shouted, "God take me, I am ready!" in my head, I was telling God, "No, she is not. Do not listen to her. She is just upset. Do not take her words seriously." I held onto her arms to prevent her from bowing to the empty room, but it was as if I was not there.

I heard footsteps rushing up the stairs. I turned my head towards the front door. It was wide open, and my younger brother ran through it and towards us. That is when I noticed the front door of our apartment had been left wide open. I asked him what was happening. He said mom was not feeling well, and he had called the ambulance, which had just arrived. I was still half-shocked and confused, sitting on the living room floor in my pajamas. I did not know what was going on, and all I could remember was that I came home from work and did not even ask my mom about the previous night's incident.

My mother was still screaming loudly, asking for her life to end or for the pain to be taken away. I ran to the bedroom and grabbed my jacket. My brain was working too fast for my half-asleep body to react. As I walked out of the bedroom with my jacket, my older brother walked into the living room along with the paramedics. They sat down and asked my younger brother to translate. They immediately began to take her vitals, and soon they transferred her to the ambulance. My younger brother went to the hospital with the ambulance since his Turkish was better than mine and he wanted to be there in case they needed to translate.

My oldest brother and I got into a taxi and followed the ambulance to the hospital. First there was a silence, then he said that mom had gone to the emergency room the night before because she had a stomachache and she was having the same symptoms but with more pain this time, so they decided to call the ambulance. I felt so guilty for not checking on her after I had gotten home that day, and I was worried that I might lose my mother.

Imagine your loved one is having an emergency in a country where you do not know any medical terms, the location of any hospitals, or have a family member who can help out. I did not know how to say stomachache, headache, or any other ailment. I did not cry the whole time we were in the taxi, I was trying to act strong in front of my oldest brother. It was maybe a ten minute drive since it was in the middle of the night and the streets were empty, but the journey seemed never ending. The ambulance itself was in such bad shape that even if there was a chance for my mother to survive her pain, she would probably succumb due to the horrendous journey.

We arrived at the emergency room and found my mother on a bed. She did not have much energy to scream anymore, but she sure was trying to express her pain. My younger brother tried to explain to the nurses that my mother was brought to the Emergency Room the previous night, and the doctors told her she had most likely eaten bad food and it was just a severe stomachache.

I was just staring at my mom, trying to help translate, and shaking with fear. I did not want to think of the worst. My mother was just so strong and patient that I could not imagine her ever in so much pain that she would scream. Shortly after our arrival at the hospital, nurses began to connect her to some medical devices and they started an IV for her. I just stared at my mom's pale face and stood by her bed.

I wanted to do something to calm down and help the situation, so I began to recite one of the Baháʼí healing prayers in my head. I was standing on my mother's right, and there was a set of windows on her left. My brothers were standing around her bed as well. I was crying quietly and reciting a healing prayer. I could hear myself in my head, asking God to help my mother, the only one who would be there for me. It was a loud Emergency Room, and we were only separated by a curtain from the other patients.

I was almost done with the prayer in my head when another patient was rushed into the Emergency Room. It was a young boy, maybe ten or eleven years old. I was facing my mother but had turned my head towards the little boy and watched him through the small opening of the curtain. He was pale and could not breathe or talk. It seemed like he was choking to death. His parents were concerned and were begging the doctors to attend to him. One of the doctors walked over to the little boy, examined him for a few seconds, and out loud announced in Turkish, "No one dies in this hospital," and then proceeded to grab a surgical knife from a tray and cut the little kid's throat open. There was blood everywhere.

I turned around and faced the little boy completely, pushed the curtain aside and started to recite the healing prayer for the little boy instead of my mother. It seemed like he needed my prayers more than my own mother needed them at the time. The doctor inserted some tube into the little boy's throat and the boy began to breathe through the tube. The little boy's parents were in shock after the quick reaction of the doctor. I guess that is why he was the Emergency Room doctor! They transferred the little boy out of the Emergency Room and most likely to an operating room. The same doctor walked over to my mother's bed.

The doctor stood by the window and looked at my mother's EKG and said in Turkish "Kalp krizi geçiriyor." We did not know what he was saying exactly. He had said kalp, which means heart in Turkish. Then as he saw that we were confused and our faces showed almost no reaction, he pointed to my mother's chest and said "kalp." The doctor knew that we did not understand, nor did he wait for our permission to proceed with the next step. They moved her to the operating room immediately, and we still did not know what was wrong with her. It was her heart, and we gathered that she was having some heart problems. My younger brother stayed with her that night, and the rest of us went home since there was nothing to do but wait.

No one was able to sleep that night; I prayed all night and cried my eyes tired. There was not much to talk about with my brother. The next morning could not have come any faster. I called the salon as I was walking the long, cold, and windy path to the hospital and told them that my mother had heart issues, and that we had taken her to the hospital so I would not be able to come to work that day. They were understanding and offered prayers. My mother was in the ICU. She had suffered from a heart attack, and had two stents implanted in her arteries the night before. She had to stay on a lot of heart medications, but I was just happy that she was alive.

They did not allow us to go into the ICU, but I saw her through the large windows. She was unconscious for hours after the surgery, and as I waited in the hospital to get more news on her health, I could not believe she had just had a heart attack in a foreign country. I would have been so lonely if anything would have happened to her. I began to learn the medical terms in Turkish at the hospital. They kept her at the hospital for at least a week. I slept at the hospital one night after they let her out of ICU. I remember that night I read that day's newspaper in Turkish and was very proud of myself for understanding the article, which was about Iran and Ahmadinejad's insane claims on nuclear energy. I felt like I was growing up so fast and had to be a strong woman for my ailing mother.

Soon after my mother's surgery I informed the salon that I needed to stay home with my mother in order to care for her. They understood and told me that they would miss me. We had no idea who would pay for the hospital bills. We never received any money from the UN during our time as refugees, and they never offered us healthcare. We contacted the UN office in Istanbul, and they said they would file paperwork for the hospital, and we should not make payments to anyone until our case was finalized.

After she was released to go home, we made her bed in the living area because she wanted to be close to the TV, and the kitchen, and watch us as we went in and out of our rooms. I cooked heart-healthy food every day and spent more time at home, cherishing my mom. I was her full-time nurse and had to watch her diet and medication regimen. I had learned a few haircuts while I worked at the salon and was happy that after years of having my hair cut by my mother, I could return the favor, so she did not have to leave the house in this cold weather for a haircut. We had the heaters on all the time; the hospital warned us to be very careful to prevent her from catching a cold, which would have been horrible for her heart.

My grandmother would come and visit, though I wished she would have stayed over more often, but she needed her independence. I really needed more help in the house. I was in charge of too many things, and on top of that I was stressed because I had no idea how long we would be living in Turkey and what would happen to us. I spent most of the winter and spring pencil painting and nursing my recovering mother. I was not very experienced at taking care of others since my mother was the one who had always fulfilled that role.

TWENTY-TWO KILOGRAMS
OF MEMORY

A month after my mother had returned home from the hospital, she was already doing much better. She was tired of her healthy diet and would hide sunflower seeds under her bed to snack on when we were not looking. I had to police her old habits and make sure she was gaining her health back. I started a new painting based on a Turkish postcard that I had bought from the small store next to the bread bakery. It was a scene of a Turkish alley with some houses that had flowers hanging from the windows.

It was around the same time that the UN informed my younger brother, and then shortly all of us, including my grandmother, that we had been accepted by the ICMC to move to New Mexico, United States. We had our second interview before my mother's heart attack, and I had gone to Istanbul with her. The UN had combined our two cases because I was under twenty-one, so, as the adult, my mother had done most of the talking.

My mother was still weak, and the doctor did not approve of her flying because he said it was too risky and she could develop more serious complications during the long flight to America. We had been given the flight date by the UN in late June and if we were to delay, we could have been stuck in Turkey for a very long time, maybe even another cold winter, and we would most likely run out of money by then. It was too risky to re-schedule the flight. Consequently we decided to move forward with the flight date.

We were all so happy that we had been approved to move to America. My youngest brother had spent two years and the rest of us fifteen months in Kayseri by the time we would fly to America. My second brother had to stay there longer since he was over twenty-one years old, had his own case, and had joined us six months after we had moved there. I was happy that my future was clear, and that we were no longer in limbo, but I was not happy that I had to leave Kayseri, my new home, and would never get to see my Iranian or Turkish friends again.

At that time, I still did not know that the world was smaller than I thought it was. I promised my Turkish friends to come back and visit after I received my green card. My mother was so moved by the refugee experience that she wanted to come back to Kayseri and help the refugees by making them food and giving them shelter. She wanted to help all refugees but especially the young, because she could see that they struggle without their family and sometimes they make poor decisions with long-lasting consequences.

Overall, we were happy. I was excited about being able to reunite with my cousins after so many years. I wanted to find out what they had been up to for the past six years and wanted to share with them my life events and future plans. I wanted to study a degree that would let me work at NASA. I knew that I had to begin attending a university as soon as I got there. I felt like I was behind since I would be almost twenty years old by the time I would get to America. I was not looking forward to learning another language from scratch, but I had hope that my courage and love for learning would help along the way.

In preparation for our move, we spent the last three months in Kayseri getting rid of everything we owned, only keeping the necessary items for my second brother. He would be moving to a different apartment with a roommate to save some money. I was trying to soak in as much of the country as I could because I did not know when I would be able to return. There was a lot of coordination between all of us during this time, but we had to stay alert and make sure we were monitoring my mother's health condition at all times. We made sure she was well rested and everything in the house was calm and organized so she would not get stressed out at all. As the weather got warmer, she visited her old jewelry-making classmates for the last time and said her goodbyes.

The most important part of our upcoming journey was to stay alert about potential flight changes, which would be communicated through mail. We were told that during our flight to America we needed to look for UN employees in every airport near the gates, holding up signs to lead us from one flight to the next. The UN had bought the cheapest flights for us, therefore there were multiple connections from Istanbul to New Mexico and they were one after the other. I do not blame them for wanting to save money, but the layovers between flights were very short and we had to rush from one gate to the other. The first flight was from Istanbul to Germany, then Florida, Colorado, and finally New Mexico.

All four of us, my oldest brother, mother, grandmother, and I had the same flight, and we had to make sure nothing happened to my grandmother or mother during the layovers. The whole family was looking to my brother and me to bring my grandmother to America in complete health. No pressure at all.

Prior to the flight date, we had to go to Istanbul for finger printing and physical health assessment, including drug tests. We were given the all cleared and confirmed for the flight date confirmed. We were allowed to take only two pieces of luggage, each weighing up to twenty-three kilograms. I had some items of sentimental value. Among them were the CDs that were sent by Roy, some gifts from my Turkish and high school friends, my nail polish bottles, my hand-written poetry and other writings, my pillow, blanket, and family photographs.

The family pictures were sentimental to all of us and very important to my mother, therefore, we had to make sure they did not get lost. We took the photos out of the albums and wrapped them up between our clothes. They added a lot of weight to our luggage but were worth taking along. I tried to get rid of as much clothing as possible because clothes could always be replaced with something better, but sentimental objects could not.

It is hard to get a one-way ticket from one continent to another and not be able to take much with you, especially not knowing what the most beneficial thing is to take with you. It is a strange feeling not knowing whether you will ever be able to return home again. Many refugees left Iran and had to pack their entire lives into just two twenty-three-kilogram bags. We were the lucky ones. At least our homes had not been invaded like many others, and we were not forced to leave our home on foot.

My maternal aunt and her family had lost most of their family pictures by putting them in the luggage six years prior to our move. Out of eight pieces of luggage they checked at the airport, the one with all of their family photos was the one that went missing. Therefore, years of family memories were lost during their immigration to America.

In order for each of us to abide by the rule of only two pieces of luggage per person, we bought the lightest luggage available. We purchased the luggage that was most durable, made from a very strong polyester, and had a reinforced bottom that made the bag stronger. Being a refugee had initiated the survival part of our brains and taught us to think wisely. Get the lightest luggage and fill it with twenty-two kilograms of memory.

SILENT
BARBECUE CHICKEN

My youngest brother, upon his approval to move to America, had asked my father to come to Kayseri and visit to say goodbye, though we feared what my father was capable of. This time all four of us would take care of my mother and not let anything happen to her. I did not think that he could legally take her from us, take her back to Iran, but this was a risk, and we were scared.

No one had talked to my father after what he had done to my mother right before she had left Iran. In addition to all the pain and emotional suffering he had caused us, my mother just had recently endured a heart attack, and I did not want her to be stressed or hospitalized again. I was afraid that this stress would aggravate her symptoms, but she reassured us that, after the many difficulties she had experienced in her life, she knew my father better than anyone else and could tolerate him for another two weeks if he decided to visit to say goodbye.

I did not want him to do anything that would raise the risk of losing my mother, either by forcing her to go back to Iran or by giving her another heart attack. I had just sent him my first painting because I wanted him to know that I loved him, and that I forgave him. My mother always reminded us to forgive him and to let go of what he had done, which was more harmful to himself than to others. I know it was not just my mother to whom he had been bothersome and unfair. He had been unfaithful and unfair to all of us, my mother, my brothers, and me. He just did not know that he had also been unfaithful to himself and to his beliefs.

I grew up in Iran, a Muslim country, and not once had I ever read anything anywhere that would justify my father's actions. Islam does not teach us to cheat or be unfaithful to ourselves and others; it teaches one to love, to forgive, and to be kind and truthful to others and to ourselves. Which Islam was he following? The one in the books, or the one he had made up to justify his harmful choices?

The Islamic law for marrying a second or third woman is very clear. It states that one needs his first wife's permission to marry the second wife, and if one wants to marry the third wife, he will need permission from the first two wives, and so on. Now, what woman would give her husband permission to lay with another woman? What woman would allow her husband to take on another lover and be sure that he loves and treats them both equally, as the Quran requires? If he loved the first one, he would not need the second one. Islam also states that a man who takes on more than one wife should be able to afford to provide a decent and comfortable lifestyle to all of them, equally.

In older days, there had been some cases where the man was encouraged by his first wife to marry the second wife for reproductive purposes, as did Ms. Zandi, our first-floor neighbor in Iran, when she suggested to Mr. Zandi to take on another woman to produce a child. Nowadays this only happens in movies and the story never ends well because no man is capable of loving two women the same way, equally. In some cases, if the husband is the only son in the family and needs someone to carry the name, there is a lot of pressure on him to have a son of his own. In older days, it was always the woman's fault if a couple did not have children after a few years of trying and the man would be pressured to divorce her; the "sterile" women would never get re-married because they would be considered useless, fruitless, and unworthy.

In any case, my father did not have any genuine reason, permission, or blessing from God, religion, the government, or his wife and children to marry another woman. Even though he knew he made a mistake, he never apologized or undid it. He actually made everything worse by leaving us with a horrible reputation in the family and the neighborhood, and a terrible financial situation that drove us to leave our home. Last but not the least, he tried to separate my mother from us by taking her to court, preventing her from exiting the country.

We were a little scared of my father coming to Turkey for a visit. I did not know what he was capable of, but it was risky to have him around right before our flight to America. My youngest brother's flight was two weeks before ours, and my father came to visit us ten days before my brother's flight.

My mother did not have any complaints about my father's visit, and I knew deep down she missed him and wanted to see him one last time. Love is so interesting; your lover could be as horrible and abusive as my dad had been to my mother, and yet you would still love him. I did not understand it then. I do not understand it now.

My parents were used to seeing each other on a regular basis in Iran, either during the court visits or when they spied on one another, but now that my mother was in Kayseri, separated from him, they were not able to even do that. I know they had missed one another, and yet it was painful for them to face one another knowing it would be the last time.

Prior to his arrival in Kayseri by train, we had all decided to be nice and patient with him. We wanted it to be a peaceful goodbye. I did not believe in everything being perfect. I strive for perfection in relationships, but if something is not meant to happen or does not align with my beliefs, I do not act or pretend otherwise. In other words, if I do not believe in something, I will not agree to it just to seek a calm relationship. I have never been a conflict-avoiding individual.

My father arrived by the train that he forbade my mother to ride. It was past 1:00 in the morning, and there was a nice summer breeze. He stepped out of the train car and hugged my youngest brother first and told him that he missed him. Then he looked at the rest of us, with reluctance, and then he proceeded to hug us as if we had done something bad and he was the bigger man by forgiving us. He was especially very cold towards me, maybe because I was now a woman, and by not wearing my hijab, he knew that I was determined and hardheaded.

My father always wanted us to know that one of us siblings was doing better than the others and we should learn from that one. For example, now that he was invited to Turkey by my youngest brother, he was the perfect one and we were all corrupt and needed to be tamed.

As soon as he arrived in our apartment, he started bickering with my mom. We laughed at the fact that their arguments never ended. Every day during his visit, he would tell me to cover my head with a head scarf, or wear less makeup or longer pants. I was very tired of his orders, trying to make a Muslim out of me when I was clearly a refugee because of my religious beliefs and had run away from the Islamic government of Iran. He would make statements such as, "A well-behaved and beloved Muslim girl would cover her hair and body." He was in complete denial about my Faith, acted as thought I were a Muslim who was misbehaving by not covering her hair.

I was rejected from the university and had to move from my home and everything that I loved at the age of nineteen because I was not Muslim. I was developing into a strong, determined woman and would not let my father's comments go unanswered. To his requests of obedience, I replied, "No, Dad, remember? I am not Muslim, and I do not believe that covering my hair is beneficial to others or to me. Why do not men cover their eyes if my hair excites them?"

Of course, he did not like my comments. My brothers would glare at me as if to tell me to stop making open-minded comments to our close-minded father. He just wanted me to pretend I was his little Muslim daughter, but that was never going to happen. It was not that I had anything against Islam; I had an issue with pretending I was someone I clearly was not. He pretended he was Muslim many times, but he was unfaithful to himself and God.

It made him feel powerful to question where I was going every day or to make comments about the clothes I would wear while he was visiting. He wanted to show that he was my father, but he did not understand that I had lived without him for years, and for six months I did not even have my mother beside me because of his selfish desire to torture her.

Where was he when I did not know Turkish and needed to pay my bills? Where was he when my mother was screaming in pain on the floor as she had a heart attack in that same apartment? He had no right to tell me what to wear or how to behave. Maybe it broke his heart that his little girl had grown up and was now a strong, independent woman who did not take orders from her father anymore. He needed to remember that it was he who left us, not the other way around, despite his attempts to make us feel otherwise. He was not the victim; by definition, he was a narcissist.

He had not tried to contact us, not even to send us any messages, while we lived in Turkey. He had completely forgotten about us. I could not believe that my father came to say goodbye to me but did not bring me a small parting gift to remember him by or at least have a nice attitude towards me during our last days. The least he could do was to accept who I was and what religion I had chosen for myself.

My oldest brother showed my father the small city of Kayseri and introduced him to our Turkish friends. Because he knew some Azeri, he could understand some of the conversations we had with our Turkish friends. He was shocked that the tables had turned, and now I was the one who spoke Turkish and could translate for him. This was no longer his secret language. Now that I had learned Turkish, I could understand Azeri as well, due to their similarity. He never said he was proud of me for learning a whole new language in such a short period of time. He never wished us well for our life in America.

Visiting us in Turkey was the first time my father had left Iran. We showed him the famous Ataturk square and took many pictures to capture the memories. One day we went to a major bazaar on the edge of the city. He shopped for his mother and asked me to help him shop for his second wife. It made me feel uncomfortable to witness him shop for his second wife, the woman who tore apart our family. He knew that living with this other woman had hurt me so much, and yet he was vulgar and rude about his relationship with this woman who was not my mother. As he shopped for his second wife, he bought me a couple of pieces of clothing. It felt cheap, but I did not reject his offer because I wanted to have something from him, to remember him by.

During one of the days when my father was visiting us, we barbecued a marinated chicken, Turkish style, on the balcony for lunch. My brothers and I wanted to have a lunch with mother and father, even though it would most likely be a fake event. We wanted to pretend that everything was beautiful and nothing unusual had ever happened. I set the sofre[43] and sat between Mom and Dad so they would not fight.

As we were barbecuing the chicken on the balcony, my second brother was taking pictures of all of us. We wanted to record a moment when everyone was having a good time, even if it was a pretend moment. We set the large sofre on the floor, on the Persian rug we had brought from Iran, in the small living room. We placed rice, salad, delicious Turkish olives, and Ekmek in the middle of the sofre and the plates with forks and

---

43 A tablecloth that is traditionally used to eat on the floor, it can be made of plastic or fabric.

spoons around it. Mom sat on my left, closer to the living room door, and dad sat on my right, closer to the balcony's glass door, which was left wide open and would let in the smoke from the burning coals. I think we were all happy to have this meal as a family, with the second woman out of the picture, and out of our minds, for the first time in a long time.

I was overwhelmed with emotion. We had not eaten a meal together as a family for years. We all posed for the camera, fake, fearful smiles, as we sat on the floor surrounding the deliciously barbecued chicken. We were scared of being in the same room with Mom, Dad, years of disagreements and an unfortunate and irreversible infidelity. I took mental pictures of that lunch since I knew in my heart that this would probably be the last time we would eat as a family.

It was a very quiet meal as my brothers and I were afraid that our mom or dad would say something to trigger the impending and delayed fight. The summer breeze entered the living room through the balcony and passed through my thoughts, and I forgave my father. I felt bad for the things my father had done, and I thought maybe he had too much pride to say that he was sorry for his actions. The Persian rug was a witness to our fake smiles, small jokes, and the silent barbecue chicken that was holding its breath, knowing that just one wrong comment could ruin the last meal.

During my father's visit to Kayseri, I knew that he was talking to my mother secretly, when we were not around. I am not sure what they talked about, but it was never followed by a fight, so that was good news. I think they both had realized that it was finally over, even though they were still legally husband and wife.

My father was proposing to come to Istanbul with us and visit some more before we caught our flight. We did not feel too safe with him coming to Istanbul, and we were not sure if he was trying to stop us from leaving. It was too close to our flight to risk anything like that. He changed his mind and decided to take the train back to Tehran once he saw we were not entertaining the idea.

The day my father took the train back to Tehran he was crying with pride, and we took many pictures with him. My youngest brother had already left for America, and I was sad that my father was leaving too. It was as if I were losing him all over again. When his train arrived to pick up Kayseri's passengers, my brothers helped him put his luggage on the train, and then he said goodbye with a sense of superiority. I went up on the train to hug him, one last time, and he held onto me. He said, "No, I am not letting go of you. You have to come back with me."

I was scared and did not know if he was joking or if he was serious. He was holding onto my arms, and my brothers were standing by the train, laughing hard. I was terrified and said, "No, I am going to America.

I can always visit you later." He let go of my arms but hugged me hard and pressed me to his chest and gave me a kiss. The train was about to take off, and I quickly jumped off and stared back at him.

As the train started moving, we walked beside it, next to his train car, then ran as the train sped up. I saw him crying, which made me cry too. Deep down I knew it was a good decision, not taking him to Istanbul with us. I felt bad that he probably would have to live without his children for the rest of his life. Was that a punishment or a reward? Did he get what he wanted out of his life? He would not have anyone to help him or take care of him as he grew old, and if we were ever to get married and have children, he would not be around them unless he came to visit us.

I was hoping the regime would change soon and all of us could go back to Iran and serve our own country. I wanted to gain an education so I could go back and serve my people, the Bahá'ís, the underprivileged, and other minorities. My father had made his decision years ago, leaving his wife and all of his children for another woman. Now, he would get to live with his mistress wife, and I hoped he was happy with his decision, though I felt bad for his second wife. My father would not have us around anymore, and we would not be there to distract him from his new love. Now she would have him all to herself, and he would have just one person to blame for all of the unfortunate events in his life on. She would have to hear him nag about losing his children, wife, family, and close friends. Did she get what she wanted?

I was relieved when he left as my life felt under control again and I was in charge of the decisions I was making. I wanted to build a new life for myself and take care of my mother, the most important person in my life.

FLIGHT TO THE UNKNOWN

My father left, and we all went back to packing, weighing our luggage, and getting rid of anything that was unnecessary. We were checking our emails to see if my younger brother had made it to America. He let us know of his arrival by posting a funny video of New York's airport.

The last day in Kayseri, I took a long and steamy shower and got dressed for the journey to Istanbul and America. We said our goodbyes to my second brother, and to our refugee and Turkish friends and took the night train, arriving in Istanbul twelve hours later in the early morning. It was the same train that was coming from Tehran, and we had always gotten off the train at Kayseri, but this time we continued on to Istanbul.

At the center of Istanbul, the European part of the city, people dressed nicely, walked fast, talked loudly, and seemed to have fun. The clubs were loud until four in the morning, and people would go in and out of the shops throughout the day and well into the night. It was Tehran, but with no mandatory hijab law, and men and woman expressed themselves freely.

We spent most of the day in the hotel, resting, and then went to the airport lobby earlier than necessary for an international trip, we did not want to miss our flight. My mother had given me five dollars and her older sister's home phone number, in case of an emergency.

There were butterflies in my stomach, and I felt uneasy as we got closer to the flight time.

Our luggage was a little over the weight limit, so we ended up taking some items out and stuffing them into our backpacks before we could check the bags. We all had large bags and backpacks hanging from our shoulders as we navigated through the airport to the departure gate. Our check-in and security processes happened swiftly, and I did not have enough time to make peace with each portion of the trip. Saying goodbye to Iran, to my refugee life and to Turkey, the country that hosted us for over a year. At the time I thought I was emotionally ready for a change so extreme, going from East to West but none of us was ready.

Finally, it was time to get on the plane, and as I was walking towards the airplane, I took a sleeping pill. I was exhausted and needed to relax and not feel anything until I got to see my family members in America. I just wanted to sleep and wake up on the other side of this long journey, which had at times felt like a nightmare, and had taken us fifteen months to complete. I do not remember anything of our flight from Turkey to Germany. My brother woke me up when we landed and told me to gather my belongings and get off the airplane to catch the next flight. I had slept for hours and had not even eaten the meal that was brought for me.

We exited the plane and followed the signs to the connecting gate. It was difficult to make sure that my elderly grandmother and my mother were both walking fast enough to make the next flight, especially because they had brought along a mixture of backpacks and bags. With the little English we knew and with the help of the UN and airport staff, we made it to the next plane, and I knew that our next stop would be in America. I immediately fell asleep on the next flight and again did not even wake up for meals.

We were part of a large group of refugees who had left Turkey and were on the same flight to America. We were all more scared than excited by this trip, a flight to the unknown. The large refugee group had been divided into two flights in Germany, those flying to southern states were with us, and those headed to northern states had taken another flight to New York. We were supposed to take two more flights after we arrived in the United States, and at each gate there were UN volunteers helping us navigate.

I wonder if others were as unsure as I was about this ideal destination, America, the land of opportunities. My mother's uncle, who moved there in the 1950s, told us once, "There are jewelry and diamonds on the streets of America; you just have to bend and pick them up." I did not know what that meant, but I was about to find out. I was about to meet family members I had never met before and re-unite with the ones I had lost several years earlier.

I was wearing a pair of denim shorts, a short-sleeved navy blue t-shirt, and All-Star navy-blue and white shoes for comfort. I had put together these clothes so I would look decent when I entered America and was welcomed by my family members. I saw how Americans dressed in movies and wanted to look as nice as they did.

On the second flight, I was sitting in the aisle seat. My oldest brother was on my left next to the window, and my mother was sitting across from me in the aisle seat, in the middle of the large plane. I do not remember where my grandmother was sitting, but I think it was away from us three.

I woke up to un-recognizable voices and felt disorganized. I opened my eyes and saw my mother laying down across the row of seats. Adrenaline kicked in. I quickly opened my seat belt and jumped out of my seat. I approached my mother; her face and lips were pale, and she had her right hand on her chest. I was so scared and immediately remembered that this whole time while we were rushing from one gate to the other, I never stopped to check and see if she was doing okay.

She started talking to me. "Donya, my heart is hurting."

I said, "How bad is it hurting, mom? Can you handle it?"

She replied in a soft voice, "I feel like I am having another heart attack." My eyes grew big. I could not believe that we were thousands of feet in the air, over the Atlantic Ocean, and she was having a heart episode. The flight attendants were definitely trying to talk to me in English and some other language that I did not recognize. I did not understand a word they said. They were worried about my mother and wanted to know where she was hurting, but I did not know any medical terms in English, and I was unable to translate my mom's condition.

Beyond the tears in my eyes, I saw my grandmother and brother sitting still and looking up to me to do something; magically speak fluent English and save my mother's life! I leaned towards my mom and whispered, "Mom, not now. I do not know English. I do not even know how to say, "heart attack." Please do not have this episode right now."

She stared back at me and said, "My heart is hurting like it was when I was in Kayseri." I stared back at her for a few seconds, still high on the sleeping pill, licked my dry and dehydrated lips, stood up and stared at the flight attendees as a mute. They were speaking, so fast, and I had no idea what they were saying. I looked around again. My brother was moving his lips, trying to communicate with me. I read his lips; he wanted to know what was going on.

I had no good news for him, so I leaned down again and said to my mother, "Mom, I do not know any English. I know Persian and Turkish. I can explain your problems in Turkish, but I cannot do anything for you in English." It was heart breaking that I could not communicate my mother's symptoms and was struggling to save her life. She did not say anything to me, she just reached out to my hand and held it.

I closed my eyes and tried to remember a key word that would help us communicate with the flight attendants. I had listened to a lot of Enrique Iglesias, Britney Spears, and Shakira love songs. I knew it was "heart," where you feel love, and that it breaks, and it hurts. I opened my eyes, stood straight, and said out loud "heart," as I pointed at my mother's chest. They asked me something in English, and I had no idea what it was. I was not going to be weak; I had learned Turkish in a short period of time and now I had to communicate in English, I just had to think hard and remember as many useful words as I could. I said, "Before. Turkey. She. Heart. Problem."

They were still talking to each other, and I was just trying to get words out. I said, "She go to hospital, ICU, in Turkey."

That time I think they got the hint. I sat next to my mom and said, "I wish this had not happened here. I do not know their language. I spent the past fifteen months learning Turkish and now it is not helping me. I tried to translate; I think they got the point." My mother was still pale and had no energy to speak. She calmly squeezed my hand as an acknowledgment.

The flight attendants announced something in the microphone to all of us, and then directed me to sit down at my designated seat and put my seatbelt on. My mom was still pale and trying to keep looking at me out of the corner of her eyes. One of the flight attendants sat close to her and kept an eye on her. The plane began to descend, and I had no way to ask if this was an emergency landing or our final flight destination in America. My mother did not look healthy, and I had no sense of time or place. I had no idea what time it was, what day it was, or where we were landing. America? An island? Europe?

The plane landed, and everyone stayed seated, most likely because they were instructed to do so. Nurses and paramedics rushed onto the plane and examined my mother. I could not translate much and even asked if any of them knew Persian or Turkish, since I could only translate the symptoms in those two languages.

They were going to transfer her to the hospital. I was terrified. I had lost so much and so many people in the past several years that I could not lose another one. I could not lose my mother now that she was free from my father and from religious persecution. I could not lose the only person who was always consistent in my life, my only friend. I almost lost her in Turkey, and I did not want to think that this was it, that this is how it would end. I held tightly onto her cold pale hands and kept my eyes on her face. She had shortness of breath and could barely talk. I told my brother to take care of grandma and that I would go to the hospital with mom. I was not sure which city we were in, much less country or even continent. I was not sure when or how, but I would find a way to call my brother, since he would most likely continue the journey to New Mexico and inform our family of our situation.

The paramedics transferred her to the ambulance. As we stepped outside of the plane, the hot and humid air hit me in the face. Where were we? I had never experienced such hot and humid weather; I could smell the ocean and see the palm trees in the distance. I immediately remembered that New Mexico was far from the ocean and most likely had a hot and dry climate. The famous Wile E. Coyote and the Road Runner cartoon, being from New Mexico, were surrounded by tumble weeds and dry looking rocks, not palm trees and humidity.

With only five American dollars in my pocket, no extra clothes, and little identification, I followed the paramedics to the ambulance, facing my biggest fear, losing the person who gave birth to me.

To be continued…